UNIX® AND WINDOWS® 2000 INTEROPERABILITY GUIDE

Alan R. Roberts

ISBN 0-13-026332-X

90000

9 780130 263322

Hewlett-Packard® Professional Books

Operating Systems	
Fernandez	Configuring CDE: The Common Desktop Environment
Lund	Integrating UNIX and PC Network Operating Systems
Madell	Disk and File Management Tasks on HP-UX
Poniatowski	HP-UX 11i System Administration Handbook and Toolkit
Poniatowski	HP-UX 11.x System Administration Handbook and Toolkit
Poniatowski	HP-UX 11.x System Administration "How To" Book
Poniatowski	HP-UX System Administration Handbook and Toolkit
Poniatowski	Learning the HP-UX Operating System
Poniatowski	UNIX User's Handbook
Rehman	HP Certified, HP-UX System Administration
Roberts	UNIX and Windows 2000 Interoperability Guide
Sauers, Weygant	HP-UX Tuning and Performance
Stone, Symons	UNIX Fault Management
Weygant	Clusters for High Availability: A Primer of HP Solutions, Second Edition
Online/Internet	
Amor	The E-business (R)evolution: Living and Working in an Interconnected World
Greenberg, Lakeland	A Methodology for Developing and Deploying Internet and Intranet Solutions
Greenberg, Lakeland	Building Professional Web Sites with the Right Tools
Klein	Building Enhanced HTML Help with DHTML and CSS
Werry, Mowbray	Online Communities: Commerce, Community Action, and the Virtual University
Networking/Communications	
Blommers	OpenView Network Node Manager: Designing and Implementing an Enterprise Solution
Blommers	Practical Planning for Network Growth
Bruce, Dempsey	Security in Distributed Computing: Did You Lock the Door?
Lucke	Designing and Implementing Computer Workgroups
Enterprise	
Blommers	Architecting Enterprise Solutions with UNIX Networking
Cook	Building Enterprise Information Architectures
Missbach/Hoffmann	SAP Hardware Solutions: Servers, Storage, and Networks for mySAP.com
Pipkin	Halting the Hacker: A Practical Guide to Computer Security
Pipkin	Information Security: Protecting the Global Enterprise
Thornburgh	Fibre Channel for Mass Storage
Thornburgh, Schoenborn	Storage Area Networks: Designing and Implementing a Mass Storage System
Todman	Designing a Data Warehouse: Supporting Customer Relationship Management

PROGRAMMING

Blinn	Portable Shell Programming
Caruso	Power Programming in HP OpenView
Chaudri, Loomis	Object Databases in Practice
Chew	The Java/C++ Cross-Reference Handbook
Grady	Practical Software Metrics for Project Management and Process Improvement
Grady	Successful Software Process Improvement
Lewis	The Art & Science of Smalltalk
Lichtenbelt, Crane, Naqvi	Introduction to Volume Rendering
Mellquist	SNMP++
Mikkelsen, Pherigo	Practical Software Configuration Management
Norton, DiPasquale	Thread Time: The Multithreaded Programming Guide
Tapadiya	COM+ Programming: A Practical Guide Using Visual C++ and ATL
Wadleigh, Crawford	Software Optimization for High Performance Computing
Ward	Qt Programming for Linux and Windows 2000
Yuan	Windows Graphics Programming: Win32 GDI and DirectDraw

IMAGE PROCESSING

Crane	A Simplified Approach to Image Processing
Day	The Color Scanning Handbook
Gann	Desktop Scanners: Image Quality

OTHER TITLES OF INTEREST

Kane	PA-RISC 2.0 Architecture
Markstein	IA-64 and Elementary Functions

UNIX® AND WINDOWS® 2000 INTEROPERABILITY GUIDE

Alan R. Roberts

PH PTR

PRENTICE HALL PTR
UPPER SADDLE RIVER, NJ 07458
WWW.PHPTR.COM

Library of Congress Cataloging-in-Publication Data

Roberts, Alan
UNIX and Windows 2000 interoperability guide / Alan Roberts.
p. cm.
Includes bibliographical references and index.
ISBN 0-13-026332-X
1. UNIX (Computer file) 2. Microsoft Windows (Computer file) 3. Operating systems (Computers) I. Title.

QA76.76.O63 R6217 2001
005.4'32--dc21

2001021493

Editorial/Production Supervision: *Jan H. Schwartz*
Acquisitions Editor: *Jill Harry*
Marketing Manager: *Dan DePasquale*
Manufacturing Manager: *Alexis R. Heydt*
Buyer: *Maura Zaldivar*
Cover Design Director: *Jerry Votta*
Cover Design: *Talar Agasyan*
Art Director: *Gail Cocker-Bogusz*
Interior Series Design: *Meg VanArsdale*
Editorial Assistant: *Justin Somma*
Composition: *Vanessa Moore*
Manager, Hewlett-Packard Retail Book Publishing: *Patricia Pekary*
Editor, Hewlett-Packard Professional Books: *Susan Wright*

Published by Prentice Hall PTR
Prentice-Hall, Inc.
Upper Saddle River, NJ 07458

Prentice Hall books are widely used by corporations and government agencies for training, marketing, and resale.

The publisher offers discounts on this book when ordered in bulk quantities.
For more information, contact
Corporate Sales Department, Prentice Hall PTR, One Lake Street, Upper Saddle River, NJ 07458
Phone: 800-382-3419; FAX: 201-236-7141; E-mail: corpsales@prenhall.com

Printed in the United States of America

10 9 8 7 6 5 4 3 2 1

ISBN 0-13-026332-X

Pearson Education Ltd.
Pearson Education Australia PTY, Limited
Pearson Education Singapore, Pte. Ltd
Pearson Education North Asia Ltd.
Pearson Education Canada, Ltd.
Pearson Educación de Mexico, S.A. de C.V.
Pearson Education — Japan
Pearson Education Malaysia, Pte. Ltd.
Pearson Education, Upper Saddle River, New Jersey

To my son Dylan,
whose eternal optimism kept me going
during a turbulent time.

CONTENTS

PREFACE

There is a debate raging among many computer professionals over the merits (or demerits) of the UNIX operating system versus those of Microsoft's Windows 2000 (formerly NT). I address the fact that there is more than one version of UNIX in the first chapter, but for ease of communication I will simply say "the UNIX operating system" for now. This type of debate, often bordering on a religious war, is not a new phenomenon. There was once one concerning MVS and VMS, then VMS and UNIX, then UNIX and DOS, then UNIX and Windows NT. All the while, we have seen similar battles pitched over Windows, OS/2, and Mac OS.

Quite frankly, I don't care which of these operating systems and their variants is "better." Nor do a lot of businesses. The reality is that most businesses run either some form of UNIX or some form of Windows in their environments. Typically, they run both. Presumably, then, each type of operating system offers something the other does not. Granted, much of what was once considered the domain of UNIX—the Internet, for example—Windows 2000 is relatively new at. Also, Windows 2000's legacy is that of the PC world, one which most people associate with DOS, Windows, and Intel processor-based computers. So, a dichotomy has naturally developed in the last several years, and many IT departments reflect this dichotomy: They maintain independent workgroups and staffs based upon operating systems. Administrators in these camps often know little of how the "other side" works.

The times, however, they are a-changin'. Increasingly it is the network that really matters, and for that, the world has standardized on TCP/IP and the applications that run on top it: FTP, Telnet, HTTP, DNS, NFS, CIFS, and SMNP. Web servers offer applications that clients can access with a browser, regardless of what platform that browser runs on. NFS products are available for Windows systems; you can install CIFS servers on UNIX systems. IT departments typically deploy any number of platforms to support these and other network services. So the key is finding ways to minimize the impact of operating system differences so that administrators can concentrate on higher-level technical issues.

The goal of this book is to do just that. It is aimed at experienced system administrators who already know concepts such as DNS, directory services, and file systems. It also assumes that they are already familiar with one or the other respective operating systems—UNIX or Windows 2000—and that all they need is a jump start to do key tasks with the operating system that is new to them. Finally, it does indeed provide interoperability tips. It is important to note that "interoperability" is not just how the two operating systems can work together, but how they can coexist. So this book simply helps an administrator understand just how things are done, where the files and directories (or folders) are, how similarly named commands behave, what commands and utilities are equivalent. Ultimately, I hope the book will help the administrator make peaceful coexistence and interoperability a reality.

Organization of This Book

With the exception of the first two chapters, each chapter of this book contains material pertaining to Windows 2000, UNIX (usually with HP-UX examples), and interoperability. We use the four-layer TCP/IP model as the model of this book, starting with the network interface layer, the Internet layer, the transport layer, and then the application layer. Application layer issues comprise the majority of chapters.

- Chapter 1, "What Is UNIX?," is a good Chapter for administrators with mostly Windows backgrounds to read. While not a comprehensive introduction to UNIX, it will help these administrators to make sense of the examples in the book.
- Chapter 2, "What Is Windows 2000?," is for UNIX-oriented administrators. Again, it is designed to help UNIX administrators understand the Windows 2000 examples in this book rather than to be a definitive overview.
- Chapter 3, "The Network Interface Layer," examines network interface cards and drivers, and looks briefly at Ethernet and Fibre Channel technologies.
- Chapter 4, "The Internet Layer," examines a few key topics found at this layer, including ARP, ICMP, IP, routing, and Ping.
- Chapter 5, "The Transport Layer," concentrates on comparing tunable TCP parameters between Windows 2000 and HP-UX. We also look at UDP and network application programming interfaces.
- Chapter 6, "Name Resolution," begins the application layer discussion. Name resolution is a key component to network application interoperability. We look at things such as computer names, resolver, DNS, BIND, and NetBIOS.
- Chapter 7, "DHCP and DNS," looks more closely at these two technologies. Of particular importance is whether HP-UX DHCP clients can have their IP addresses registered with Microsoft's dynamic DNS.
- Chapter 8, "User Authentication," looks at topics such as NTLM, Kerberos, NIS, and pluggable application modules.

- Chapter 9, "Basic TCP/IP Utilities," compares the Windows 2000 and HP-UX versions of Finger, Ftp, Tftp, Rsh, Rcp, Rexec, and Telnet, and describes to what degree these utilities interoperate.
- Chapter 10, "Windows Services for UNIX," describes this optional product for Windows 2000, concentrating on the Telnet client and server and Server for NIS.
- Chapter 11, "NFS File Sharing," looks at employing NFS as a file sharing mechanism between Windows 2000 and HP-UX. The Windows 2000 NFS component is part of Windows Services for UNIX.
- Chapter 12, "CIFS File Sharing," compares CIFS and NFS and looks at Hewlett-Packard's CIFS/9000 product, available in both client and server versions.
- Chapter 13, "Miscellaneous Interoperability Topics," briefly describes network-attached storage, X Window, and Lpr as interoperability tools.

Acknowledgments

Many folks helped me complete this book. First, I must thank Bob Vomaske, Hewlett-Packard manager. In addition to being the best manager I've ever had, Bob offered me both time and support in abundance for this book. Right behind him is Eric Sperley, EMC manager, who encouraged me to finish the book despite having changed jobs. Then there is Jill Harry of Prentice Hall, who didn't drop this project even though it was late—several times. Also important was Rob Lucke, my technical mentor at Hewlett-Packard and fellow author, who inspired me with his work ethic and professionalism. Thanks also go to Jim Kelly, who did a technical review of the book. Finally, I must acknowledge and thank all my friends and family for their love and support, especially my son Dylan, to whom this book is dedicated.

CHAPTER 1

What Is UNIX?

Formally, the name UNIX is a registered trademark of The Open Group, an international consortium of vendors and customers dedicated to the advancement of open systems. In everyday use, however, UNIX means any variant, derivative, or clone of the operating system first developed by AT&T's Bell Laboratories in the 1970s. These variants include the commercially available HP-UX from Hewlett-Packard, AIX from IBM, Solaris from Sun Microsystems, UnixWare from SCO, and Tru64 UNIX from Compaq. These UNIX systems run mostly on RISC-based or Intel-based processors and usually contain modifications, additions, or other "enhancements" to make each of them different from the other, sometimes significantly different. Also available, for free on the Internet, are NetBSD, FreeBSD, OpenBSD, and Linux. FreeBSD runs exclusively on Intel processor-based computers, while the others run on several different platforms. Such operating systems are developed and maintained by volunteers who believe strongly in open systems and some form of open source software.

Obviously, then, there is no such thing as *the* UNIX operating system; there are many. While each has its own distinct characteristics, these operating systems have enough in common to warrant the designation of UNIX operating system. So, why is this the case? Where did UNIX come from anyway? Well—please don't groan—to answer these questions, we have to look at a little history.

1.1 In the Beginning

UNIX began as an in-house project within AT&T's Bell Telephone Labs (BTL) in 1969. Two BTL staff members, Ken Thompson and Dennis Ritchie, began writing an operating system on a DEC PDP-7, in part to run a simulation program (and game) called Space Travel. Originally, Space Travel ran on a mainframe operating system called Multics (Multiplexed Information and Computing Service), and it is as pun on this acronym that the new operating system eventually became called UNIX.

UNIX underwent several editions in the early 1970s, but it remained primarily an internal operating system to BTL until 1974. In that year, Ritchie and Thompson published a paper describing UNIX in a computer science journal, and as a result, a number of academic institutions began requesting copies of it for educational purposes. AT&T agreed to do so for a small fee, just enough to cover the cost of reproducing the tape and documentation. AT&T, operating under a consent decree at the time and really not in the computer operating system business, decided that releasing UNIX to universities in this manner *and without support* would be permissible.

So, institutions receiving a copy of UNIX in those days got not only the compiled version but the source code as well. And because AT&T provided no support for UNIX, these sites felt free to fix bugs and make changes and additions on their own. Sometimes these changes made their way back to BTL and became incorporated into the next release of UNIX. One significant source of change came from the University of California-Berkeley. In 1975, Ken Thompson went to Berkeley, his alma mater, as a visiting professor, bringing with him the latest version of UNIX. Two graduate assistants, Bill Joy and Chuck Haley, quickly started hacking on the operating system, and this work eventually led to a separate distribution of UNIX, called BSD (Berkeley Software Distribution), first appearing in 1978.

Meanwhile, work continued at AT&T, which released version 7 of UNIX in 1979. The two releases of UNIX—one from AT&T and one from Berkeley—each had enough differences to warrant the widely growing view that they were two separate entities. In reality, though, contributions to UNIX came from many sources and grew tremendously in the 1980s. Sometimes, individuals passed on their contributions to BSD, and then some of BSD's were passed on to AT&T. Companies like SCO and Microsoft got into the act, releasing a version of UNIX called Xenix in 1980. Others, like Hewlett-Packard, Sun Microsystems, DEC, Apollo, and IBM began offering UNIX systems for their hardware, each containing elements of both AT&T and BSD forms of UNIX, as well as their own enhancements.

The result is that today there are many flavors of UNIX, all of which have their roots in the work that began about 30 years ago. Over time, there have been literally hundreds of individual and corporate contributors to UNIX, creating something of an operating system mélange. While this diversity has resulted in robust and flexible operating systems, it has also led to a great deal of criticism for the lack of standards. The 1990s saw efforts to create a unified UNIX operating system, but commercial pressures have caused these efforts to fail. In 1993, AT&T sold its UNIX business to Novell, and Novell in turn sold it to SCO two years later, where the UNIX source code continues to reside. However, Novell did pass ownership of the UNIX trademark and specification to the X/Open Company, one of the groups formed to create UNIX standards. In 1996, X/Open merged with the Open Software Foundation (OSF) to form The Open Group, where the trademark resides today.

1.2 The New Face of UNIX

Technically speaking, UNIX is proprietary software. SCO owns the UNIX originally created by AT&T. The Open Group owns the UNIX trademark and governs the UNIX name. Hewlett-Packard owns HP-UX, IBM owns AIX, Sun Microsystems owns Solaris, SGI owns IRIX, SCO owns UnixWare, and Compaq owns Tru64 UNIX. You cannot use, copy, or distribute any of these operating systems without a license (which you pay for) from these vendors. This fact irritates a lot of folks, particularly those who were involved in the early days of the modern computer revolution, which I date back to the early 1970s. (Yes, this is a moot point.) One such individual is Richard Stallman.

In 1983, Stallman, then an employee of the MIT Artificial Intelligence Lab, announced to a couple of newsgroups that he was going to "write a complete UNIX-compatible software system called GNU (for Gnu's Not UNIX), and give it away free to everyone who can use it." You can find the original message on the Free Software Foundation's Web site at *www.fsf.org*. He was discouraged by the shrinking world of cooperative programming that typified his computing experience in the 1970s. In those days, according to Stallman, programmers, or more accurately, hackers, willingly shared software with each other just because it was the right thing to do. He and other programmers had become increasingly dismayed by the trend on the part of many of the large computer companies to maximize their profits by restricting the use of their software, particularly operating systems. So, in January 1984, Stallman left his job and began writing GNU software.

The GNU was, in effect, to be a system that looked like UNIX, acted like UNIX, and smelled like UNIX, but was in fact *not* UNIX. Stallman said in his announcement, "GNU will be able to run UNIX programs, but will not be identical to UNIX." In other words, he was not going to take AT&T's source code and modify it. Instead, he and others would simply redevelop all the features of a UNIX system. This meant not only a fully functional kernel, but all the utilities and programs one would expect from a UNIX system: compilers, editors, shells. So, the first pieces of GNU software he created included GCC, a C compiler, and GNU Emacs, a text editor.

In 1985, Stallman and others founded the Free Software Foundation (FSF), a tax-exempt organization dedicated to free software development and distribution. FSF has written a number of pieces of GNU software, slowly building up the packages that typify a UNIX distribution. By 1990, the GNU suite was nearly complete, but without a key component: a kernel. Though the FSF had (and still has) a kernel under development, the GNU system has since linked up with, quite successfully, the kernel developed by Linus Torvalds, known as Linux. Torvalds began writing his kernel in 1991, using GNU tools to flesh out his system. Today, GNU tools are important parts of any Linux distribution. For this reason, the FSF rightly claims that references to Linux be designated as GNU/Linux.

1.3 UNIX and Open Source Software

GNU and Linux systems, as well as others such as NetBSD and FreeBSD, are the result of efforts to provide free software to the public. To what extent *free* means depends on who does the talking. In this context, however, free means software offered to the public free of charge and that can be modified and distributed by anyone in any manner. This, in my opinion, is the essence of the *open source software* movement. The FSF's GNU *General Public License* (GPL) parallels this description. Software covered by the GPL

- may be distributed and used free of charge.
- may in turn be distributed by others for a fee, provided that those who do so do not restrict further distribution and use.
- can be modified to create new versions of the software, but these new versions are also covered by the GPL.
- is copyrighted to the developers of the software and is not in the public domain.
- either must have the source code included in a distribution or have it available for download.

Linux is covered by the GPL, so it can be considered open source software. Also, because it was not derived from any licensed source code and is not registered with The Open Group, it *cannot* in the strictest sense be accurately designated as a UNIX system. Rather, it is a UNIX *clone*, meaning that it looks and smells like UNIX, but it really just "mimics the form and function of a UNIX system." (See "What about All Those Flavors?" at The Open Group's Web site at *www.opengroup.org*.)

1.4 The Elements of UNIX

So, we now know, more or less, the origins of UNIX. As you can see, there really is no such thing as *the* UNIX operating system. For convenience, I use only one form of UNIX for this book, namely HP-UX version 11. HP-UX is based on the UNIX System V Release 4 operating system and includes important features from the Fourth Berkeley Software Distribution. Most HP-UX commands are the same as most UNIX implementations. However, you may have to consult the *man* pages for your particular system.

All UNIX implementations share some general characteristics, and so what follows is a brief description of those characteristics. If you are mostly a DOS/Windows person, you should read through this section before looking at later chapters.

1.4.1 The Kernel

Every UNIX system has a file, loaded into memory upon system startup, called the *kernel*. HP-UX calls this file */stand/vmunix*; Red Hat Linux calls it */boot/vmlinuz*. In one sense, the kernel can be considered the operating system itself, since it talks directly to the hardware, schedules processes, handles interrupts, and the like. However, most people think of an operating system as being more than just the kernel; it also includes utilities, commands, compilers, libraries, and editors. So, in another sense, the kernel can be thought of as the memory-resident portion of the operating system.

But there is no doubt that the kernel controls the interaction between user programs and the hardware. You, as a user, do not access the kernel directly. Instead, you run a command or application that can do so by making a *system call,* one of the kernel routines residing in memory. To access certain pieces of the hardware, such as a tape drive, the driver for that device must be built into the kernel and must have at least one *device file* serving as a kernel pointer to the driver somewhere on disk.

Traditionally, UNIX systems have required drivers for all the devices you use to be built directly into the kernel, creating a single, *monolithic* kernel. Adding new devices to this kind of kernel requires you to compile a new one that includes the new drivers, moving it into the appropriate location on disk, and then rebooting. Recently, however, UNIX systems have seen the emergence of *dynamically loadable kernel modules,* modules that can be added to the running kernel to support devices that may be used only sparingly. Having dynamically loadable kernel modules keeps the size of the kernel proper small, using fewer computing resources. HP-UX 11 supports such modules.

1.4.2 The Shell

A shell is an interface between you, the user, and the kernel. It enables you to "do things" with the system. Traditionally, UNIX users have thought of the shell as a *command-line interpreter.* In other words, the shell would provide a command prompt, waiting for you to issue some kind of command. The command may be a built-in shell command (thus residing in memory when the shell is loaded) or it may be found on disk. The shell would then run these commands on your behalf. (If you are a long-time DOS user, then you know that its shell is *COMMAND.COM.*) More recently, however, the shell can take the form of some kind of *graphical user interface* (GUI), enabling you to carry out functions without having to issue something on a command line. However, even these functions often require a traditional UNIX shell to execute.

There are many shells available to UNIX users. Each flavor of UNIX usually has what is known as the *default shell*, the shell used by system management scripts. The default shell is also what users get when their account is first created, unless they specify differently. Available shells include the Bourne shell, the C shell, the Korn shell, the POSIX shell, and BASH (the Bourne-again shell, similar to the Bourne shell). Each shell has its own built-in commands, scripting language, command prompts, and special features. Which one you use is up to you, but to keep you from having to learn all the shells and then choosing, consider the following:

- The Bourne shell is nearly universal on all versions of UNIX but is being obsoleted on HP-UX because it lacks many features contained in the POSIX and Korn shells.
- The Korn shell is a superset of the Bourne shell, with some nifty features like command history recall and editing.
- The POSIX shell is the default shell on HP-UX, and is similar to the Korn shell.
- BASH is the default shell for Linux and combines the best features of the Bourne and C shells. It is not available on HP-UX.
- The C shell incorporates a command history buffer, C language-like syntax, and job control facilities. It is offered on all UNIX systems.

1.4.2.1 Terminal Emulators

So, how do you access a shell? When you create a UNIX account, one of the things you must specify is the path name of the shell that will run when the newly created user logs in. On older UNIX systems, you logged into some kind of text-based terminal, after which the login prompt disappeared and a blank screen with either a *$* or a *%* command prompt took its place. This is frequently still the case on large server systems, where fancy graphics displays are usually unnecessary. If you use a current UNIX workstation, however, you are likely to login to some kind of graphical user interface based on the X Window System. Here, once you login, you get a number of windows, including something usually called a *terminal emulator.* A terminal emulator is a window that mimics one of the older terminals, most often the DEC vt100 terminal.

Figure 1–1 displays an example of an *xterm,* a vt100 emulator. This example comes from a Linux system; therefore the default shell is BASH. The default prompt for BASH is *bash$,* but here it has been set to reflect the current user name and base name of the current working directory. Of course, *xterm* can run any of the other shells, and there are other terminal emulators out there, depending on the flavor of UNIX you run.

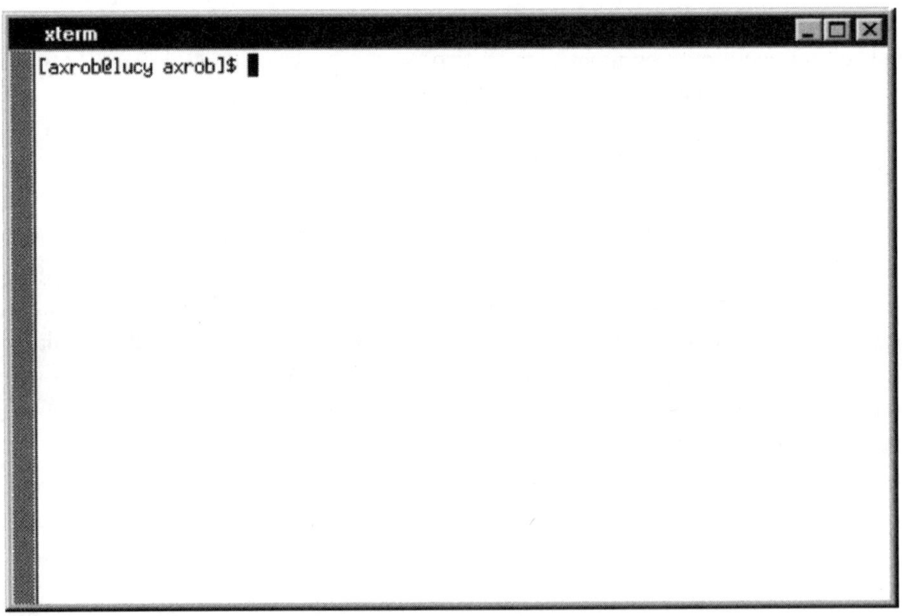

Figure 1–1 An *xterm* terminal emulator.

1.4.2.2 Entering Commands

If you want to administer a UNIX system efficiently, with lots of power and flexibility at your fingertips, then it is a good idea to master one of the shells. Although some folks might scoff at a command-line method of system administration, you can do so much more, *and do so quickly,* if you get good at a shell. This is one of the golden rules of UNIX system administration.

When you type a command, remember that in UNIX all names are *case sensitive*. So, if you type *LS*, thinking that it is the same as the *ls* command, you will be sorely disappointed. Also, most UNIX command options are preceded by a minus sign (–). For example, the command *ls –l* at a command line prompt will give you a detailed listing of the files and directories contained in your current working directory. Finally, like DOS, UNIX has the concept of a command path, so if you get some kind of "not found" message after typing a command (assuming you spelled it correctly and had the right case), then you will have to find the full path name of the command and type that.

1.4.2.3 Getting Help

At a shell prompt, you can get online documentation of any command by using the *man* command. For example, if you wanted more information on the *ls* command, you would type *man ls* at the command prompt. This will provide you with the official "manual page" (hence the name of the command) for that command. So, if I say, "Check the *man* page for the *chown* command for more information," I mean to type *man chown* at the command line. A word of warning about *man* pages, however: They tend to be written so that only programmers can understand them. Once you slog through enough of a *man* page to get the basic idea of what a command can do, scroll to the bottom of the page and look at the examples that are usually provided. Doing so can save you a lot of time in trying to get something done.

1.4.2.4 A Note on File Editing

Effective UNIX system administration depends not only on using a lot command-line stuff, it also requires a good deal of text file editing. With the exception of AIX, which has a configuration database somewhat analogous to Windows 2000's Registry, UNIX systems get configuration data from text files. To customize UNIX, you edit files. Usually, a vendor's system management tool will do a lot of this for you, but sooner or later, you will have to edit a file yourself. There are often religious debates over the merits and demerits of the various UNIX text editors, *vi* and *emacs* being the most popular. Which one you choose does not really matter. Although the fancy GUIs that come with UNIX systems today usually have very easy-to-use editors, using something like *vi*, though archaic at first glance, makes managing a mixture of UNIX systems a lot easier. To get really good at UNIX, learn a good editor. This is another golden rule.

1.4.3 File Systems

The term *file system* (sometimes spelled as one word: filesystem) can refer to either the layout of files and directories on a system or to how the files are actually stored and referenced on a single disk or partition of a disk.

1.4.3.1 Directory Tree

Files and directories are located in a hierarchical tree structure that most people are familiar with, even if their only experience is with DOS or Windows systems. One significant difference on UNIX systems is that file and directory path names are delineated with forward slashes (/)

rather than back slashes (\). Also, path names do not have drive letters or server names associated with them. Why that is the case, I'll explain in a minute. Table 1–1 lists some of the more significant directories in HP-UX.

Table 1–1 Important HP-UX Directories

Directory	Contains
/bin	Essential command binaries for all users. In HP-UX this is a link to */usr/bin.*
/stand	System-specific kernel configuration and binary files.
/dev	Device files.
/etc	Host-specific system and application configuration files.
/home	Default location for user home directories.
/lib	Essential shared libraries and kernel modules. In HP-UX this is a link to */usr/lib.*
/opt	Optional applications.
/sbin	Commands and scripts essential to booting and shutting down a system.
/tmp	Temporary files.
/usr	The bulk of the operating system, including commands, libraries, and documentation.
/var	Multipurpose log, temporary, transient, variable-sized, and spool files.

1.4.3.2 File System Formats

The term *file system* can also refer to a formatted area on some type of media for the purpose of storing files. This media can be CD-ROMs, floppy drives, hard disks, or partitions of hard disks. There are many different file system formats, but to a user, these formats are transparent, as long as the operating system knows how to access them. HP-UX recognizes the following file systems:

HFS, the High-Performance File System. The HFS physically resides on a mass storage device, usually on a hard disk. Earlier versions were known as the UNIX File System (UFS).

NFS, the Network File System. NFS is a remote file system accessed over a network. The local system treats NFS as local.

CD-ROM, also known as the ISO 9660 file system, makes the files and directories on a compact disk available to the local system.
JFS, the Journaled File System. JFS is an extent-based journaling file system that offers fast performance and file system recovery.

Linux recognizes NFS and ISO 9660 file systems, as well as many others. The default file system on Linux is the Second Extended file system, also known by the abbreviation *ext2*. Linux can also access MS-DOS, Windows 98, Windows NT, OS/2, and Apple Macintosh file systems.

Hard disk file systems are formatted areas that can encompass one or more entire disks, a single partition on a single disk, a single partition spanning more than one disk, or a collection of small units that collectively form a *logical partition*. These file systems are the physical containers of files. To access these files, the entire file system must be attached, or *mounted,* to a directory in the root partition. If there is a single file system for a single file hard disk in a system, then the entire contents of the file system are mounted to the */* directory. If there are multiple file systems on one or more hard disks, then each of these file systems, once mounted, form physical pieces of the virtual file system tree. In this way, UNIX avoids the use of drive letters in its file system tree, because each file system is mounted on a directory in the root partition, *regardless of its location, be it a logical volume, partition, or remote file system.*

If this seems confusing, then consider this simple example. Let's say you have a UNIX system with a single hard disk sliced up into three partitions. One file system contains the *root partition*, one contains all the files and directories belonging to the */usr* directory, and one contains something call a *swap partition*. When this system boots, the first partition to be mounted is the root partition. If for some reason the partition containing the */usr* directory does not mount, you would have access to nothing in */usr*. Assuming that all the commands you need to access the system can be found in the root directory, then a listing of the files in */* would show things like */bin, /etc, /tmp, /opt, /sbin*—and even */usr*! But whereas all these directories would contain files, */usr* would not. Why? Because the physical location of those files, the file system, is not mounted. Mounting this file system, either by rebooting or doing so from the command line, would then result in a */usr* directory full of stuff. By the way, the swap partition does not contain a file system. Rather, it contains space for the operating system to page memory.

1.4.4 Permissions

One of the hallmarks of a UNIX system has been its multiuser capability: More than one user can access a UNIX system, and it has been that way for a long time. So, UNIX has always had a permission scheme to keep users from stepping on each other's toes and to keep them from destroying the system by messing with essential system files. The basic permission scheme is the same for all types of UNIX, though other pieces of software, such as NFS, can add to them. Permissions can be a complex topic, but you do need to know the following basics. The rest of the permissions section is derived from Hewlett-Packard's manual *Using HP-UX*, which says pretty much the same thing here but talks about the *ll* command, which does the same thing as *ls –l* but is only an HP-UX command.

When a user logs into a system, usually one of two mechanisms authenticate that user: the password and group files (*/etc/passwd* and */etc/group*) or the Network Information Service (NIS). Both of these mechanisms establish the user and group identifiers (UIDs and GIDs) of each authenticated user. Among other attributes, the file system stores the UID and GID of the owner of each file and directory in an on-disk structure called an *inode*, sometimes called *file system metadata*. Also stored for each file is its permissions.

Three classes of users can access files and directories: *owner, group,* and *other.* Owner is usually the person who created the file, group is several users grouped together and who share permissions, and other is all other users. For each of these classes there are three types of access permissions: *read, write,* and *execute*. These permissions mean different things, depending on whether you are talking about files or about directories. Table 1–2 describes these differences.

Table 1–2 Standard UNIX Permissions

Permission	Means This for a Directory	Means This for a File
read (r)	Users can view names of files and directories in that directory.	Users can view the contents of the file.
write (w)	Users can create, rename, or remove files or directories contained in that directory.	Users can change the contents of the file.
execute (x)	Users can view the contents of files within the directory, and run commands, scripts, and programs within that directory.	Users can run the file (execute it) by typing the file name at the command prompt.

To determine a file's permissions, you use the *ls –l* command, which displays the following information:

- Whether the item is a file or directory
- The access permissions for each of the three classes of users (owner, group, and other)
- Number of links
- Name of the owner
- Name of the group
- Size in bytes
- Date and time of last modification

For example, if you type the following command:

```
$ ls -l myfile
```

you will get output something like this:

```
-rw-r--r--  1  leslie  users  154  Nov 4 10:18 myfile
```

The first dash on the left indicates that *myfile* is a file. Were it a directory, you would see a *d* in place of the dash. Each of the other items is explained in the Table 1–3.

Table 1–3 Explanation of *ls –l* Output

Output	Meaning	Explanation
`rw-r--r--`	Permissions	Permissions are displayed in groups of three. Owner *leslie* has read and write permission. Group *users* and others have read-only permission. If a permission is not allowed, a dash appears in place of the letter.
`1`	Number of links	Each entry has at least one link.
`leslie`	The owner of the file	*leslie* is owner.
`users`	Group	These are the permissions of the *users* group.
`154`	Size of the file in bytes	A very small file.
`Nov 4 10:18`	Modification date	If the time of last modification was more than six months ago, the year is substituted for the hour and minute.
`myfile`	The file name	*myfile* is the item being listed.

If you use the *ls –l* command by itself, you will see a listing of files in the current working directory. If you supply that command with the name of a directory as an argument, then you will get a listing of the contents of that directory. If you want to see the permissions on a directory without seeing a listing of all its files, use the *ls –ld* command.

HP-UX supports commands that alter permissions: *chown* to change a file's ownership, *chgrp* to change a file's group, and *chmod* to change the actual permissions. However, the way in which each of these commands behaves differs between the two operating systems. Check the *man* pages on the respective system for more information.

1.4.5 Networking

UNIX and TCP/IP are blood brothers. In the mid 1970s, the Defense Department's Advanced Research Projects Agency (DARPA) funded Bolt, Beranek, and Newman (BBN) to develop TCP/IP for UNIX, and the University of California-Berkeley later integrated this software into BSD UNIX. Since then, UNIX networking has meant TCP/IP, and, until recently, TCP/IP was driven by the spread of UNIX and the Internet.

Modern UNIX systems support a variety of network interface layer devices and protocols: Ethernet, Token Ring, ATM, ISDN, and others. They also support either SLIP or PPP. Networking applications include NFS for file sharing, and NIS for the sharing of key information, such as passwords.

One extremely important application is the X Window System. Though it is often thought of as a graphical system, it really is a networking protocol because it separates the client application from the display server. The client runs natively on a system and connects to its display via the network, even if the display is on a separate system. All current forms of UNIX support X Window, and it is the basis for all GUIs in use today, including the Common Desktop Environment found on HP-UX, AIX, and Solaris, and the GNOME and KDE found on Linux.

1.4.6 System Management Tools

Even though I've sung the praises of command-line system administration, there is much to be said about the graphical system administration tools provided by most versions of UNIX. HP-UX has SAM, the System Administration Manager. AIX has SMIT, System Management Interface Tool. Many Linux distributions include a similar tool called Linuxconf. These tools can help you do tasks for which you know *what* needs to be done (for example, mount a file system) but you are not sure exactly *how* it should be done. Since I will be using HP-UX for most of my UNIX examples, I will refer to the SAM tool frequently.

1.5 Is There More?

Oh, yes. A lot more. But this gives you a rough idea of what UNIX is about. If you are a UNIX newbie and have read all of this chapter, then you should be able to comprehend what follows. Remember, this book is designed to get you functional in a hurry. If you need more information, please consult the references at the end of each chapter.

References

1. Morris I. Bolsky, David G. Korn, *The KornShell:Command and Programming Language*. (Prentice Hall, 1989).
2. Charles Fernandez, *Configuring CDE: The Common Desktop Environment.* (Prentice Hall PTR, 1996)
3. Don Libes & Sandy Ressler, *Life with UNIX: A Guide For Everyone*. (Prentice Hall, 1989).

4. Evi Nemeth, Garth Snyder, Scott Seebass, Trent R. Hein, *UNIX® System Administration Handbook,* 2nd ed. (Prentice Hall PTR, 1995).
5. Uresh Vahalia, *UNIX Internals: The New Frontiers.* (Prentice Hall, 1996).
6. Matt Welsh, Matthias Kalle Dalheimer, and Lar Kaufman, *Running Linux,* 3rd ed. (O'Reilly, 1999).

CHAPTER 2

What Is Windows 2000?

If you are a long-time UNIX system administrator, Windows 2000 may seem like a fortified version of Windows 98. Or, you may think that Windows 2000, installed mostly on Intel processor-based systems, is directly descended from the old DOS world. Windows 2000, built on NT technology, however, is a completely different beast from both DOS and Windows 98. So how did it come to be? Again, let's look at a little history.

2.1 A New Operating System

For a long time (in computer-industry time), when someone thought of a PC, he or she usually thought of an Intel processor-based computer running some form of DOS. Even Windows 95 and Windows 98 were based on DOS. However, to say that Windows 2000 is a PC operating system is somewhat misleading. For one thing, it is not based on DOS. For another, Windows 2000 can run on more than just an Intel processor. In 1988, Microsoft began working on a new operating system that would have a number of highly desirable features:

- The ability to run on different processors
- Be multiuser and multitasking
- Meet C2-level security
- Be scalable for the enterprise
- The ability to support legacy DOS and Windows applications

It was designed to be an operating system for high-end workstations and servers where UNIX had long dominated. (Today, Windows 2000 runs on "everyday" PCs and laptops.) To lead this effort, Microsoft recruited David Cutler from Digital Equipment Corporation (DEC). Cutler was an experienced operating system designer who knew a lot about things like multitasking, but it took him and his team five years to release the first version of what was to become Windows NT.

Microsoft released two flavors of its operating system, Windows NT 3.1 and NT Advanced Server 3.1, in the summer of 1993. The version number 3.1 was chosen to coincide with that of the 16-bit Windows operating system prevalent throughout the world at the time. It also implied that this new operating system was not an unstable 1.0 release. It was slow, using a lot of memory and requiring much in the way of computer hardware, but it was a significant achievement, nonetheless. It was the first 32-bit Windows operating system, and it could run on non-Intel-based processors: MIPS, Alpha, and Power. Though not a big commercial success, it was a propitious start in the effort to create an alternative to UNIX.

From 1993 to 1996, Microsoft released three major versions of NT: versions 3.5, 3.51, and 4.0. Version 4.0 has been by far the most successful version of NT. It offered more device support, default TCP/IP networking, Internet services, and a Windows 95 interface. These and other features have made Windows NT 4.0 the operating system of choice for business desktops, cutting severely into the UNIX desktop business since its release in 1996.

The next generation of NT technology is Windows 2000, known unofficially as Windows NT 5 until a few months before its official release in February 2000. There are several versions of Windows 2000:

- **Windows 2000 Professional.** Designed for business desktops and laptops.
- **Windows 2000 Server.** Designed for workgroup and small business network services.
- **Windows 2000 Advanced Server.** Designed for e-business and line-of-business applications.
- **Windows 2000 Datacenter Server.** Designed for large systems running critical applications such as OLTP and datawarehousing.

Table 2–1 comes from the Microsoft Windows 2000 Web site and summarizes the features of the operating systems.

2.2 Windows 2000 Architecture

Figure 2–1 depicts the major components of Windows 2000. At the lowest level is the hardware itself, most often an Intel processor-based system. Above that is the Hardware Abstraction Layer (HAL), a layer of software designed to hide hardware differences from the rest of the operating system. At the next level, we have both device drivers and the kernel. Herein is an important difference between most versions of UNIX, including HP-UX, and Windows 2000. The Windows 2000 kernel is a microkernel; it does not include device drivers. Therefore, the kernel remains small, taking care of the most basic of operating system functions. As pointed out in Chapter 1, "What Is UNIX?," most UNIX kernels require that a device's driver be compiled into the kernel. Moreover, whereas UNIX kernels handle I/O and memory management, in Windows 2000, these functions are separated into *subsystems*.

Table 2–1 Differences Between Windows 2000 Versions

	Windows Professional	Windows Server	Windows Advanced Server	Windows Datacenter Server
Target audiences	Business desktops, notebooks	File, print, intranet, networking	Line of business, e-commerce	Large critical applications: OLTP, data warehouses, ASPs, and ISPs
CPUs supported by 1 system	2	4	8	32
Memory supported	4 GB	4 GB	8 GB	64 GB
Clustering	None	None	Two-node failover, 32-node network load balancing	Cascading fail-over among four nodes, 32-node network load balancing

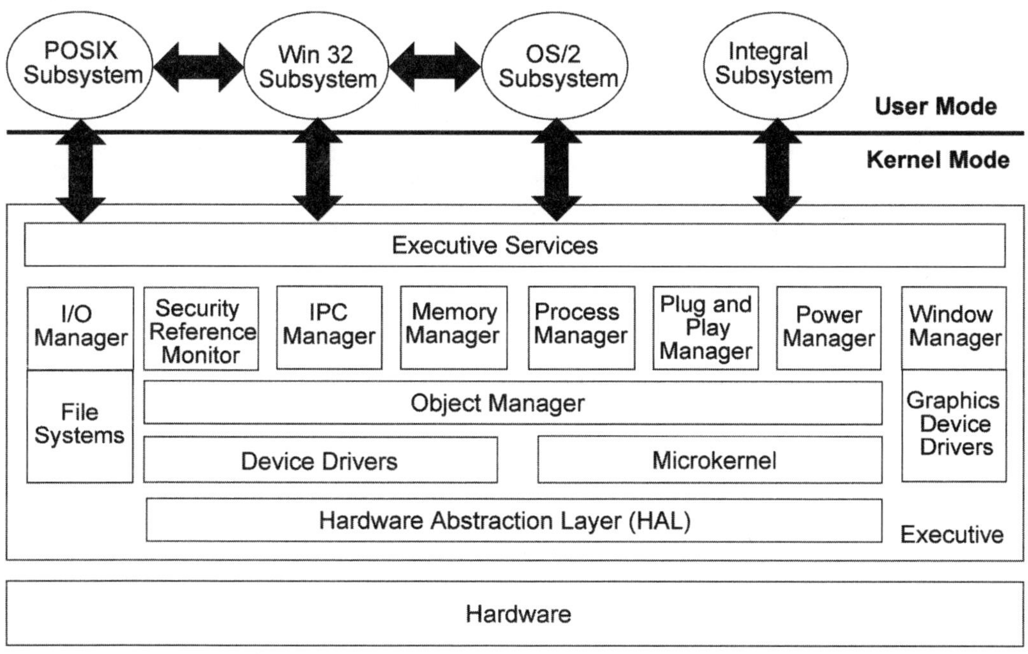

Figure 2–1 Windows 2000 architecture.[1]

Therefore, while it is possible to refer to the kernel as the operating system in UNIX (which a lot of people do), in Windows 2000, the operating system is more than just the kernel. It consists of the HAL, the microkernel, device drivers, and several kernel-mode components, such as the I/O Manager, Memory Manager, and the Process Manager.

Running in user mode are the POSIX, Win 32, and OS/2 subsystems. The POSIX subsystem provides APIs to enable POSIX-based applications to run. The OS/2 subsystem provides a set of APIs for 16-bit, character-based applications. Win 32 is a subsystem that provides an environment for running Win 16 and MS-DOS applications, as well as Win32-based applications. Also running in user mode are several integral subsystems. These subsystems perform essential operating system functions such as security services and the server and workstation services.

2.3 Elements of Windows 2000

Please note that in this book, the term *directory* is used interchangeably with the term *folder*. (I will also use the terms *login* and *logon* interchangeably.)

2.3.1 The Registry

Windows 2000, like NT, keeps hardware and software settings in a hierarchical database called the Registry. Other versions of Windows kept this information in text files, often ending in *.ini*. UNIX systems, with the exception of AIX, still rely heavily on configuration files. However, you cannot change the contents of the Registry using a text editor. Instead, you must use the Registry Editor, *regedt32.exe*.

In Windows 2000, the Registry contains information about virtually everything installed on a particular system, things such as hardware (for example, CPU and bus type), device drivers, applications, and network settings. The following describes the components that use the Registry. (Taken from the *Microsoft Windows 2000 Beta Training Kit*, pp. 117–118.)[2]

> **Windows NT Kernel**
>
> During system startup, the kernel, *ntoskrnl.exe*, reads information from the Registry, including the device drivers to load and the order in which they should be loaded. The kernel writes information about itself to the Registry, such as the version number.
>
> **Device Drivers**
>
> Device drivers receive configuration parameters from the Registry and also write information to it. A device driver informs the Registry which system resources it is using, such as hardware interrupts or DMA channels. Device drivers also report discovered configuration data.

Setup Programs
A setup program can add new configuration data to the Registry when it installs hardware or software. It can also query the Registry to determine whether required components have been installed.

Ntdetect.com
On Intel-based computers, *ntdetect.com* scans the system for hardware. It adds configuration information to the Registry for components it discovers. RISC-based computers extract such data from the computer firmware.

Hardware Profiles
Computers with two or more hardware configurations use hardware profiles. When Windows 2000 starts, the user selects a hardware profile. Windows 2000, with the Registry, then configures the system accordingly.

User Profiles
Windows 2000 creates and maintains user environmental settings in a user profile. When a user logs on, the system caches the profile in the Registry. Windows 2000 first writes user configuration changes to the Registry and then to the user profile.

2.3.2 Active Directory

Active Directory is Windows 2000's directory services. Directory services enables users and applications to locate network resources, including user data, servers, and printers. Active Directory uses the Domain Name System (DNS) to locate network names and Lightweight Directory Access Protocol (LDAP) or Hypertext Transfer Protocol (HTTP) for obtaining resource information. Because of its reliance on DNS, Active Directory domain names coincide with DNS names, though an Active Directory domain is not exactly the same thing as a DNS domain.

2.3.3 User Interfaces

In Chapter 1, we saw that UNIX traditionally has provided a default shell with which to run commands and applications. In recent years, HP-UX, AIX, and Solaris have provided a graphical user interface (GUI) called the Common Desktop Environment (CDE), which makes a number of day-to-day user tasks easier. Additionally, all major forms of UNIX provide some kind of system management tool, such as SAM in HP-UX and SMIT in AIX, to help simplify system administration. Windows 2000 provides similar tools: a command interpreter, a GUI, and a system administration tool known as the Microsoft Management Console (MMC).

2.3.3.1 Command Interpreter

The Windows 2000 application *C:>%SystemRoot%/System32/cmd.exe* starts a window running what looks like an MS-DOS command prompt. (See Figure 2–2.) Actually, though, it is a 32-bit program that, according to the Help page, "retains and enhances almost all the functionality of

Figure 2–2 The Windows 2000 command interpreter.

MS-DOS." However, a number of MS-DOS commands are not available on the Windows 2000 command line. Though not fully scriptable, the Windows 2000 command interpreter supports batch commands, including *if* and *for.* For more information, see the Windows 2000 Command Reference Main Page in the Help utility.

Windows 2000 is *not* case sensitive when you enter commands. If you type *DIR* at a command prompt, you will get a directory listing. You will get the same thing if you type *dir.* However, Windows 2000 *is* case retaining. In other words, if you were to type *mkdir BoB* at the prompt and then do a directory listing, you would see a directory named *BoB*. However, if you were to change your directory to *BoB* by typing *cd bob*, your command prompt would show *C:\BoB>*. Therefore, Windows 2000 retains the case of a file or directory name for display purposes only.

As in UNIX, you must be aware of what your PATH variable is set to. If, for example, the following command is not in your command path, you will see something like:

```
C:\>QTW_203.EXE
'QTW_203.EXE' is not recognized as an internal or external command,
operable program or batch file.
```

You can set the PATH variable by right clicking on **My Computer,** selecting **Properties,** clicking on the **Advanced** tab, and then selecting the **Environmental Variables** button. The PATH variable is found in the System Variables box. See Figure 2–3.

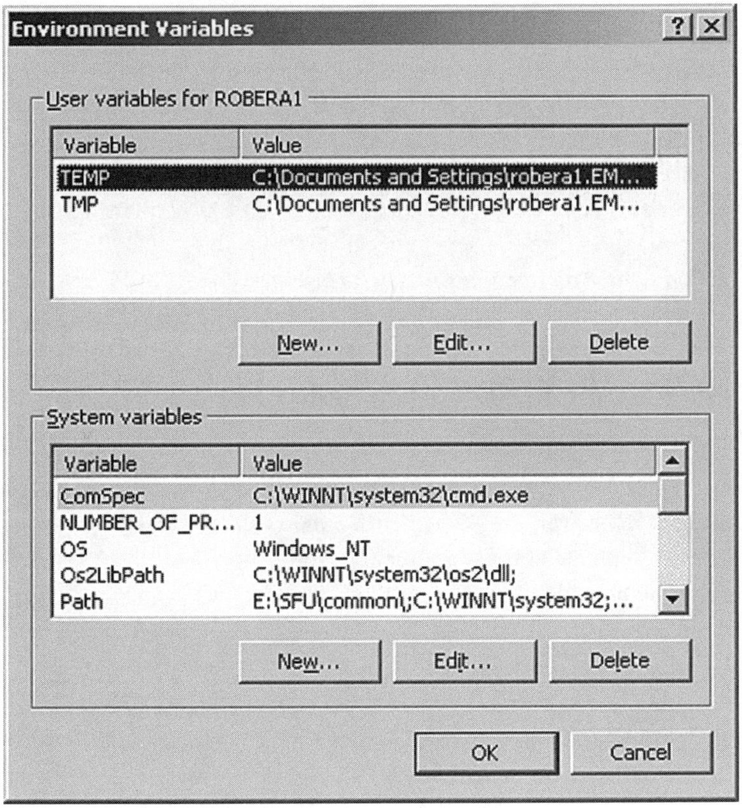

Figure 2–3 The Environmental Variables box.

Windows 2000 commands, like UNIX commands, take options (sometimes called *flags* or *switches*). Normally, these commands follow the DOS convention: Options are designated by forward slashes (/). However, the following TCP/IP utilities, perhaps reflecting their UNIX roots (for most of the commands, at least), have options designated by the minus sign (-):

- arp
- ftp
- finger
- hostname
- lpq
- lpr
- rcp
- rexec
- route
- ipconfig
- nbtstat
- netsh
- netstat
- nslookup
- ping
- rsh
- tftp
- tracert

2.3.3.2 Windows 2000 GUI

One of the great appeals of Windows NT and Windows 2000 is that they employ GUIs similar to those found on Windows 95 and Windows 98. Most user and administrative activities do not require a command-line interface. However, while both UNIX and Windows 2000 systems provide easy-to-use GUIs, the graphical subsystems are vastly different. As you might recall, UNIX GUIs are based on the X Window system, a network-based display system, while Windows 2000 employs its own Window Manager as a component of the Executive. With X Window, "a client program executing natively on computer A can run separately from its windowing GUI on computer B across a network." (Taken from *Architecting Enterprise Solutions with UNIX Networking* by John Blommers.) In Windows 2000 this is not the case; both the client and server functionality of Window Manager run on the same computer. Therefore, you cannot run an application on one system and display it on another, *unless* you deploy Windows 2000 Terminal Services.

Terminal Services provides similar functionality to X Window: It runs on a server (any of the Windows 2000 server family) and provides a client system with an application that runs on the server but displays on the client. However, only Microsoft Windows-based clients can connect to Terminal Services without a separate software purchase. You simply load the Microsoft Remote Desktop Protocol (RDP) client available on the server. Other clients, such as Macintosh and UNIX systems, require the purchase of a client from Citrix Systems.

2.3.4 The MMC

The MMC provides a way to centralize Windows 2000 administrative tools, including third-party tools. The MMC itself does not do any administrative tasks; it is simply an interface. Figure 2–4 shows a predefined MMC called Computer Management. Predefined consoles are created when you install Windows 2000. Each of the applications displayed in a console is known as a *snap-in*. You can create custom consoles containing only those tools you want to use or those that certain users can use. Also, you can use MMCs to administer remote systems.

2.3.5 Getting Help

To get help on basic Windows 2000 operation, do a **Start→Help**. You will get a graphical help system that includes topics like the ones you see in Figure 2–5. The equivalent of UNIX *man* pages is the *help* command you type at the command prompt. The syntax is *help [command]*. For example,

```
C:\>help diskcopy
Copies the contents of one floppy disk to another.

DISKCOPY [drive1: [drive2:]] [/V]

  /V   Verifies that the information is copied correctly.

The two floppy disks must be the same type.
You may specify the same drive for drive1 and drive2.
```

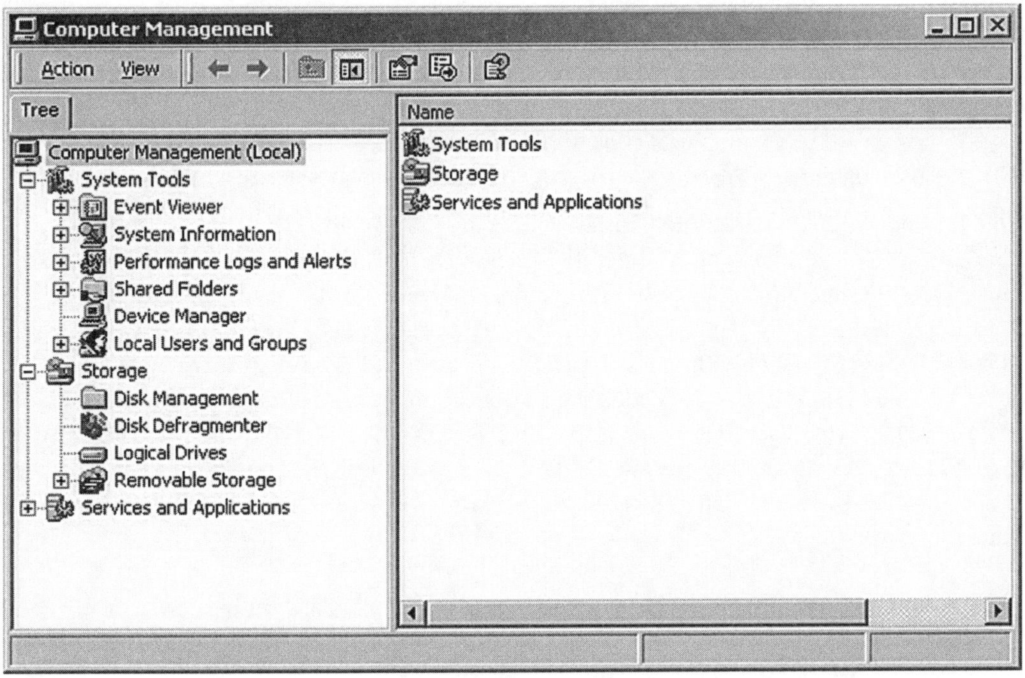

Figure 2–4 A sample MMC. This one is predefined and is called Computer Management.

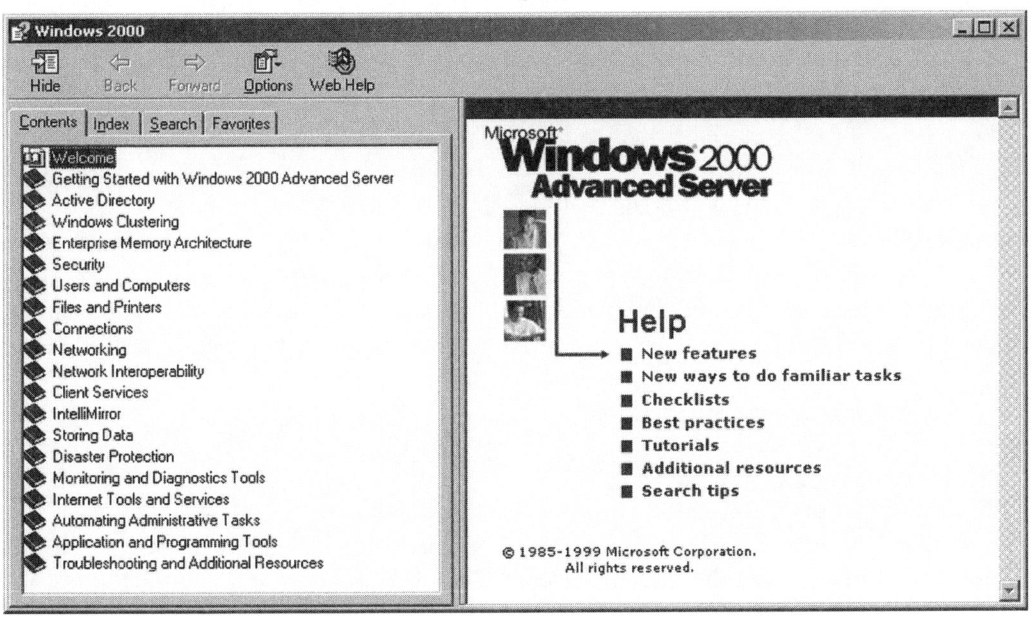

Figure 2–5 The Windows 2000 help screen.

You can also see commands using the Windows 2000 Command Reference, accessible through the **Help** utility. To get to the Command Reference, **Start→Help**, choose the **Contents** tab, click on **Troubleshooting and Additional Resources**, and the select **Additional Resources**.

2.3.6 Directory Tree

Though Windows 2000 is an entirely different operating system than DOS, it has inherited many of its characteristics, including a directory structure that has a drive letter at the root level. Unlike in UNIX, there is no single root directory; there are, in fact, many root directories, 24 altogether (represented by the letters C–Z). This drive scheme goes back to the days when PCs did not have hard drives, only floppies. Typically, a system had two floppy drives, one labeled *A:* and one labeled *B:*. You usually loaded your application, such as WordStar, from a floppy in drive A and kept your data files on the floppy in drive B. When hard disks began to show up on these systems, they did not replace the A and B floppy drives. Therefore, the hard disk became the *C:* drive. The A and B letters are still reserved for floppies. Commonly found directories include

Documents and Settings. This directory contains user data and settings on the local computer. However, because of Microsoft's IntelliMirror technology, both of these items can exist somewhere else on the network.

Program Files. This contains applications installed on the local system. However, you can put applications on any drive and in any directory.

The value of the %SystemRoot% variable. This is the directory that contains the Windows 2000 system files. You specify this location when you install the operating system; otherwise, the directory will be *\WINNT*.

2.3.7 File System Formats

Windows 2000 supports the NTFS and two file allocation table (FAT) file systems: FAT16 and FAT32. The latter two are available primarily to allow for dual booting of systems. However, the real workhorse of Windows 2000 file systems is NTFS. This file system offers a number of features and benefits and is the only one you should consider if you are not dual booting and are managing a network of more than just a few machines. Features of NTFS include the following:

File and folder-level security. You can apply permissions on both files and directories, much like you do in UNIX.

Disk compression. You can set an NTFS volume to be compressed to save disk space. Not all NTFS volumes have to be in a compressed state, however.

Disk quotas. UNIX file systems have long supported quotas to keep a few users from eating most of a group's disk space. Windows 2000 NTFS allows you to do the same. You can set quotas for all users or for individuals.

Encryption. Encryption is available for physical volumes and helps protect you if disk drives are stolen from any of your systems. It provides an additional security mechanism to access control lists (ACLs).

2.3.7.1 NTFS Security and Permissions

When a user logs into a Windows 2000 system, the user is either authenticated locally or by a domain controller, depending on the account the user has. If the user is properly authenticated, the operating system creates an *access token* containing the user's security identifier (SID) and security settings. NTFS stores an ACL for each file and directory, much like an inode in a UNIX file system. Each ACL contains an *access control entry* (ACE) for the user or group to which the user belongs and the associated permissions. Therefore, for a user to access an object in the file system, the ACL for that object must contain an ACE for that user or his or her group. That ACE in turn specifies what kind of access is to be granted.

As in UNIX file systems, NTFS permissions vary, depending on whether you apply them to folders or to files. Tables 2–2 and 2–3 summarize NTFS permissions. (Taken from the *Microsoft Windows 2000 Beta Training Kit*, pp. 384–5.)

Table 2–2 NTFS Folder Permissions[3]

NTFS Folder Permission	Allows the User To
Read	See files and subfolders in the folder and view the folder ownership, permissions, and attributes.
Write	Create new files and subfolders within the folder, change folder attributes, and view folder ownership and permissions.
List Folder Contents	See the names of files and subfolders in the folder.
Read & Execute	Move through folders to reach other files and folders, even if the users do not have permission for those folders, and perform actions permitted by the Read permission and the List Folder Contents permission.
Modify	Delete the folder *plus* perform actions permitted by the Write permission and the Read & Execute permission.
Full Control	Change permissions, take ownership, and delete subfolders and files *plus* perform actions permitted by all other NTFS folder permissions.

Table 2–3 NTFS File Permissions[4]

NTFS File Permission	Allows the User To
Read	Read the file and view file attributes, ownership, and permissions.
Write	Overwrite the file, change file attributes, and view file ownership and permissions.
Read & Execute	Run applications *plus* perform the actions permitted by the Read permission.
Modify	Modify and delete the file *plus* perform the actions permitted by the Write permission and the Read & Execute permission.
Full Control	Change permissions and take ownership *plus* perform the actions permitted by all other NTFS file permissions.

2.3.8 Networking

"In the beginning, there was LAN Manager. This product provided part of the foundation of Windows NT 3.1 Advanced Server." (Taken from *Introducing Microsoft Windows 2000 Server*, p. xiii.)[5] Microsoft announced LAN Manager in 1987. This networking product ran natively over the NetBIOS Frames Protocol (NBF), which is actually a set of protocols also known as NetBEUI. The term NetBIOS refers to a networking API developed by Sytec, Inc., for IBM. LAN Manager provided a number of network services for the PC that utilized the NetBIOS API and ran over NetBEUI.

RFC 1001, "Protocol Standard for a NetBIOS Service on a TCP/UDP Transport," was published in 1987. When Microsoft released Windows NT 3.1 in 1993, its networking services were based on LAN Manager. In other words, they were NetBIOS services. These services ran over not only NetBEUI, but IPX/SPX and TCP/IP as well. Because NetBEUI was designed for a LAN—it was not routable—and because of the growing interest in inter-LAN communication and the Internet, the default transport mechanism for Windows NT 4.0 networking services was TCP/IP.

Windows 2000 offers something new with regard to NetBIOS over TCP/IP. According to the *TCP/IP Core Networking Guide,* "Windows 2000 uses NetBIOS over TCP/IP to communicate with prior versions of Windows NT and other clients, such as Windows 95. However, the Windows 2000 redirector and server components now support direct hosting for communicating with other computers running Windows 2000. With direct hosting, NetBIOS is not used for name resolution. DNS is used for name resolution and the Microsoft networking communication is sent directly over TCP without a NetBIOS header. . . . By default, both NetBIOS and direct hosting are enabled, and both are tried in parallel when a new connection is established." (Taken from the *Microsoft Windows 2000 Server TCP/IP Core Networking Guide*, p. 112.)[6]

One of the more important networking applications that runs on NetBIOS is the Server Message Block (SMB) protocol. SMB enables network file and print sharing and messaging among Windows-based systems. It was a part of LAN Manager and has since evolved into the Common Internet File System (CIFS). We will look more closely at NetBIOS, SMB, and CIFS later in this book.

2.4 Conclusion

We have attempted to summarize some key features of Windows 2000 for those who have very little knowledge of it. I fully acknowledge that this is no more than a cursory look at the operating system and that there are other resources that can provide a more complete introduction. However, I have touched on enough to give you an idea of what Windows 2000 is, and this provides us with a basis to move forward. We talked a little about networking in the first two chapters; let's now move on to some more detail.

References

1. John Blommers, *Architecting Enterprise Solutions with UNIX Networking* (Prentice Hall, 1998).
2. Jerry Honeycutt, *Introducing Microsoft Windows 2000 Professional.* (Microsoft Press, 1999).
3. Anthony Northrup, *Introducing Microsoft Windows 2000 Server.* (Microsoft Press, 1999).
4. Microsoft, *Microsoft Windows 2000 Beta Training Kit.* (Microsoft Press, 1999).
5. Microsoft, *Microsoft Windows 2000 Server TCP/IP Core Networking Guide.* (Microsoft Press, 2000).

Endnotes

1.–4. From *Microsoft® Windows® 2000 BETA Training Kit* by Microsoft Corporation. Reproduced by permission of Microsoft Press. All rights reserved.

5. From *Introducing Microsoft® Windows® 2000 Server* by Tony Northrup. Reproduced by permission of Microsoft Press. All rights reserved.

6. From *Microsoft® Windows® 2000 Server Resource Kit* by Microsoft Corporation. Reproduced by permission of Microsoft Press. All rights reserved.

CHAPTER 3

The Network Interface Layer

Now that we have a basic understanding of both UNIX and Windows 2000, let's move to the foundation of interoperability: networking. In recent years, the computing market place has moved to a number of standards that make networking between disparate operating systems much easier than in the early days of LANs. With the explosive growth of the Internet, one of these standards is the TCP/IP protocol suite. TCP/IP is often described using a four-layer model, depicted in Figure 3–1. Using that as our guide, we will begin our discussion with the lowest layer, the layer upon which all the other layers depend to function: the network interface layer.

3.1 Network Interface Cards and Drivers

From the viewpoint of the system administrator, the network interface layer deals primarily with network interface cards, cabling, and the operating system drivers that make these physical components work. It concerns the physical and electrical properties of a network medium, such things as voltages, currents, impedances, cable shielding, and distance limitations. It also is concerned with sending data to and receiving data from a network medium, usually in the form of frames (data encapsulated between headers and trailers). Each network interface technology in use today defines these and related characteristics. These technologies, found on both UNIX and Windows 2000 systems, include

Ethernet
Token Ring
FDDI
ATM
ISDN
PPP over RS-232
Fibre Channel

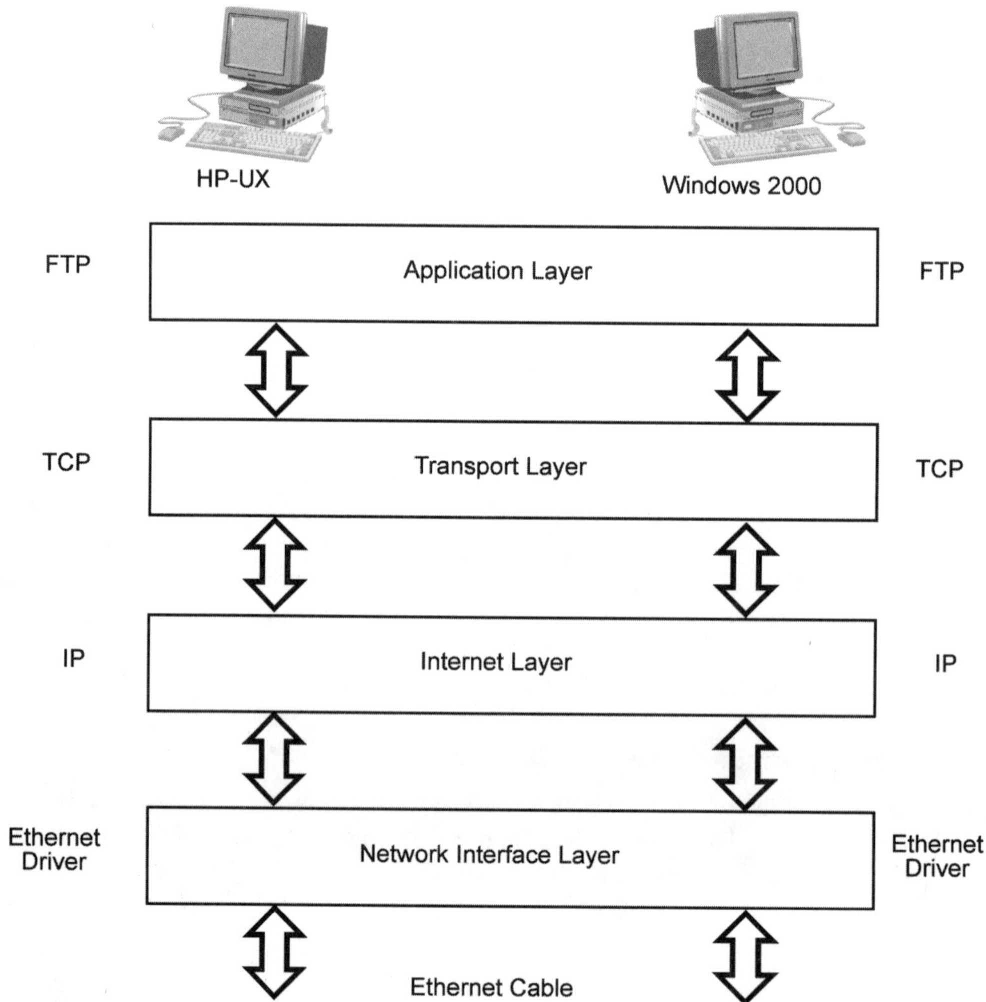

Figure 3–1 The four-layer TCP/IP model. Each protocol on one system communicates with its counterpart on the other.

Details on how each of these technologies works can be found in a multitude of computer networking and data communications books, so there is no need to describe them in detail here. However, I would like to discuss two a little more: Ethernet, because of its importance today, and Fibre Channel, because of its increasing importance.

3.1.1 Ethernet

It seems that today the network interface layer of choice for LANs is some form of Ethernet. Though adequate for most business desktop use, the 10-Mbs shared technology has been supplanted by various forms of 100-Mbs networking, such as 100Base-T4 (running on 4-pair UTP, Category 3, 4, or 5 cable at half-duplex), 100Base-TX (2-pair Category 5 UTP or Type 1 STP cable at full duplex), or 100Base-FX (2 strands 62.5/125 micron multimode fiber at full duplex). Gigabit Ethernet (1000Base-SX) is also making a strong showing these days, usually for use in servers. Most desktops, however, come installed with a 10/100-Mbps auto-sensing Ethernet card so that you can upgrade from 10-Mbps to 100-Mbps networking without buying a new adapter.

Digital Equipment Corp., Intel, and Xerox (DIX, for short) published the Ethernet II (sometimes called DIX Ethernet) standard in 1982, based on Xerox's original technology. A few years earlier, the IEEE published another Ethernet standard, commonly known as IEEE 802.3, which, combined with the 802.2 Logical Link Control standard, defined a different frame format for Ethernet. Both types of frames can exist on the same network, but if your systems' network adapters cannot read both, then you will have to standardize on a frame format or separate your systems with an IP router.

3.1.2 Fibre Channel

Fibre Channel is a data communications technology that can interconnect storage devices with servers as well as provide high-speed networking. A Fibre Channel adapter can serve either as a disk I/O adapter or a network adapter because both SCSI and IP can run on top of it. Currently its most prevalent use is for connectivity to storage. Transfer rates are currently 133 Mbps, 266 Mbps, 530 Mbps, and 1 Gbps, with rates up to 4 Gbps coming soon. This technology is becoming increasingly important as the growth in Storage Area Networks (SANs) and Network-Attached Storage (NAS) continues.

A SAN is a network of shared storage, connecting servers of different types to high-capacity disk arrays, either through the use of Arbitrated Loop technology (up to 126 nodes) or Switched Fabric technology (theoretically, more than 16 million nodes). A conceptual view of a SAN is shown in Figure 3–2. Client systems can in turn access the information stored in these arrays over an existing IP network using a file server running some kind of file-sharing protocol such as Network File System (NFS) or Common Internet File System (CIFS), or both.

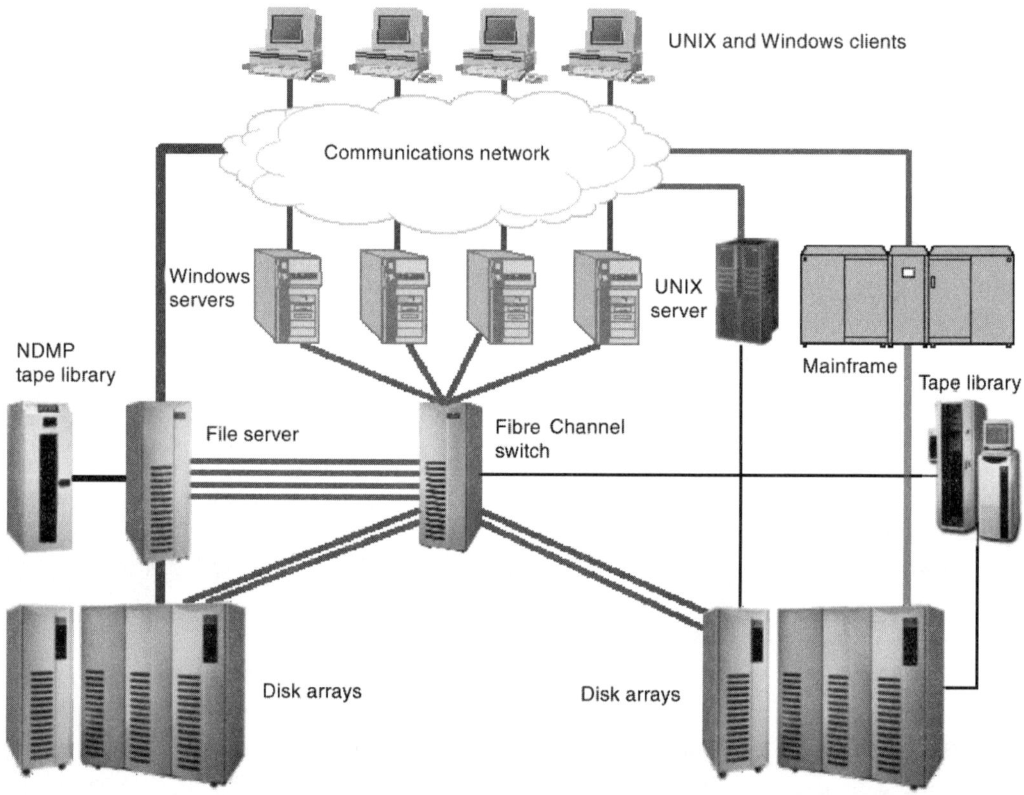

Figure 3–2 A conceptual view of a SAN. Multiple servers can connect to high-capacity disk arrays using components like those used in networking. A popular way of connecting all these devices is through Fibre Channel technology running on fiber-optic cable. SANs and the use of network-attached storage will play an increasingly important role in operating system interoperability.

NAS is currently based on specialized file servers hooked up to a storage array. These servers do nothing but share the volumes of the array (again using NFS, CIFS, or both) by connecting to a network using the currently popular technologies of Ethernet (from 10 Mbps to 1 Gbps), Fiber Distributed Data Interface (FDDI), and Ansynchronous Transfer Mode (ATM). Fibre Channel can play an important role here as well, as shown in Figure 3–3. This figure shows a file server running EMC's Multiplex File System (MPFS). Clients can connect to the file server using only the network via NFS or CIFS, or they can use both the network and a channel connection. In the latter, the client accesses a file's metadata over the network, but gets the actual data over a SCSI or Fibre Channel.

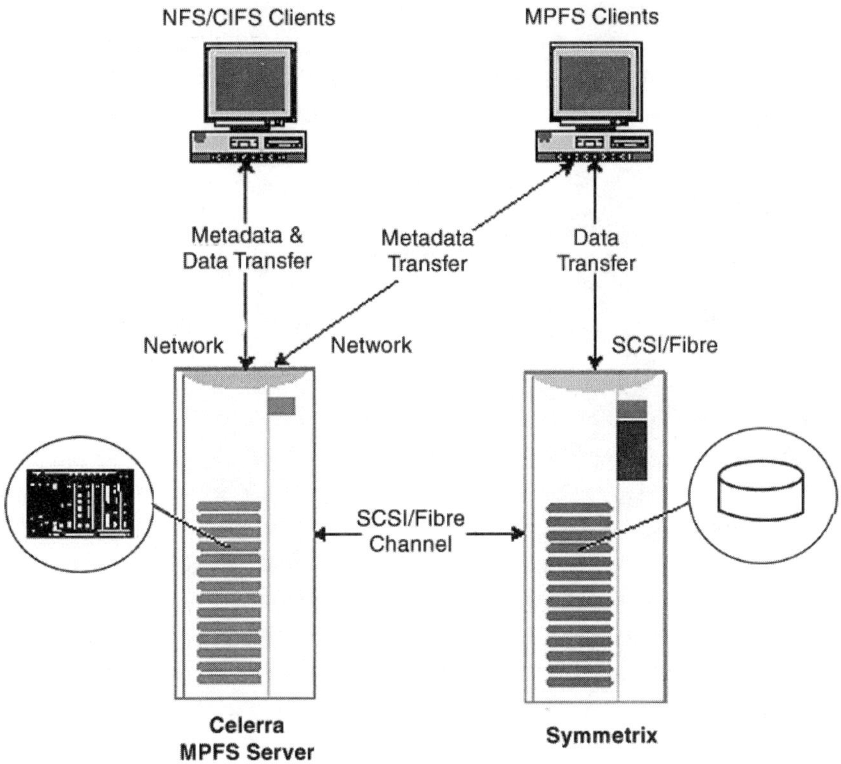

Figure 3–3 Network-Attached Storage and Direct-Attached Storage combined. Traditional NAS consists of a file server running NFS or CIFS. MPFS provides metadata transfer over the network and actual data transfer via SCSI or Fibre Channel.

3.1.3 Network Interface Drivers

Ethernet, Token Ring, FDDI, Fibre Channel, and the like are standards—important, to say the least. For example, DIX Ethernet frames are of the same format for both UNIX and Windows 2000 systems. What this means is that the lower levels of internetworking are already taken care of for you, provided you standardize on a particular technology. For example, you cannot expect to easily integrate your Ethernet-based Windows 2000 system into your existing Token Ring network of UNIX systems. You can, however, plug your Windows 2000 computer into a 10Base-T network with Ethernet-based UNIX systems and not have to buy special cabling or connecting hardware like hubs.

The differences, of course, lie in the drivers for these adapters. If a particular network adapter is to work on both Windows 2000 and UNIX systems, it must have an appropriate driver for the operating system. Many network interface card (NIC) vendors, though, will design cards only for Intel processor-based systems, which confines their functionality to only those operating systems that run on such architectures, such as Linux, SCO UNIX, or some version of Windows. Yet, whether the NIC is designed for a Reduced Instruction Set Computing (RISC)-based UNIX system or an Intel-based Windows system, as long as you standardize on a particular technology, such as 100Base-T Ethernet, and as long as all your systems support it, you will have basic network interconnectivity right out of the box.

If your system, be it UNIX-based or Windows-based, comes with the operating system preinstalled, then the appropriate driver for the network card is already present. If you install the operating system yourself, the install process will detect your NIC (if it is a popular one) and ensure that you have the right driver in place. RISC-based UNIX systems ship only with NICs supported by the appropriate operating system. Windows 2000 systems come with a wider variety of NICs. However, you may wind up installing some systems with cards not found on Microsoft's Hardware Compatibility List (HCL). Microsoft supplies as many of the NIC drivers in existence as it can on the installation CDs, but sometimes you will have to go to the card vendor's Web site to get an updated driver for Windows 2000.

HP-UX systems can automatically detect newly installed hardware and create device files for them, but usually the device drivers still need to be present in the kernel. (With HP-UX 11 and Linux, you can employ dynamically loadable kernel modules. These are precompiled kernel modules that can be loaded into memory as needed. However, such modules are usually reserved for less frequently used devices, not NICs.) Because the Windows 2000 kernel is a *microkernel,* device drivers are not built into it, making it possible for you to add devices dynamically without building kernel modules. Windows 2000 supports Plug and Play (PnP), which provides for automatic hardware detection and configuration.

An important element in networking interoperability is the ability of an operating system to run multiple protocol stacks on a single network card. UNIX systems have been able to handle multiple stacks easily because of their protected memory model. (John Blommers, *Architecting Enterprise Solutions with UNIX Networking*, p. 168.) Windows 2000 accomplishes the same thing, using something called an *NDIS wrapper.* NDIS stands for the Network Device Interface Specification, which provides for an interface that, among other things, allows multiple protocols to bind to a single NIC driver. What this means is that both UNIX and Windows 2000 systems can concurrently run protocols such as TCP/IP, IPX/SPX (or NWLink for Windows 2000), or AppleTalk. For a look at how Windows 2000 network architecture accomplishes this, see Figure 3–4. This capability is something we will come back to later in this book.

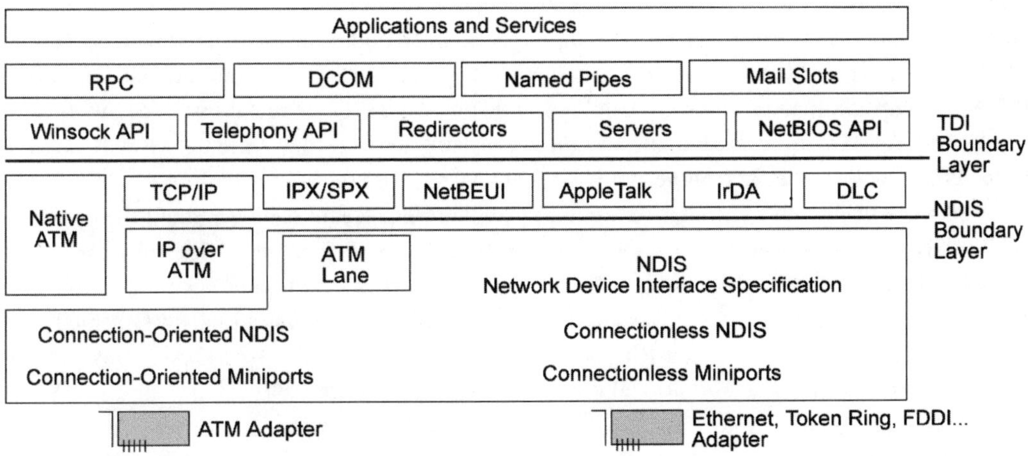

Figure 3–4 Windows 2000 network architecture. Note that the NDIS layer is an interface between higher-level networking protocols and the network adapter, be it ATM, Ethernet, Token Ring, etc. Source: *Microsoft Windows 2000 Server TCP/IP Core Networking Guide*, p. 762.[1]

3.1.4 Configuring Your Network Interface Card

3.1.4.1 Windows 2000

When you install Windows 2000, your network adapter is automatically detected for you. If you are doing an interactive install, you will have to supply networking information like the IP address, subnet mask, and gateway. If you use Dynamic Host Configuration Protocol (DHCP), most of this information will be configured into the LAN adapter automatically. At this point, the process will install the appropriate driver and then *bind* the adapter to TCP/IP. If you later install another protocol, such as NWLink (IPX/SPX), then it will bind the adapter to both TCP/IP and NWLink. Some drivers will ask for card-specific configuration information when they install. If you want to change these settings later, start the Device Manager, expand the Network adapters entry, right-click the icon representing your adapter, and then choose Properties.

If you change NICs or add additional ones, Windows 2000 will automatically detect the new cards via PnP and will install the drivers from the installation media or from a source you specify. Again, you may be asked to provide some additional configuration information.

Most systems transmit Ethernet frames in DIX format, which Windows 2000 does by default. To set the default transmitting format to 802.2/802.3, edit the Registry and set the following parameter to 1:

```
HKLM\SYSTEM\CurrentControlSet\Services\Tcpip\Parameters\ArpUseEtherSNAP
```

3.1.4.2 HP-UX

HP-UX 11 supports multiple *logical interfaces* per NIC. IP addresses associated with the logical interfaces can be on the same or different subnets. If you require both Ethernet and IEEE 802.3 (SNAP) encapsulations on the same NIC, you must configure two logical interfaces with separate IP addresses in different subnets. The interface name for Ethernet is *lan*; for IEEE 802.3 it is *snap*. The loopback interface name is always lo0.

If you had your NIC in place when you installed your HP-UX system, then the operating system installation process installed its driver into the kernel, created device files for it, and installed the appropriate networking software. For Ethernet, this software is called LAN/9000. Because of its popularity, we will assume you are installing an Ethernet card. (Other HP networking software includes Token Ring/9000, FDDI/9000, and 100VG-AnyLAN Link.) If you switch Ethernet cards or add additional ones, follow the procedure below.

It is much easier to configure your NIC using Hewlett-Packard's System Administration Manager (SAM) than to do everything through commands and startup files. The same is probably true about other forms of UNIX. Make sure the LAN card and driver are installed in the system before you use SAM to configure the software. (These steps come from Hewlett-Packard's *Installing and Administering LAN/9000 Software*, pp. 32–34.) Log in as *root* and do the following:

1. At the HP-UX prompt, type **sam.**
2. Select the **Networking and Communications** item of the SAM main window.
3. Select the **Network Interface Cards** item from the **Networking and Communications** window.
4. Highlight the LAN card that you want to configure from the object list.
5. Verify that the hardware path is correct for your LAN card.
6. If you are configuring the first logical interface for a card type (also called the *initial interface*), choose **Configure** from the *Actions* menu to open the **Configure LAN Card** window.

   If you are adding logical interfaces to a card type, choose **Add IP Logical Interface** from the *Actions* menu to open the **Configure LAN Card** window.

   a. Enter the information about the LAN card. To do so, press the Tab key to move through the data entry fields.

   NOTE: SAM displays the Card Name, Hardware (H/W) Path, and Station Address fields with the appropriate values. These fields cannot be modified.

   b. Choose the **Card Type** of your LAN card. The default is Ethernet. SNAP802.3 can be selected.

   *NOTE: The **Enable DHCP** button specifies that the system is a DHCP client. If you activate this button, the IP parameters for this system will be set using DHCP.*

c. Enter the Internet address for your LAN card. Upon exiting the Internet Address field, SAM checks to make sure that the IP address you entered is correctly formatted and is not currently in use.

d. Specify whether your LAN card will be on a subnet or supernet. The **Subnet Mask** field can contain a fixed-length subnet mask, a variable-length subnet mask, or a supernet mask. Enter the appropriate type of mask for your network-addressing scheme.

e. Optionally, enter comments about your LAN card.

f. Choose **Modify Host Name Aliases** to open the **Add Aliases** window. You must complete this step if you have more than one LAN card installed in your system.

g. Add, modify, or remove alias host names for your logical interface.

h. Activate the **OK** button to perform the task and return to the **Configure LAN Card** window.

i. Optionally, activate the **Advanced Options** button. This will allow you to modify the Station Address and configure an Internet Broadcast Address. The Maximum Transmission Unit (MTU) field is display only.

7. Activate the **OK** button at the **Configure LAN Card** window to enable your LAN card. If the software is correctly configured, SAM displays the Network Interface Cards object list with the status Enabled for your LAN card; otherwise, SAM displays an error message.
8. Choose **Exit** from the *File* menu.
9. At the Networking and Communications window, choose **Exit SAM** from the *File* menu.

3.2 Conclusion

The network interface layer performs the same function on both Windows 2000 and HP-UX. How they are actually implemented and configured differ, however. Two of the more important technologies at this layer are Ethernet and Fibre Channel. Whereas Ethernet is ubiquitous in today's LANs, both play an important role in the new SAN and NAS technologies.

References

1. John Blommers, *Architecting Enterprise Solutions with UNIX Networking*. (Prentice Hall, 1998).
2. Gilbert Held, *Ethernet Networks: Design, Implementation, Operation, Management,* 3rd Ed. (John Wiley & Sons, 1998).
3. Hewlett-Packard, *Installing and Administering LAN/9000 Software.* (Hewlett-Packard, 1997).
4. Microsoft, *Microsoft Windows 2000 Server TCP/IP Core Networking Guide.* (Microsoft Press, 2000).
5. Ralph H. Thornburgh, *Fibre Channel for Mass Storage.* (Prentice Hall, 1999).

Endnotes

1. From *Microsoft® Windows® 2000 Server Resource Kit* by Microsoft Corporation. Reproduced by permission of Microsoft Press. All rights reserved.

CHAPTER 4

The Internet Layer

We now proceed to the next level of the four-layer TCP/IP model, the internet layer, sometimes called the network layer. (If the word internet is not capitalized, it refers to the *internetworking* of networks in a generic sense. The word *Internet* (with a capital *I*) refers to the now famous worldwide public internetwork.) The internet layer enables pieces of data, usually called *datagrams*, to find their correct destination, even if the destination is several networks away. Within the TCP/IP protocol suite, IP, the Internet Protocol, is responsible for the routing of these datagrams. Because of the recent Internet phenomenon, TCP/IP is omnipresent these days, making it a key to system interoperability. TCP/IP runs on a wide variety of platforms: mainframes, Macs, VAXs, and of course UNIX and Windows 2000 systems. Therefore, though your desktop computer may run Windows 2000, you can connect to a Web server running HP-UX 11 or Linux, since the Web relies on Hypertext Transfer Protocol (HTTP), a TCP/IP application. So let's look at TCP/IP, concentrating in this chapter on IP, the network layer.

TCP/IP began as part of a project of the Defense Department's Advanced Research Projects Agency in 1969. It was incorporated into BSD UNIX in the early 1980s and is part of every current implementation of UNIX. Microsoft released a completely rewritten TCP/IP suite with the release of Windows NT 3.5 in 1994. Whatever the source, any vendor claiming to provide TCP/IP must ensure that it adheres to the Internet Standards set forth in the Request for Comments (RFC) document series. According to RFC 2026, The Internet Standards Process – Revision 3, p. 3, "The Internet Standards process is an activity of the Internet Society that is organized and managed on behalf of the Internet community by the Internet Architecture Board (IAB) and the Internet Engineering Steering Group (IESG)." RFCs are the official means of these bodies to regulate Internet standards. You can find the RFCs in a number of locations on the Internet, one of which is the Internet Engineering Task Force's Web site at *www.ietf.org*.

A first step in internetworking is to standardize on TCP/IP. Older Windows network applications often used NetBEUI (NetBIOS Extended User Interface) to communicate with each other. Similar applications on Windows NT and Windows 2000 can use NetBEUI, IPX/SPX, AppleTalk, and of course TCP/IP. However, all Windows network applications default to TCP/IP, and UNIX networking is practically synonymous with it.

In Chapter 3, "The Network Interface Layer," we looked briefly at the network interface layer, mentioning Ethernet and Fibre Channel in particular, and talked about that layer's drivers. Now we move up the "stack," if you will, to the major protocols that exist at or near the internet layer.

4.1 ARP

IP uses a 32-bit addressing scheme to send datagrams. However, these addresses are *logical;* in other words, they are not tied to a particular system. In fact, in Dynamic Host Configuration Protocol (DHCP) environments IP addresses for particular machines change all the time. (We will talk more about DHCP later.) IP must rely on a protocol that sits between it and the network interface layer to find the actual *physical* address of a machine. That protocol is the Address Resolution Protocol, or ARP.

Let's assume your network is Ethernet. Ethernet sends frames to other systems using the 48-bit hardware address burned into the NIC (the MAC address). When IP sends a datagram to Ethernet for delivery, that datagram contains the destination IP address. Since Ethernet does not understand IP addresses, it uses ARP to determine the appropriate hardware address of the machine owning the destination IP address, and once it does so, delivers the frame. ARP then caches the mapping of IP and hardware addresses so that frequently used destinations do not have to go through the broadcast mechanism again. Cache entries last up to 10 minutes on Windows 2000 system, five minutes on HP-UX. Static entries do not expire.

ARP sends an *ARP request* in the form of a broadcast in order to find the hardware address of the destination system. All systems on the network hear this request, but only the owner of the destination IP address will respond with an *ARP reply* containing its hardware address. If the IP address belongs to a system on a remote network, then usually the first-hop router will reply to the ARP request, even though the ultimate destination may be several routers away. This service is known as *proxy ARP.*

4.1.1 Viewing the ARP Cache

4.1.1.1 Windows 2000

To view the ARP cache in Windows 2000, use the *arp –a* command. For example,

```
C:\>arp -a

Interface: 10.0.0.3 on Interface 0x2
  Internet Address      Physical Address      Type
  10.0.0.4              08-00-09-83-31-b1     dynamic
  10.0.0.5              08-00-5a-d8-1e-a9     dynamic
  10.10.1.1             00-60-b0-6a-8e-9c     dynamic
```

Here you see that all four cache entries are labeled *dynamic;* that is, they are acquired automatically, without user intervention. Dynamic entries last for a maximum of 10 minutes. You can set the expiration time of unreferenced entries by changing the value of the following Registry entries in

```
HKLM\SYSTEM\CurrentContolSet\Services\Tcpip\Parameters: ArpCacheLife\
    ArpCacheMinReferencedLife
```

Notice that the hardware addresses are given as six hexadecimal bytes separated by *dashes*. HP-UX requires the use of colons.

4.1.1.2 HP-UX

HP-UX also has the *arp –a* command, but the output is different. For example,

```
# arp -a
houyhnhnm.book.local (10.0.0.3) at 0:8:0:a0:36:f7 ether
aix1.book.local (10.0.0.5) at 8:0:5a:d8:1e:a9 ether
```

Notice here that HP-UX provides the host name as well as the IP address for each entry. Also, note that the hardware addresses are given as six hexadecimal bytes separated by *colons*. By default, dynamic ARP cache entries stay in the cache for five minutes. To change this parameter, use the *ndd -get /dev/arp arp_cleanup_interval* command, specifying the interval in milliseconds. For example, the first command below will set the ARP cleanup interval to six minutes; the second will display the new value:

```
# ndd -set /dev/arp arp_cleanup_interval 360000
# ndd -get /dev/arp arp_cleanup_interval
360000
```

4.1.2 Deleting ARP Cache Entries

4.1.2.1 Windows 2000

In Windows 2000, do an *arp –a* to find the entry you want to delete and then supply only the IP address to the *arp –d* command. For example,

```
C:\>arp -a

Interface: 10.0.0.3 on Interface 0x2
  Internet Address      Physical Address      Type
  10.0.0.5              08-00-5a-d8-1e-a9     dynamic
  10.0.0.4              08-00-09-83-31-b      dynamic
  10.10.1.1             00-60-b0-6a-8e-9c     dynamic

C:\>arp -d 10.0.0.4

C:\>arp -a
```

```
Interface: 10.0.0.3 on Interface 0x2
  Internet Address      Physical Address      Type
  10.0.0.5              08-00-5a-d8-1e-a9     dynamic
  10.10.1.1             00-60-b0-6a-8e-9c     dynamic
```

4.1.2.2 HP-UX

HP-UX requires that you provide the host name of the entry to be deleted, not the IP address, as in Windows 2000.

```
# arp -d w2kserv.book.local
w2kserv.book.local (10.10.1.1) deleted
```

4.1.3 Adding a Static Entry to the ARP Cache

4.1.3.1 Windows 2000

In Windows 2000, use the *arp –s* command. You must supply both the IP address and the hardware address.

```
C:\>arp -a

Interface: 10.0.0.3 on Interface 0x2
  Internet Address      Physical Address      Type
  10.10.1.1             00-60-b0-6a-8e-9c     dynamic

C:\>arp -s 10.10.1.1 00-60-b0-6a-8e-9c

C:\>arp -a

Interface: 10.0.0.3 on Interface 0x2
  Internet Address      Physical Address      Type
  10.10.1.1             00-60-b0-6a-8e-9c     static
```

4.1.3.2 HP-UX

HP-UX also has the *arp –s* command.

```
# arp -s w2kserv.book.local 0:60:b0:6a:8e:9c
# arp -a
w2kserv.book.local (10.10.1.1) at 0:60:b0:6a:8e:9c ether permanent
houyhnhnm.book.local (10.0.0.3) at 0:8:0:a0:36:f7 ether
aix1.book.local (10.0.0.5) at 8:0:5a:d8:1e:a9 ether
```

Note that static entries in HP-UX are noted as *permanent*.

4.1.4 Gratuitous ARP

4.1.4.1 Windows 2000

Windows 2000 supports *gratuitous ARP*, sending ARP requests upon system startup that check to see if the IP address being configured already exists on the local network. The number of requests sent is specified in the following Registry entry:

```
HKLM\SYSTEM\CurrentControlSet\Services\Tcpip\Parameters\ArpRetryCount
```

If a duplicate exists, Windows 2000 disables the network interface of the booting machine.

4.1.4.2 HP-UX

HP-UX also supports gratuitous ARP. However, if upon booting ARP discovers a duplicate IP address, ARP sends a message like the following to the system console:

```
Duplicate IP address!! Sent from Ethernet address: x:x:x:x:x:x:
```

where *x:x:x:x:x:x* is the hardware address of the offending system. Unlike Windows 2000, HP-UX does not disable the network interface of the booting machine when it discovers a duplicate IP address.

4.2 IP

At the internet layer, IP is the key protocol. It sends and receives packets, known as *datagrams*, using a 32-bit addressing scheme. As a system administrator, you should already know something about IP addressing and subnet masking, so we won't go into any details about such here. However, if you'd like more information about addressing, two excellent references are W. Richard Stevens', *TCP/IP Illustrated, Volume 1* (Addison-Wesley Publishing Company, 1994) and Microsoft Corporation's, *Microsoft Windows 2000 Server TCP/IP Core Networking Guide* (Microsoft Press, 2000).

4.2.1 Configuring IP

4.2.1.1 Windows 2000

Windows 2000 Professional defaults to using DHCP when you install the system. DHCP typically provides each client with an IP address, subnet mask, and a default gateway, as well as other parameters. However, if you are not using DHCP—for example, when installing a domain controller—then you must enter the IP information in the **Internet Protocol (TCP/IP) Properties** box. (See Figure 4–1.)

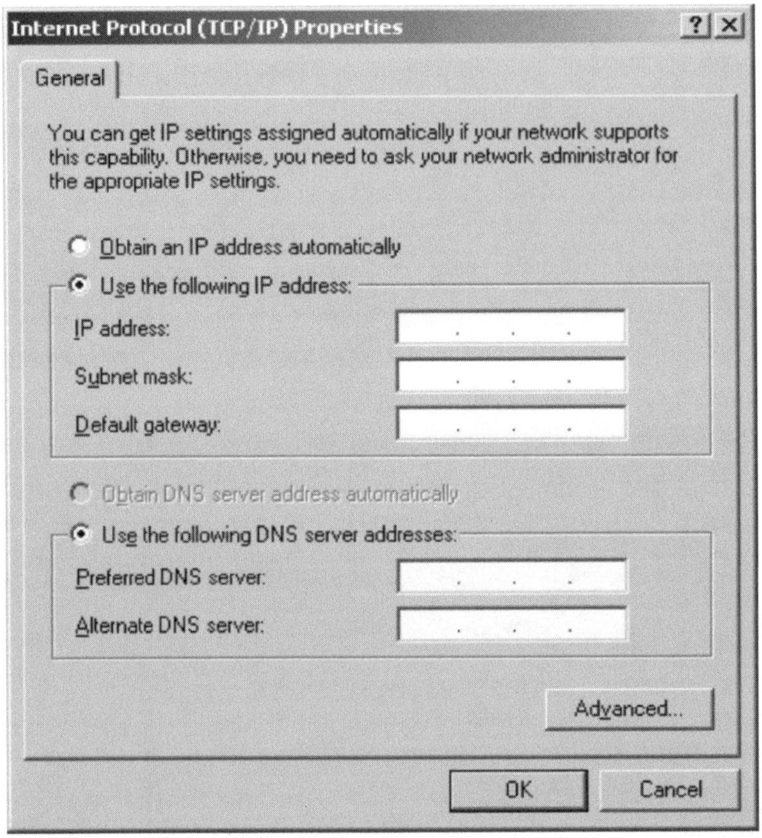

Figure 4–1 Configuring IP on Windows 2000. To get to this box, open the **Network and Dial-up Connections** window from the **Control Panel**, right-click on **Local Area Connection,** and choose **Properties**. In the **Local Area Connection Properties** window, select **Internet Protocol (TCP/IP)** and choose **Properties**.

4.2.1.2 HP-UX

You can do the following to configure IP on HP-UX:

1. Use the command line. Command-line changes are not permanent.
2. Edit system startup files. Changes you make to these files do not take effect until after you reboot the system.
3. Use SAM. This will make changes to the system and ensure the proper entries are placed in the startup file.
4. Use the *set_parms* script.

The startup script */sbin/init.d./net* runs a couple of the commands you would use on the command line: *ifconfig* and *route*. The *ifconfig* command sets the IP address, subnet mask, and local loopback interface; *route* configures the routing table. You don't edit the */sbin/init.d/net* script; rather, you change the value of variables found in */etc/rc.config.d/netconf*. These values include:

```
HOSTNAME
LOOPBACK_ADDRESS
INTERFACE_NAME[0]
IP_ADDRESS[0]
SUBNET_MASK
BROADCAST_ADDRESS
INTERFACE_STATE[0]
DHCP_ENABLE[0]
ROUTE_DESTINATION[0]
ROUTE_GATEWAY[0]
ROUTE_COUNT[0]
```

The values of the variables become the arguments of the *ifconfig* and *route* commands that are run at system startup.

Because it is easy to make a mistake when editing files, it is usually best to use either SAM or *set_parms* to set the variables in */etc/rc.config.d/netconf*. After starting SAM, select the **Networking and Communications** item from the main menu to configure your IP parameters. The *set_parms* command runs right after you install HP-UX, but you can run the script at any time. Running the *set_parms ip_address* command will set your IP address; *set_parms addl_netwrk* will set the subnet mask, default gateway, DNS domain name, DNS server, Network Information Service (NIS) domain name, and NIS server.

You can set your system to be a DHCP client with the *set_parms initial* command or by using SAM. If you set your system up as a DHCP client, do not make any changes to */etc/rc.config.d/netfconf* or set new parameters with *set_parms*. Doing so will most likely hose your system's communications.

4.2.2 Viewing IP Configuration

4.2.2.1 Windows 2000

You can view all the essential IP configuration of a Windows 2000 system by typing the *ipconfig /all* command at the system prompt. For example,

```
C:\>ipconfig /all

Windows 2000 IP Configuration

        Host Name . . . . . . . . . . . . : houyhnhnm
        Primary DNS Suffix  . . . . . . . :
        Node Type . . . . . . . . . . . . : Mixed
        IP Routing Enabled. . . . . . . . : No
        WINS Proxy Enabled. . . . . . . . : No
        DNS Suffix Search List. . . . . . : book.local
```

```
Ethernet adapter Local Area Connection:

        Connection-specific DNS Suffix  . : book.local
        Description . . . . . . . . . . . : HP 10/100TX PCI LAN Adapter
        Physical Address. . . . . . . . . : 00-60-B0-6A-8E-9C
        DHCP Enabled. . . . . . . . . . . : Yes
        Autoconfiguration Enabled . . . . : Yes
        IP Address. . . . . . . . . . . . : 10.0.0.5
        Subnet Mask . . . . . . . . . . . : 255.0.0.0
        Default Gateway . . . . . . . . . :
        DHCP Server . . . . . . . . . . . : 10.10.1.1
        DNS Servers . . . . . . . . . . . : 10.10.1.1
        Primary WINS Server . . . . . . . :
        Secondary WINS Server . . . . . . :
        Lease Obtained. . . . . . . . . . : Monday, May 15, 2000 9:11:44 AM
        Lease Expires . . . . . . . . . . : Tuesday, May 16, 2000 9:11:44
```

4.2.2.2 HP-UX

You may have to do more to see similar information on an HP-UX system. To see the host name of a system, use the *uname* command:

```
# hostname
hpux1
```

To see the physical address of your NIC, use the *lanscan* command. Please note that *lanscan* is unique to HP-UX.

```
# lanscan
Hardware Station        Crd  Hdw    Net-Interface  NM  MAC    HP-DLPI  DLPI
Path     Address        In#  State  NamePPA        ID  Type   Support  Mjr#
2/0/2    0x0800098331B1 0    UP     lan0 snap0     1   ETHER  Yes      119
```

To get the IP address, netmask, and broadcast address for an interface, use the *ifconfig* command. Remember that *lan0* is the default name of the NIC logical interface, indicating that the encapsulation method is DIX Ethernet.

```
# ifconfig lan0
lan0: flags=843<UP,BROADCAST,RUNNING,MULTICAST>
    inet  10.0.0.4 netmask ff000000 broadcast 10.255.255.255
```

To get additional information, such as whether the DHCP client is enabled and what your DNS configuration is, run SAM and select **Networking and Communications** from the main menu.

4.2.3 Viewing the Route Table

4.2.3.1 Windows 2000

In Windows 2000, use either the *route print* command or the *netstat –r* command. For example,

```
C:\>route print
===========================================================================
Interface List
0x1 ........................... MS TCP Loopback interface
0x2 ...00 08 00 a0 36 f7 ...... LAN/Fax/Modem PCMCIA Card
===========================================================================
===========================================================================
Active Routes:
Network Destination        Netmask          Gateway       Interface  Metric
         10.0.0.0        255.0.0.0         10.0.0.3        10.0.0.3       1
         10.0.0.3  255.255.255.255        127.0.0.1       127.0.0.1       1
   10.255.255.255  255.255.255.255         10.0.0.3        10.0.0.3       1
        127.0.0.0        255.0.0.0        127.0.0.1       127.0.0.1       1
        224.0.0.0        224.0.0.0         10.0.0.3        10.0.0.3       1
  255.255.255.255  255.255.255.255         10.0.0.3        10.0.0.3       1
===========================================================================
Persistent Routes:
  None

C:\>netstat -r

Route Table
===========================================================================
Interface List
0x1 ........................... MS TCP Loopback interface
0x2 ...00 08 00 a0 36 f7 ...... LAN/Fax/Modem PCMCIA Card
===========================================================================
===========================================================================
Active Routes:
Network Destination        Netmask          Gateway       Interface  Metric
         10.0.0.0        255.0.0.0         10.0.0.3        10.0.0.3       1
         10.0.0.3  255.255.255.255        127.0.0.1       127.0.0.1       1
   10.255.255.255  255.255.255.255         10.0.0.3        10.0.0.3       1
        127.0.0.0        255.0.0.0        127.0.0.1       127.0.0.1       1
        224.0.0.0        224.0.0.0         10.0.0.3        10.0.0.3       1
  255.255.255.255  255.255.255.255         10.0.0.3        10.0.0.3       1
===========================================================================
Persistent Routes:
  None
```

Each route consists of a destination host or network, a netmask, and a gateway (router address) to use in forwarding datagrams. These three items are displayed along with the interface used for the route and the hop count (metric). The hop count usually indicates the number of routers that must be crossed to reach the network ID.

The first line, the *Active Routes* section of this command's output, is the *default route address*, designated with a 0.0.0.0 network destination and a 0.0.0.0 netmask. The second line is the *loopback network address*, for IP addresses in the form of 127.x.y.z. The next line is an entry for the *directly attached network address* for datagrams staying on the same local network. Following that is the *local host address*. All datagrams with the host's IP address are forwarded to 127.0.0.1 (the loopback address). Next is the *network broadcast address*, which corresponds to the all-subnets broadcast address. Then comes the *multicast address*, which is used to route multicast IP datagrams. The last line contains the *limited broadcast address*

4.2.3.2 HP-UX

It is common to use the *netstat –r* command to display the routing table in HP-UX. Using the *–n* option with this command displays IP addresses instead of host names. (Use *–v* to display the network masks in the route entries.)

```
# netstat -nr
Routing tables
Dest/Netmask     Gateway          Flags     Refs     Use     Interface     Pmtu
127.0.0.1        127.0.0.1        UH        0        570     lo0           4136
10.0.0.4         10.0.0.4         UH        0        905     lan0          4136
10.0.0.0         10.0.0.4         U         2          0     lan0          1500
127.0.0.0        127.0.0.1        U         0          0     lo0           4136
```

In addition to displaying the destination host or network, netmask, and gateway addresses, this command has a few more fields. The *Flags* field shows whether the route is up (U), whether the route is to a gateway (G), or whether the route is a host or network route (with or without H). The *Use* field shows a count of the number of packets sent using this route. The *Interface* field identifies which network interface (logical name instead of IP address) is used for the route. The *Pmtu* field displays the path maximum transmission unit (PMTU).

The first line indicates the route for the *loopback host address.* Notice the command displays the loopback interface's logical name, not IP address. The next line is for the *local host address,* which has the system's IP address instead of the loopback address as the gateway. Following that is the *directly attached network address;* this line is similar to the one displayed in Windows 2000. The fourth line is the *loopback network address* for IP addresses in the form of 127.x.y.z., just as it is in Windows 2000. The last line is the default gateway.

4.2.4 IP Routing Process

On a given system, IP can receive datagrams from either some other protocol running on the local host or from another system on the network through the NIC. In the first case, IP forwards the datagram according to the local routing table. This is known as *host routing*. In the second case, IP will discard datagrams not addressed to the local host *unless the local host is configured to be a router.* In the former, IP sends routing error messages to the upper protocols. In the latter, it sends them in the form of Internet Control Message Protocol (ICMP) messages to the sending host.

The routing algorithms for Windows 2000 and HP-UX are nearly the same. In both systems, IP performs a bit-wise logical AND between the netmask in the routing entry and the IP datagram's destination address and then compares the result with the destination address in the routing entry. If they match, then IP selects that route. If there is more than one route selected as a result of this process, IP selects the route with the longest netmask. This results in a more specific route because the longer the netmask, the narrower the range of IP addresses. With Windows 2000, if more than one route matches at this point, IP selects the route with the lowest metric. If there is still more than one match, IP randomly selects the route.

The default route is the least specific route and is selected only if there is none more specific. If the chosen route's gateway is the same address as the interface, the destination is local and IP sends the datagram directly. If the route's gateway is not the same as the interface, IP forwards the datagram to the gateway.

Using the routing table, IP on HP-UX takes the following actions:

1. Look for a matching complete-destination IP address. This is an IP address on the same network and with the host ID. If the entry has the *G* flag set, IP forwards the datagram to the next-hop router. If the *H* flag is set, IP sends the datagram directly to a system on the local network.
2. Find an entry that matches the network ID. If found, IP sends the datagram either to the next-hop router or the locally attached system. Again, IP checks for the appropriate flag for this.
3. Use the default route, appropriately labeled "default." IP sends the datagram to the next-hop router.

4.2.5 Configuring Routes

4.2.5.1 Windows 2000

If you are using DHCP, then the default route is automatically provided. If you use static IP information, then you specify the default gateway in the **Internet Protocol (TCP/IP) Properties** box. (See Figure 4–2.) By clicking on the **Advanced** button of this box, you can enter additional default gateways.

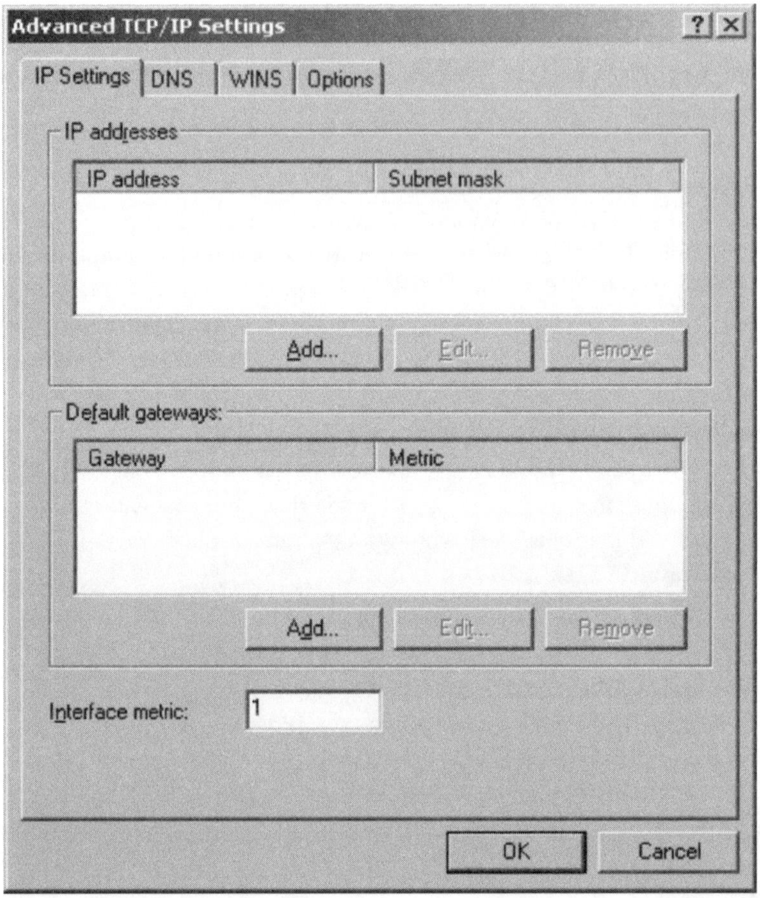

Figure 4–2 Adding default gateways. To get to this box, open the **Network and Dial-up Connections** window from the **Control Panel**, right-click on **Local Area Connection,** and choose **Properties**. In the **Local Area Connection Properties** window, select **Internet Protocol (TCP/IP)** and choose **Properties**. Then, click on the **Advanced** button.

To add a route on the command line, use the *route* command. The syntax for the command is

```
route [-f] [-p] [command [destination] [mask subnetmask] [gateway]
   [metric costmetric]]
```

For example,

```
C:> route add 10.0.0.0  mask 255.0.0.0  10.10.1.1  metric 1
```

If you use the *–p* option with *route add*, then you make the route *persistent;* in other words, you make it permanent even between reboots. Windows 2000 stores persistent routes in

```
HKLM\SYSTEM\CurrentControlSet\Services\Tcpip\ParametersPersistentRoutes
```

4.2.5.2 HP-UX

Both default and persistent routes are normally set in startup files. You can use SAM and *set_parms* to configure a default gateway, or you can issue the following command:

```
# /usr/sbin/route add default gateway_address 1
```

The *gateway_address* argument is the IP address of the gateway host. Then, set the following environment variables in the */etc/rc.config.d/netconf* file:

```
ROUTE_DESTINATION[0]="default"
ROUTE_GATEWAY[0]="gateway_address"
ROUTE_COUNT[0]="1"
```

If the default gateway is your own host, set the ROUTE_COUNT variable to 0. Otherwise, set it to 1.

To set up additional routes, type the following command for each network you need to reach:

```
#/usr/sbin/route add net network_address gateway_address
```

Then, create a new set of routing variables in the */etc/rc.config.d/netconf* file for each new route. Whenever you create a new set of variables, increment the number in the square brackets.

```
ROUTE_DESTINATION[n]="network_address"
ROUTE_GATEWAY[n]="gateway_address"
ROUTE_COUNT[n]="1"
```

4.2.6 Multihoming and Routing

Windows 2000 and HP-UX differ in their concepts of multihoming. According to Windows 2000 documentation, any system with multiple *IP addresses* is a multihomed machine. Therefore, multihoming can mean multiple IP addresses for a single NIC. However, HP-UX views multihoming as a system with multiple *NICs*, each of which has a separate IP address. On HP-UX, having multiple IP addresses on a single physical interface requires the use of a *logical interface*. Logical interfaces are configured at system startup using the *ifconfig* command.

To enable IP forwarding on Windows 2000, you must configure and start the Routing and Remote Access service. Among other things, this service enables you to convert your Windows 2000 Server into a router. Routing and Remote Access is installed by default on Windows 2000 Server but is not enabled until you run **Start→Programs→Administrative Tools→Routing and Remote Access**. By default, HP-UX will automatically route across multiple NICs. Both Windows 2000 and HP-UX support RIP and OSPF.

4.2.7 ICMP Redirects

Both Windows 2000 and HP-UX support ICMP redirects. For both systems, the ICMP redirect must come from the current first-hop router, and the new router must be directly attached to the network of the originating host. Also, the new routing table entry created by an ICMP redirect must be a host route, not a network route. For Windows 2000, the new route has a 10-minute lifetime. For HP-UX, this lifetime is five minutes. To set a different value for HP-UX, use the *ndd –set /dev/ip ip_ire_redirect_interval* command. For example, to set the value to six minutes, type the following:

```
# ndd -set /dev/ip ip_ire_redirect_interval 360000
```

4.2.8 Router Discovery

4.2.8.1 Windows 2000

Windows 2000 supports ICMP router discovery, a dynamic method of determining the best default gateway. Routers configured with ICMP router discovery periodically broadcast router advertisements from which clients can choose the most appropriate default route. Hosts configured to be router discovery clients join the all-hosts multicast group of 224.0.0.1 in order to listen to these advertisements upon system startup. Clients choose a default gateway among the advertisements it receives. In addition to listening for routing advertisements, hosts can actually solicit routers using the 224.0.0.2 multicast address. You can configure Windows 2000 hosts for router discovery by setting the following registry entry to a value of 1:

```
HKLM\SYSTEM\CurrentControlSet\Services\Tcpip\ParametersPerformRouterDiscovery
```

4.2.8.2 HP-UX

HP-UX implements ICMP router discovery on clients via *rdpd*, the router discovery daemon, preferring to call it the Router Discovery Protocol (RDP). RDP on the client works the same way as ICMP router discovery does on Windows 2000 clients. Clients listen for router advertisements over the all-hosts multicast address of 224.0.0.1 or the NIC's broadcast address. The client also sends solicitations to the all-routers multicast address of 224.0.0.2.

You can start *rdpd* either by setting the RDPD variable in */etc/rc.config.d/netconf* to 1 and rebooting (or running the */sbin/init.d/net start* command) or by configuring *gated*. *gated* is a routing daemon that handles multiple routing protocols, including Routing Information Protocol (RIP), Border Gateway Protocol (BGP), External Gateway Protocol (EGP), the Hello Protocol (HELLO), Open Shortest Path First (OSPF), and RDP. To configure *gated*, edit the */etc/gated.conf* file and change the GATED variable in */etc/rc.config.d/netconf* to 1. For more information, run the following commands:

```
# man gated
# man 4 gated.conf
```

Do not, however, start RPD using *both* methods.

4.2.9 MTU and Path MTU

4.2.9.1 Windows 2000

Windows 2000 systems have Path MTU discovery enabled by default for all interfaces. If you disable it, Windows 2000 defaults to a Maximum Transmission Unit (MTU) of 576 bytes. Change the value of the following Registry parameter to 0 to disable Path MTU discovery:

```
HKLM\SYSTEM\CurrentControlSet\Services\Tcpip\Parameters\EnablePMTUDiscovery
```

You can set the MTU of a network adapter manually by changing the value of the following Registry parameter:

```
HKLM\SYSTEM\CurrentControlSet\Services\Tcpip\Parameters\Interfaces\
   <interface-name>\MTU
```

Setting a value for this parameter will override anything discovered dynamically (provided, of course, that you have not disabled Path MTU discovery). But, according to the Windows 2000 Server Resource Kit, if you enter a value greater than the dynamically determined MTU, the system uses the value of the dynamically determined MTU instead. You can use this entry to reduce, but not to increase, the size of the MTU.

4.2.9.2 HP-UX

By default, when a new routing entry is created for the *local subnet,* the Don't Fragment bit is never turned on. If the route is for a *remote destination*, the Don't Fragment bit is not initially set. Instead,

1. An ICMP Echo Request of full MTU size is generated and sent out with the Don't Fragment bit on.
2. The datagram that created the routing table entry is sent out immediately *without* the Don't Fragment bit set.
3. If no response to the Echo Request is received, the Don't Fragment bit is never turned on for that route. If an ICMP Fragmentation Needed message is received from the Echo Request, the PMTU is reduced accordingly, and a new Echo Request with the new PMTU is sent. This process repeats as necessary. If a response to this Echo Request is received, the Don't Fragment bit is set for all further packets.

If you want the Don't Fragment bit set on all outgoing datagrams, issue the following command:

```
# ndd -set /dev/ip ip_pmtu_strategy 1
```

If you want to disable PMTU discovery, use *0* instead of *1* for the above command.

You set the PMTU for a static route in HP-UX using the *route –p pmtu* command. According the HP-UX 11 Release Notes, "The *–p pmtu* option is useful only if you know the network topology well enough to choose an appropriate PMTU for a host or network route. IP will fragment a datagram to the PMTU specified for the route on the local host before sending the datagram to the remote. If the PMTU specified in the route command is correct, it will avoid fragmentation by routers along the path. Using the *–p pmtu* option can simplify the maintenance of *route* when the same PMTU can be applied to all hosts on a network. However, this feature can result in poor network performance or connectivity problems if a network consists of multiple media with different PMTUs. Therefore, using the *–p pmtu* for a network route should be used with some caution." (For more information, see the Release Notes for HP-UX 11.0, Section 7.18.1.)

4.2.10 The Ping Command

There are some significant differences in the *ping* command of the operating systems under discussion. The syntax of Windows 2000 *ping* is

```
ping [-t] [-a] [-n count] [-l length] [-f] [-i ttl] [-v tos]
    [-r count] [-s count] [[-j computer-list] | [-k computer-list]]
    [-w timeout] destination-list
```

The syntax of HP-UX *ping* is

```
ping [-oprv] [-i address] [-t ttl] host [-n count]
ping [-oprv] [-i address] [-t ttl] host packet-size [ [-n] count]
```

Windows 2000 uses the *–f* option (sends a packet with a Don't Fragment flag set) and the *–l length* option (sends Echo Request packets with a specified data length) to determine the PMTU manually. For example, the following two commands demonstrate that the PMTU is set to the maximum for Ethernet:

```
C:\> ping -f -l 1472 10.10.1.1

Pinging 10.10.1.1 with 1472 bytes of data:

Reply from 10.10.1.1: bytes=1472 time<10ms TTL=128
Reply from 10.10.1.1: bytes=1472 time<10ms TTL=128
Reply from 10.10.1.1: bytes=1472 time<10ms TTL=128
Reply from 10.10.1.1: bytes=1472 time<10ms TTL=128

Ping statistics for 10.10.1.1:
    Packets: Sent = 4, Received = 4, Lost = 0 (0% loss),
Approximate round trip times in milli-seconds:
    Minimum = 0ms, Maximum =  0ms, Average =  0ms

C:\>ping -f -l 1473 10.10.1.1

Pinging 10.10.1.1 with 1473 bytes of data:

Packet needs to be fragmented but DF set.
Packet needs to be fragmented but DF set.
Packet needs to be fragmented but DF set.
Packet needs to be fragmented but DF set.

Ping statistics for 10.10.1.1:
    Packets: Sent = 4, Received = 0, Lost = 4 (100% loss),
Approximate round trip times in milli-seconds:
    Minimum = 0ms, Maximum =  0ms, Average =  0ms
```

In the first command, we specified 1472 as the data length because if we add the ICMP Echo Request (8 bytes) and the IP header (20 bytes), we get 1500, the MTU of Ethernet. By adding another byte in the second command (1473), we exceeded the Ethernet MTU and received ICMP error messages to that effect. You can specify the packet size in HP-UX with the *packet_size* parameter.

- In Windows 2000, the *–t* option means the *ping* will continue without interruption. In HP-UX, *–t ttl* sets the time-to-live field in a multicast datagram.
- In Windows 2000, the *–a* option resolves addresses to computer names. There is no *–a* option in HP-UX. Windows 2000 has a *–i* option to set the time-to-live field. HP-UX uses the *–t* option.
- The *–v tos* option of Windows 2000 *ping* sets the type-of-service field to the value specified by *tos*; in HP-UX, it specifies *verbose* output, where ICMP packets other than Echo Responses are shown.
- The *–r count* option in Windows 2000 *ping* records the route of the outgoing packet and the returning packet in the record route field. In HP-UX, *–r* specifies to bypass the normal routing tables and send directly to a host on an attached network.
- Windows 2000 *ping* has a *–s count* option, specifying the timestamp for the number of hops specified by *count*. HP-UX *ping* does not have a *–s* option.
- In Windows 2000, *–j computer-list* routes in loose-source mode packets by way of the list of computers specified by *computer-list*, and *–k computer-list* routes in strict-source mode packets specified by *computer-list*. The closest HP-UX equivalent is *–o*, which inserts an IP Record Route option in outgoing packets, summarizing routes taken when the command terminates.
- Windows 2000 has a *–w timeout* option, specifying a timeout interval in milliseconds. HP-UX does not have this option.
- HP-UX has a *–i address* option. If the destination is a multicast address, the option sends multicast datagrams from the interface with the local IP address specified by *address*. If *–i* is not used, multicast datagrams are sent from the default route interface.
- Finally, if you ping from an HP-UX system and do not specify the number of pings with the *–n count* option, *ping* keeps sending packets until interrupted (using Ctrl-C). Windows 2000 *ping* will continue only four times *unless* you specify more with the *–n count* option.

4.3 Conclusion

The network layer revolves around IP. Though Microsoft has rewritten the TCP/IP stack, it does interoperate with that of HP-UX. There are a number of differences in the behavior of commands like *arp* and *ping*, but the functionality is the same. Though Windows 2000 supports NetBEUI and IPX/SPX, real UNIX and Windows interoperability begins with standardizing on TCP/IP.

References

1. W. Richard Stevens, *TCP/IP Illustrated, Volume 1.* (Addison-Wesley Publishing Company, 1994).
2. Microsoft Corporation, *Microsoft Windows 2000 Server TCP/IP Core Networking Guide.* (Microsoft Press, 2000).

CHAPTER 5

The Transport Layer

At the transport layer we have the connection-oriented Transmission Control Protocol (TCP) and the connectionless User Datagram Protocol (UDP). While both HP-UX and Windows 2000 implementations of TCP/IP interoperate, they differ significantly in the tunable parameters. This chapter briefly describes those parameters.

5.1 TCP

The TCP connection establishment process between HP-UX and Windows 2000 works per the standard:

1. The client sends a *synchronize* (SYN) segment to the server, specifying a destination port number and *initial sequence number* (ISN).
2. The server responds with a SYN segment containing its ISN and an acknowledgment (ACK) containing the client's ISN plus one.
3. The client acknowledges the server's SYN segment by acknowledging the server's ISN plus one.

TCP ports are well-defined and standardized. The common TCP ports are listed in Table 5–1. Windows 2000 networking services are often NetBIOS-based, making TCP port 139 an important one.

Table 5–1 Commonly Used TCP Ports

Service Name	Port
FTP (Data Channel)	20
FTP (Control Channel)	21
Telnet	23
HTTP	80
NetBIOS session service	139

5.1.1 Tunable Parameters

5.1.1.1 Maximum Segment Size (MSS) and Path MTU Discovery

In Chapter 4, "The Internet Layer," we talked about Path maximum transmission unit (MTU) discovery, in which the Don't Fragment bit in the IP header is sent to see if any router along the path returns an Internet Control Message Protocol (ICMP) error. TCP handles Path MTU discovery during connection setup, when each side can announce its maximum segment size (MSS). If the receiving end does not announce its MSS, TCP on the sending station will use one of 536 bytes. At that point, TCP will send IP datagrams with the Don't Fragment bit set. If a router returns an ICMP Destination Unreachable-Fragmentation Needed message, TCP will start adjusting its MSS until no more such messages are received.

By default, Windows 2000 sends TCP segments with the Don't Fragment flag set in the IP header. Therefore, Windows 2000-initiated TCP sessions automatically participate in MTU discovery. Windows 2000 will adjust the TCP MSS to the MTU of the router indicated in the ICMP Destination Unreachable-Fragmentation Needed message.

HP-UX TCP on HP-UX will also adjust its MSS from ICMP Destination Unreachable-Fragmentation Needed messages. This is the default. To disable this behavior, use the following command:

```
# ndd -set /dev/tcp tcp_ignore_path_mtu 1
```

If you run the above command, TCP will default to an MTU of 576 bytes (536-byte MSS plus 40 bytes for the IP and TCP headers).

5.1.1.2 Receive Window Size

Windows 2000 TCP does not have a set value for the receive window size; instead, it uses an algorithm to set it dynamically. This algorithm, taken from the *Microsoft Server TCP/IP Core Networking Guide*, p. 95, is as follows:

1. The first connection request sent to a remote host advertises a receive window size of 16 kilobytes (KB) or 16,384 bytes.
2. Upon establishing the connection, the receive window size is rounded up to an integral multiple of the TCP MSS that was negotiated during connection setup.
3. If the rounded-up value is not at least four times the MSS, then it is adjusted to 4 × MSS, with a maximum size of 64 KB, unless a window-scaling option (RFC 1323) is in effect.

To override this process and set the receive window size manually, edit the following Registry entry:

```
HKLM\SYSTEM\CurrentControlSet\Services\Tcpip\Parameters\
   Interface\<interface>\TcpWindowSize
```

HP-UX The default maximum size for the receive window is 32,768 bytes. To specify another value, use the following command, where *window_size* is in bytes:

```
# ndd -set /dev/tcp tcp_recv_hiwater_def window_size
```

You can also set the maximum size for the receive window of "long, fat pipes" (lfp), such as Fibre Channel, using the *ndd –set /dev/tcp tcp_recv_hiwater_lfp* command. The default for this value is 65,536 bytes. For receive windows of "long, narrow pipes" (lnp), such as PPP, use the *ndd –set /dev/tcp tcp_recv_hiwater_lnp* command. The default here is 8,192 bytes.

5.1.1.3 TCP Keep-Alive Messages

You can set the interval at which Windows 2000 TCP sends keep-alive messages on an inactive connection with the following Registry parameter:

```
HKLM\SYSTEM\CurrentControlSet\Services\Tcpip\ParametersKeepAliveTime
```

The default interval is 7,200,000 milliseconds (two hours). Often, applications like Telnet, rather than users, set up keep-alive messages.

In HP-UX, the following kernel parameters affect TCP behavior for keepalive packets:

- tcp_keepalive_interval
- tcp_ip_abort_interval
- tcp_ip_abort_cinterval
- tcp_keepalive_detached_interval

The parameter **tcp_keepalive_interval** determines the amount of time that TCP waits for an idle connection with no unacknowledged data before sending keep-alive packets. The default is two hours. You can use the *ndd* command to reset the default. The argument to this command is in milliseconds. For example, to set the keep-alive interval to three hours, you would type:

```
# ndd -set /dev/tcp tcp_keepalive_interval 10800000
```

If the remote system does not acknowledge the keep-alive packet, TCP will use one of the following retransmission timers and terminate the connection when it elapses:

State	Timer	Default
Established connection	tcp_ip_abort_interval	600000 ms (10 minutes)
Connection establishment	tcp_ip_abort_cinterval	240000 ms (4 minutes)
Connection termination	tcp_keepalive_detached_interval	240000 ms (4 minutes)

5.1.1.4 TCP Time-Wait Delay

By default, Windows 2000 maintains a socket pair for 240 seconds (four minutes) after the connection closes. To change this value, you edit the following Registry entry:

```
HKLM\SYSTEM\CurrentControlSet\Services\Tcpip\ParametersTcpTimedWaitDelay
```

The value of this parameter can be anywhere from 30 to 300 seconds.

HP-UX, by default, maintains a time interval of 60 seconds for TCP endpoints to persist in a Time-Wait Delay. This value can be changed using the *ndd –set /dev/tcp tcp_time_wait_interval* command. This command's argument is specified in milliseconds, ranging from 10 milliseconds to 600,000 milliseconds.

5.1.2 Windows 2000-Only Tunable Parameters

Windows 2000 allows tuning of TCP using the Registry for which there are no HP-UX equivalents. Following is a list of some of those Registry entries. See the Registry Reference for more information.

TcpDelAckTicks. Changes the ACK timer. The default is 200 milliseconds.
SackOpts. Enables/disables selective acknowledgments (SACKs). The default is enabled.
TcpMaxDataRetransmissions. Determines how many times TCP retransmits an unacknowledged data segment on an existing connection. TCP retransmits data segments until they are acknowledged, or until this value expires. The default is five.
TcpMaxConnectRetransmissions. Determines how many times TCP retransmits an unanswered request for a new connection. TCP retransmits new connection requests until they are answered, or until this value expires. The default is two.
TcpMaxDupAcks. Specifies how many duplicate ACKs (ACKs for the same sequence numbers) constitute a signal to retransmit a segment. The default is two.

5.1.3 HP-UX-Only Tunable Parameters

Below is a list of arguments to the HP-UX *ndd* command that do not have an equivalent Registry entry in Windows 2000. For more information, use the *ndd –h* command. For example,

```
# ndd -h tcp_conn_request_max
```

tcp_conn_request_max. Maximum number of outstanding inbound connection requests. Default is 20 connections.

tcp_ip_notify_cinterval. First threshold timer during connection establishment. Default is 10,000 (10 seconds).

tcp_ip_notify_interval. First threshold timer for established connections. Default is 10,000 (10 seconds).

tcp_ip_ttl. Time-to-live (TTL) value inserted into IP header for TCP packets only. Default is 64.

tcp_largest_anon_port. Largest anonymous port number to use. Default is 65,535.

tcp_rexmit_interval_initial. Initial value for round trip time-out, from which the retransmit time-out is computed. Default is 500ms.

tcp_rexmit_interval_initial_lnp. Same as tcp_rexmit_interval_initial, but used for devices with the LNP flag set. Default is 1,500 (1.5 seconds).

tcp_rexmit_interval_max. Upper limit for computed round trip time-out. Default is 60,000 (1 minute).

tcp_rexmit_interval_min. Lower limit for computed round trip time-out. Default is 500ms.

tcp_sth_rcv_hiwat. If nonzero, sets the Stream-head flow control high water mark. Default is 0.

tcp_sth_rcv_lowat. If nonzero, sets the Stream-head flow control low water mark. Default is 0.

tcp_syn_rcvd_max. Controls the SYN attack defense of TCP. The value specifies the maximum number of suspect connections that will be allowed to persist in SYN_RCVD state. Default is 500 connections.

tcp_status. Obtains a complete report similar to *netstat –an* on all TCP instances.

tcp_xmit_hiwater_def. The amount of unsent data that triggers write-side flow control. Default is 32,768 bytes.

tcp_xmit_hiwater_lfp. The amount of unsent data that triggers write-side flow control for fast links. Default is 65,536 bytes.

tcp_xmit_hiwater_lnp. The amount of unsent data that triggers write-side flow control for slow links. Default is 8,192 bytes.

tcp_xmit_lowater_def. The amount of unsent data that relieves write-side flow control. Default is 8,192 bytes.

tcp_xmit_lowater_lfp. The amount of unsent data that triggers write-side flow control for fast links. Default is 65,536 bytes.

tcp_xmit_lowater_lnp. The amount of unsent data that triggers write-side flow control for slow links. Default is 8,192 bytes.

5.2 UDP

A number of prominent applications on both UNIX and Windows 2000 systems use User Datagram Protocol. These applications include Trivial File Transfer Protocol (Tftp), Simple Network Management Protocol (SNMP), and DNS. On the UNIX side, NFS has used UDP as its transport mechanism, though TCP is becoming more popular to enabling file sharing over WANs.

WANs. Windows 2000 uses UDP for key networking services, something we will examine next. For now, however, keep in mind that many of these services are NetBIOS applications. Note that in Table 5–2 NetBIOS uses UDP ports 137 and 138.

Table 5–2 Commonly Used UDP Ports in Windows 2000

Service Name	Port
DNS client-to-server lookup	53
NetBIOS name service	137
NetBIOS datagram service	138
Common Internet File System	445

5.3 Network Application Interfaces

Before we move on to describing the Application Layer in the next chapter, let's look briefly at network application interfaces in both HP-UX and Windows 2000.

5.3.1 Windows 2000

There are primarily two network application program interfaces (APIs) used in Windows 2000: the Windows Sockets API and the NetBIOS API. Figure 5–1 depicts the relationship between these APIs and the TCP and UDP protocols.

5.3.1.1 Windows Sockets

Windows Sockets is based on the interface developed at the University of California Berkeley. The version shipped with Windows 2000 is 2.2 and is commonly known as Winsock2. Windows 2000 TCP/IP utilities such as Telnet and FTP, as well as applications such as Internet Explorer, are Winsock clients. Such clients resolve host names and IP addresses using tools already familiar to UNIX administrators: HOSTS files and DNS.

5.3.1.2 NetBIOS Interface

Chapter 2, "What Is Windows 2000?," briefly described the origins of NetBIOS. Windows 2000 networking services—the workstation, server, messenger, netlogon, browser—are NetBIOS applications. The term NetBIOS also refers to the protocols that support the API: the name service, datagram service, and session service. These services can run over TCP/IP in addition to IPX/SPX and NetBEUI. Windows implements NetBIOS over TCP/IP via a kernel component known as *NetBT.*

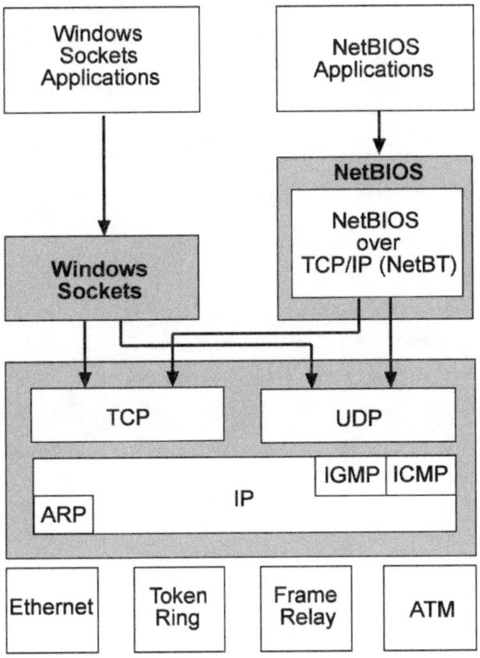

Figure 5–1 Windows 2000 application programming interfaces. Both APIs use TCP and UDP. From *Microsoft Windows 2000 Server TCP/IP Core Networking Guide,* p. 17.

NetBT utilizes a different name resolution scheme, employing things such as broadcasts, LMHOSTS files, and the Windows Internet Naming Service (WINS). Therefore, you need to manage both WinSock and NetBIOS name resolution in a Windows-based network. However, as stated in Chapter 2, the Windows 2000 workstation and server services now support direct hosting—but for computers running Windows 2000 only. With direct hosting, clients use DNS to resolve names and send communication to TCP port 445 instead of port 139 (where NetBIOS session communication normally takes place).

5.3.2 HP-UX

As late as version 10.20, HP-UX TCP/IP was Berkeley sockets-based. At version 11, it is now STREAMS-based. Uresh Vahalia, in *UNIX Internals: The New Frontiers*, (Prentice Hall, 1996), p. 548, describes it best: "A *stream* is a full-duplex processing and data transfer path between a driver in kernel space and a process in user space. STREAMS is a collection of system calls, kernel resources, and kernel utility routines that create, use, and dismantle a stream." From a networking standpoint, it enables the system to utilize any given combination of protocols and drivers.

STREAMS-based network applications resolve host names and IP addresses, using either a HOSTS file, DNS, Network Information Services (NIS), or a combination of all three. There is no need to use WINS or the equivalent of an LMHOSTS file *unless* you install a product such as Hewlett-Packard's Advanced Server/9000, which installs NetBIOS into the kernel.

5.4 Conclusion

We looked at the two protocols found at the transport layer of the TCP/IP protocol suite: the connection-oriented TCP and the connectionless UDP. You can tune TCP parameters in both HP-UX and Windows 2000, though exactly which ones depends on the operating system. NFS and NetBIOS have used UDP extensively for years, though the trend is toward TCP. Network APIs for Windows 2000 include WinSock and NetBIOS. HP-UX has transitioned from Berkeley sockets to STREAMS.

References

1. Thomas Lee and Joseph Davies, *Microsoft Windows 2000 TCP/IP Protocols and Services Technical Reference.* (Microsoft Press, 2000).
2. Microsoft Corporation, *Microsoft Windows 2000 Server TCP/IP Core Networking Guide.* (Microsoft Press, 2000).
3. Uresh Vahalia, *UNIX Internals: The New Frontiers.* (Prentice Hall, 1996).

CHAPTER 6

Name Resolution

As stated in Chapter 5, "The Transport Layer," Windows 2000 networking services are NetBIOS-based. Traditionally, this has required using the NetBIOS name cache, LMHOSTS files, and WINS to resolve NetBIOS computer and service names to IP addresses. Beginning with Windows 2000, such entities are not necessary *as long as you have only Windows 2000 systems in your network.* As of this writing, though, a Windows 2000-only network is unlikely, not to mention that this book assumes you have UNIX-based clients and servers running in your enterprise. Pre-Windows 2000 systems and the tools that make UNIX interoperate with Windows systems currently use NetBIOS. Therefore, it is highly likely that you will continue to have to manage both NetBIOS name resolution and TCP/IP host name resolution.

6.1 Windows 2000

6.1.1 Computer Names

A Windows 2000 *full computer name* is the same thing as a fully qualified domain name (FQDN). An FQDN consists of a host name plus the *primary DNS suffix*. These can be set when you install the system or by right-clicking on **My Computer**, choosing **Properties**, and then clicking on the **Network Identification** tab. Click on the **Properties** button and you will see the **Identification Changes Box**, like the one in Figure 6–1.

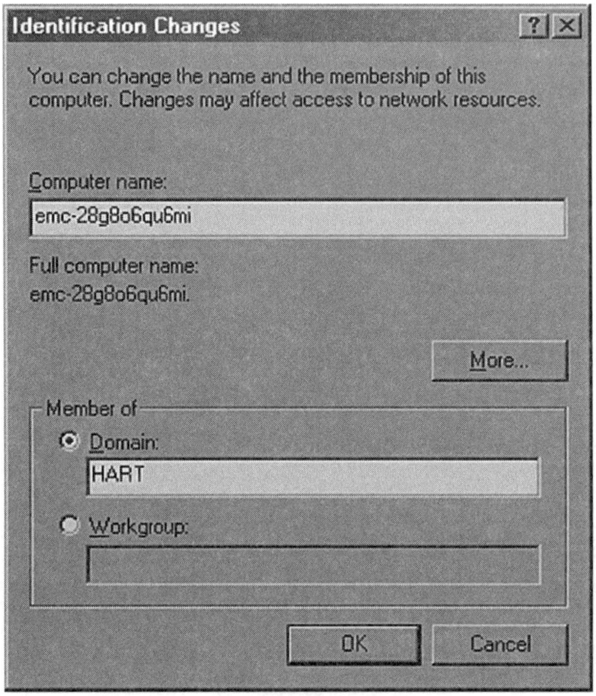

Figure 6–1 Setting the host name. In this example, the full computer name is the host name followed by a period. The primary DNS suffix has not been set. Clicking on the **More...** button enables you to set it.

Filling in the **Computer name:** box sets the host name. If you want to set the primary DNS suffix, click on the **More...** button. You will get the **DNS Suffix and NetBIOS Computer Name** box. See Figure 6–2.

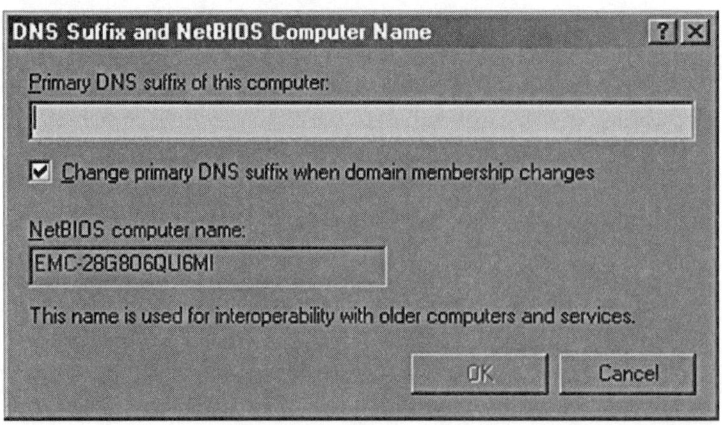

Figure 6–2 Setting the primary DNS suffix. This box enables you to set the primary DNS suffix, which, combined with the host name, creates the full computer name. The NetBIOS computer name defaults to the host name and is provided to enable communication with pre-Windows 2000 systems.

However, you can have more than one FQDN for a system, because Windows 2000 allows you to have a different DNS suffix for each adapter. Thus each adapter can have a *connection-specific DNS suffix*. This suffix can be set either manually or by a DHCP server. Microsoft provides an example of connection-specific DNS suffixes in the Resource Kit, namely that if a system is connected to both the Internet and the corporate intranet, you can have a different FQDN for each connection. (*Microsoft Windows 2000 Server TCP/IP Core Networking Guide*, pp. 338–339.)[1]

6.1.2 Lookup Process

Windows 2000 departs from the NT tradition of going through the NetBIOS name resolution process before trying DNS. Instead, it works the other way around: It goes the DNS route first and *then* NetBIOS. This assumes, of course, that you have a Windows 2000-only network. In order for Windows 2000 systems to communicate with systems that are not Active-Directory enabled, you still must use Windows Internet Naming Service (WINS).

When a user runs a Winsock-based application like Ping or FTP and specifies a host name as the target, the systems calls the **gethostbyname( )** function, which

1. Checks to see if the destination host name matches the source destination name.
2. Checks the local HOSTS file (*\%SystemRoot%\System32\Drivers\Etc*) for a matching entry.
3. Queries DNS.
4. If all else fails, and if the destination host name is 15 bytes or fewer, follows the NetBIOS name resolution method.

If a Winsock application tries to get a host name using an IP address, it calls the **gethostbyaddr( )** function, in which case the system

1. Consults the local HOSTS file for a matching entry.
2. Queries DNS.
3. Sends a NetBIOS Adapter Status Request to the target IP address, the reply to which contains the host name.

Remember, if you have an all-Windows 2000 network, the workstation and server services can use DNS exclusively for communications, eliminating the need for NetBIOS. By default, NetBIOS over TCP/IP is enabled. It is a good idea to keep this setting until all your systems are either Windows 2000 or fully compatible systems.

6.1.3 Windows 2000 Resolver

The first step the Windows 2000 resolver takes in the DNS name resolution process is to determine what kind of name is being submitted. Name types include:

- FQDNs. These are names terminated with a period (for example, *mysystem.emc.com.*) These names are immediately submitted to DNS.
- Multiple-label, unqualified domain names. These either look like FQDNs without a terminating period (for example, *mysystem.emc.com*) or are incomplete FQDNs (for example, *mysystem.emc*). In the former, the resolver appends a period to create an FQDN and then submits the name to DNS. In the latter, it appends different DNS suffixes (specifiable by the user) and periods, and submits each to DNS until resolution succeeds. The user can specify what suffixes to add on the **DNS** tab in the **Advanced TCP/IP Settings** dialog box (see Figure 6–3). If there are no entries in this tab, the resolver uses the primary DNS suffix specified on the **Network Identification** tab of the **System Properties** dialog box. (Click on the **System** icon in the **Control Panel**.)
- Single-label, unqualified domain names. These are simply host names (for example, *mysystem*). In this case, the resolver appends DNS suffixes in the manner described in the previous bullet until resolution succeeds.

For both types of unqualified domain names, the DHCP server can set the primary DNS suffix and the connection-specific DNS suffix. The DNS name resolution process can be quite complex. For more information, including some excellent flow charts illustrating the process, see the *Microsoft Windows 2000 Server TCP/IP Core Networking Guide*, pp. 344–354.[2]

The Windows 2000 resolver caches information received from a DNS query, be it positive (host name found) or negative (host name not found). After undergoing name transformation as previously described, if needed, all queries first go through this cache. The DNS cache also contains the entries in the HOSTS file, loaded automatically upon system startup. The following options to the *ipconfig* command affect the DNS cache:

/flushdns	Removes all entries from the DNS cache.
/displaydns	Displays the contents of the DNS cache.

You can set the length of time that positive and negative responses are cached by editing the following Registry entries:

```
HKLM\SYSTEM\CurrentControlSet\Services\DNSCache\ParametersMaxCache
   EntryTtlLimit
```

```
HKLM\SYSTEM\CurrentControlSet\DNSCache\ParametersNegativeCacheTime
```

The default for positive responses is 86,400 seconds (24 hours); for negative, 300 seconds.

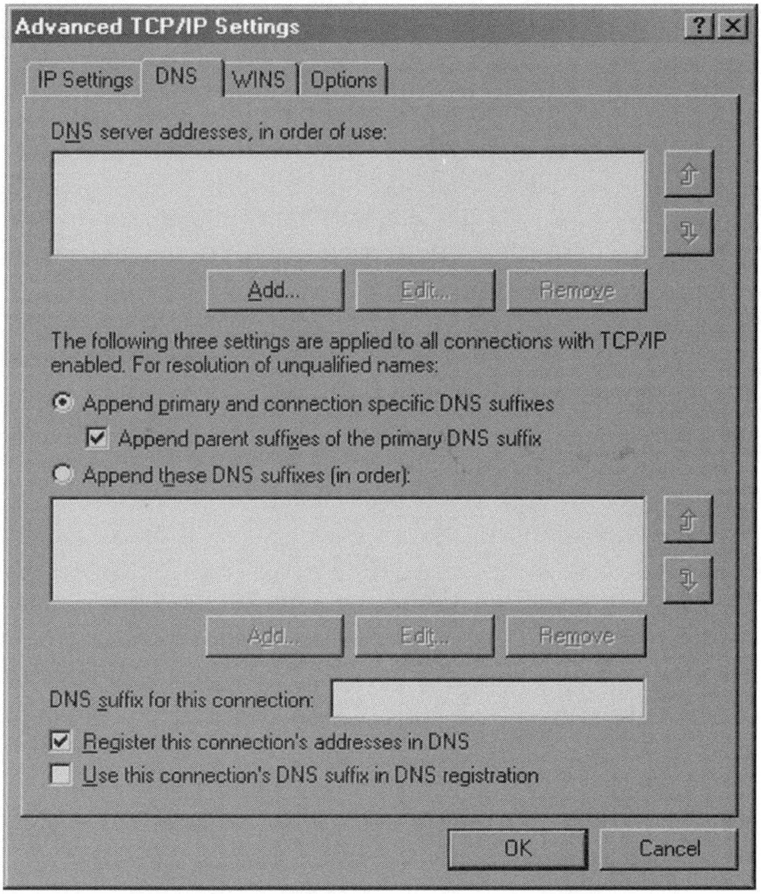

Figure 6–3 The **DNS** tab of the **Advanced TCP/IP Settings** dialog box. Right-click on **My Network Places→Properties**, right-click on **Local Area Connection→Properties.** (This assumes you have just one network adapter.) Then, select **Internet Protocol (TCP/IP)** and select the **Properties** button.

6.1.4 DNS Name Registration

Microsoft's DNS and recent versions of BIND now support dynamic updates of the DNS database. Traditionally, DNS entries have been updated manually. But now you have, in effect, a form of name registration that has long been a feature of WINS. We will come back to this topic later in this chapter. For now, let's move on to NetBIOS name registration and resolution.

6.1.5 NetBIOS

NetBT is Microsoft's implementation of NetBIOS over TCP/IP, but we will assume you use TCP/IP and the more commonly used term NetBIOS instead. NetBIOS-based applications use NetBIOS services to locate resources, establish connections, send and receive data, and terminate connections. These services are the name service, the session service, and the datagram service. Because NetBIOS uses names to identify network resources, the name service is particularly important, since it manages both the registration and resolution of names. The name service uses UDP port 137. The session service establishes, maintains, and terminates reliable, point-to-point connections between NetBIOS applications. A NetBIOS session must be established before any SMB (Server Message Block, the file-sharing protocol) transactions can take place. The session service uses TCP port 139. The datagram service, using UDP port 138, handles messaging that does not require a session.

NetBIOS identifies network resources by names, not addresses. These names are 16 characters long and usually contain a computer name, a user name, or a domain name. You can specify the first 15 characters of these names, but the sixteenth character is reserved to specify the specific network component being addressed. For example, the NetBIOS name for the workstation service (identified by 00 hex) for the computer JETHRO would be JETHRO<00>. The domain master browser (identified by 1B hex) for the domain CLAMPETT would be CLAMPETT<1B>. On Windows 2000 systems, you can view which names a computer has registered by typing *nbtstat –n* at a command prompt.

6.1.6 NetBIOS Name Registration

How are these names created? Usually, they are created when a service starts, like at system startup and when a user logs in. When a particular service starts, its associated name is registered either by network broadcast or by consulting a NetBIOS name server (usually running WINS). If a client is not configured to register its name with a name server, it will send a name service broadcast called a Name Registration Request at startup on the local subnet. After a few tries, if no other client has contested the name, the client's name is officially registered on the subnet (as can be seen by running *nbtstat -n* command). If the system is a WINS client, it sends a Name Registration Request directly to the WINS server, which does the job of ensuring the uniqueness of the name before entering it into its database. Since broadcasts are normally confined to subnets, it is wise to use WINS to enable internetwork name registration.

6.1.7 NetBIOS Name Resolution

How a system resolves NetBIOS names to IP addresses depends on its *node type*. Systems are one of five node types:

B-node	Broadcasts to resolve names.
P-node	Queries WINS to resolve names.
M-node	Broadcasts first, then queries WINS if that fails.
H-node	Queries WINS first, then broadcasts if that fails.
Enhanced	Uses the local LMHOSTS file plus DNS, in addition to the other types.

By default, Windows 2000 systems are configured as B-node unless you specify a WINS server, in which case they become H-node. A Windows DHCP client can obtain its node type from a DHCP server. As with name registration, name resolution is greatly facilitated when you employ WINS in your environment.

If you configure your Windows 2000 system to be a WINS client and it becomes an H-node, the following name resolution process takes place:

1. The client checks the NetBIOS name cache to see if there is a matching entry for the target system. The cache can be preloaded with contents of the LMHOSTS file. See the comments in that file for more information.
2. If that fails, it contacts the WINS server via a *directed datagram*, a routable message sent directly to the WINS server.
3. If that fails, it resorts to broadcasting on the local network.
4. If that fails, it checks the LMHOSTS file, if enabled.

This process greatly reduces broadcast traffic and the need for maintaining LMHOSTS files. Remember, beginning with Windows 2000, this process takes place *only* after the DNS name resolution fails.

6.2 HP-UX

6.2.1 Computer Names

You can set the host name of an HP-UX system upon installation or by running the */sbin/set_parms hostname* command. This host name can be a simple computer name of up to 64 characters, or it can be an FQDN. If it is not an FQDN, you must provide the *domain* option in the */etc/resolv.conf* file. (See the next section, "Lookup Process.") UNIX systems do not have NetBIOS computer names *unless* you install a file-sharing package, such as Samba. Most, if not all, such packages allow you to make a UNIX system a WINS client. In some, such as Advanced Server/9000, you also have the equivalent of a NetBIOS name cache.

6.2.2 Lookup Process

HP-UX systems can consult any combination of the following to resolve host names and IP addresses: a local */etc/hosts* file, an NIS *hosts* map, or DNS. Which of these sources is consulted, and in what order, is determined by the *name service switch*.

- ***/etc/hosts***. The */etc/hosts* file has the same syntax as the HOSTS file on Windows 2000 systems. Its usefulness is primarily for small networks that have little or no need to communicate beyond the local LAN. Unlike the Windows 2000 HOSTS file, a UNIX */etc/hosts* file's contents are not preloaded into a DNS cache.
- **NIS**. The NIS *hosts* map is available to all NIS clients of a particular domain. There is one copy per NIS domain, making maintenance of host name information easier. However, like */etc/hosts* files, NIS maps do not scale well if your systems need to communicate with others outside your LAN. Many UNIX systems now support NIS+, though it is recommended that you use one or the other of NIS or NIS+.
- **DNS**. Finally, DNS, usually in the form of the Berkeley Internet Name Domain (BIND) service, is available for larger scale name resolution.

6.2.2.1 The Name Service Switch

The name service switch determines where a system will search for key pieces of information, including host names and their IP addresses. You configure this switch by editing the */etc/nsswitch.conf* file.

A default version of */etc/nsswitch.conf* contains the following lines:

```
passwd:       files nis
group:        files nis
hosts:        dns [NOTFOUND=return] nis [NOTFOUND=return] files
networks:     nis [NOTFOUND=return] files
protocols:    nis [NOTFOUND=return] files
rpc:          nis [NOTFOUND=return] files
publickey:    nis [NOTFOUND=return] files
netgroup:     nis [NOTFOUND=return] files
automount:    files nis
aliases:      files nis
services:     nis [NOTFOUND=return] files
```

The first field indicates the information database to consult. To configure the name resolution process, you change the *hosts* line. The HP-UX default is to consult DNS first. If the service is not configured, then NIS is consulted. If NIS is not configured, then */etc/hosts* is consulted. If DNS does not find the host, then the lookup process stops (indicated by NOTFOUND=return). If NIS does not find the host then the process stops (also indicated by NOTFOUND=return). This is the default behavior if */etc/nsswitch.conf* does not exist.

The syntax of */etc/nsswitch.conf* is

```
database:  name_service [ status = action  status = action ...]
```

where *database* is the type of information you're seeking. In our case, we want to configure how hosts are looked up, so we would specify *hosts*. The *name_service* is one of the three services available (*files* for */etc/hosts*, *nis* for NIS, or *dns* for DNS). The lookup order is determined by the order of *name_service* entries. Thus, the simplest line for *hosts* would look something like:

```
hosts:    dns NIS files
```

The *status* keyword is what is returned by a name service query, which can be one of the following values:

SUCCESS	The requested information was found.
NOTFOUND	The name service responded but did not find an entry for the request.
UNAVAIL	The name service wasn't available.
TRYAGAIN	The name service was busy.

The *action* keyword determines what action to take given the *status* of a response. The *continue* action means to try the next name service in the list. The *return* action means to end the lookup process.

Therefore, as an example, if you want your system to consult */etc/hosts* first, and then DNS if */etc/hosts* does not find the requested information, then your *hosts* line in */etc/nsswitch.conf* would look like this:

```
hosts: files [NOTFOUND=continue] dns [NOTFOUND=return UNAVAIL=return]
```

This line also indicates that if the requested information is not found, or if the service is not configured, the lookup process stops.

If this seems too complicated to figure out, use SAM. Select **Networking and Communications→Name Service Switch**. You will see a window like the one depicted in Figure 6–4. Just select the **hosts** line, choose **Actions→Configure Name Service Switch,** and use the interface to select the order and criteria for name lookups.

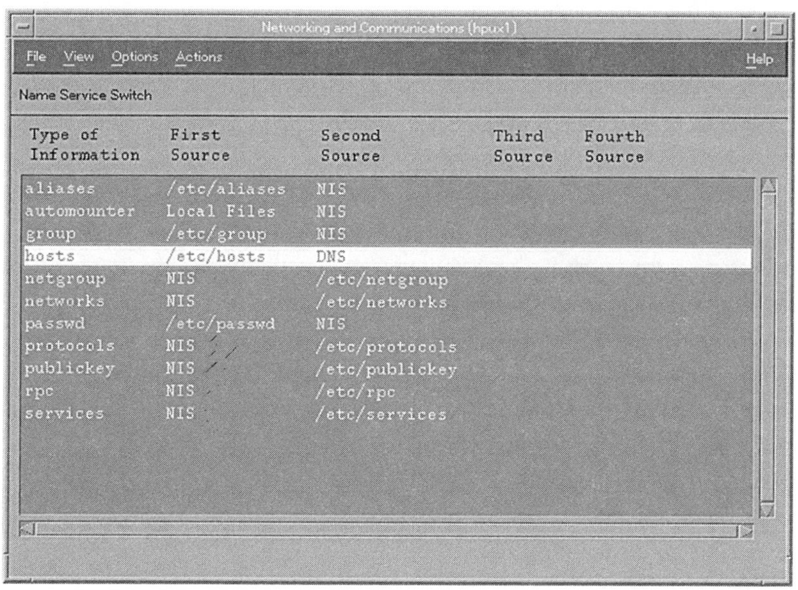

Figure 6–4 Using SAM to configure the name service switch.

6.2.3 The BIND Resolver

The */etc/resolv.conf* file configures the BIND resolver and can contain one of four options:

domain *default_domain* For example: `domain    dev.emc.com`	You need this line when the host name is not an FQDN and you have not configured the search option.
search *domain* For example: `search dev.emc.com it.emc.com`	You can have up to six domains listed, separated by spaces or tabs. If a host name request does not end in a dot, the resolver will append these domain names in order, one at a time, before submitting the query to DNS.
nameserver *name_server_IP_address* For example: `nameserver 132.22.0.4`	You can specify up to three name server IP addresses, each on a separate line beginning with the *nameserver* option name.
options *ndots:n* For example: `options ndots:2`	Sets a threshold for the number of dots which must appear in a name before an initial FQDN query is made. The default value is 1.

The resolver submits names to DNS in the following manner (taken from Hewlett-Packard's *Installing and Administering Internet Services*, pp. 65–67).

- If the target name ends with a dot, BIND looks it up as is, without appending any domains to it.
- If the name to be queried contains at least the number of dots specified by the `ndots` option in the */etc/resolv.conf* file, BIND looks it up as is, before appending any domains to it. (The default value of *ndots* is 1, so if the target name contains at least one dot, it will be looked up as is, before any domains are appended to it.)
- If the target name consists of a single component (contains no dots), and you have set up a host aliases file, BIND looks in your aliases file to translate the alias to a fully qualified host name. You can create a host aliases file for frequently typed host names, like the following example file:

```
john zircon.chem.purdue.edu
melody fermata.music.purdue.edu
```

The alias (the first field on each line) must be all one word, with no dots. To use the file, set the `HOSTALIASES` environment variable to the name of the file, as in the following example:

```
export HOSTALIASES=/home/andrea/myaliases
```

- If the input host name does not end with a dot, BIND looks it up with domain names appended to it. The domain names that BIND appends to it can be configured in four places: the `LOCALDOMAIN` environment variable, the *hostname* command, the *search* option in the */etc/resolv.conf* file, and the *domain* option in the */etc/resolv.conf* file. If a user has set the `LOCALDOMAIN` variable, as in the following example,

  ```
  export LOCALDOMAIN="nmt.edu div.inc.com inc.com"
  ```

  the `LOCALDOMAIN` variable overrides the host name and any *search* or *domain* option in */etc/resolv.conf* for BIND requests made within the context of the user's shell environment. The target host name is looked up in each of the domains in the variable, in the order they are listed.

  If the local host name is set to an FQDN, and the *search* and *domain* options are not specified in */etc/resolv.conf*, the target host name is looked up in the domain configured in the fully qualified host name.

  The *search* option specifies a list of domains to search. You can set the *search* option to any list of domains, but the first domain in the list must be the domain of the local host. BIND looks up host names in each domain, in the order they are listed. BIND uses the *search* option only if the `LOCALDOMAIN` variable is not set.

  The *domain* option specifies the local domain. If you use the *domain* option, BIND will search only the specified domain to resolve host names. BIND uses the *domain* option for host name lookups only if the `LOCALDOMAIN` variable is not set and the *search* option is not specified. (Do not use the *domain* and *search* options together in the same */etc/resolv.conf* file. If you do, the one that appears last in the file will be used, and any previous ones will be ignored.)

6.3 Nslookup Differences

The *nslookup* command works very much the same way in both Windows 2000 and HP-UX. You can run it in interactive or non-interactive mode to query Internet domain name servers. A key difference, however, is that in Windows 2000 *nslookup* queries DNS servers *only*, whereas in HP-UX it can also query */etc/hosts* and NIS. Of course, since NIS is not a Windows 2000 name service, you might expect it to consult the HOSTS file. This is not the case, however.

HP-UX, on the other hand, has the name service switch, and *nslookup* will follow the directives of the */etc/nsswitch.conf* file. Therefore, if your */etc/nsswitch.conf* file has the following entry:

```
hosts: files [NOTFOUND=continue] dns [NOTFOUND=return UNAVAIL=return]
```

then *nslookup* will consult */etc/hosts* first and then DNS. For example,

```
# nslookup hp.com
Using /etc/hosts on:  hpux1
```

```
looking up FILES
Trying DNS
Non-authoritative answer:
Name:     hp.com
Addresses:  192.151.11.32, 192.151.52.13, 192.151.52.10, 192.151.11.13
```

You can also see the order of lookups by using the *policy* subcommand when running *nslookup* in interactive mode. For example,

```
# nslookup
Using /etc/hosts on:  hpux1

> policy
        #Lookups =  2
        files [RCCR]    dns [RRRR]
> exit
```

HP-UX also allows you to keep your options to the *nslookup* command in a file in your home directory called *.nslookuprc*. Type *man nslookup* on the command line for more information.

6.4 Name Resolution Issues in a Mixed Environment

6.4.1 The HOSTS Versus the LMHOSTS File

The format of both the Windows 2000 HOSTS file and the UNIX */etc/hosts* file is the same: IP address followed by host and alias names. If you employ DNS (as most sites now do), the question often asked is, "Should I maintain a HOSTS file (Windows 2000 or UNIX)?" The answer to that is, "It depends." A HOSTS file is handy as a fallback mechanism, should your DNS server become unavailable for some reason. It can also be useful if you want to Telnet to UNIX systems on a network whose IP addresses are not entered into DNS.

If you have a UNIX system providing NetBIOS services and you have NetBIOS over TCP/IP enabled, the Windows 2000 HOSTS file will not help you. In this case, you might need to put its IP address and name into the LMHOSTS file and preload them with #PRE directive and/or make sure these systems (and your clients) are WINS clients.

6.4.2 The NetBIOS Legacy

There is a good chance that Windows 2000 systems will coexist with legacy Windows systems for a while. Also, your UNIX-based interoperability tools may continue to run NetBIOS. For these reasons it will be necessary to manage NetBIOS name resolution and all that it entails: name cache, LMHOSTS, and WINS. However, you can greatly simplify your life in this area by maintaining a WINS server in your organization and making all your clients WINS clients. This is also true of UNIX systems running NetBIOS. Tools such as Samba can make a UNIX file and print server a WINS client, which in turn will enable it to show up in browse lists.

6.4.3 The DNS Server

UNIX systems typically employ some version of BIND as their DNS server. Windows 2000 DNS is a different piece of software. While both BIND and Windows 2000 DNS are RFC-compliant, there are some important differences between the two:

- Dynamic updates support
- WINS and DNS integration
- Active Directory support

6.4.3.1 Dynamic Updates

Windows 2000 DNS supports dynamic updates, which is the ability to register new systems and their IP addresses automatically in the DNS database. BIND version 8.1.2 or later also supports dynamic updates; however, many UNIX systems still run BIND 4.9.7, which does *not*. If your current implementation of DNS does not support dynamic updates, you should disable client-side registration by clearing the **Register this connection's addresses in DNS** box in the **Advanced TCP/IP Settings** box. (See Figure 6–5.) This will keep your DNS servers from being bombarded with registration requests from your clients.

6.4.3.2 WINS

Windows 2000 DNS can be configured to query a WINS server should it fail to find a client's request. The DNS server then passes on the response to the client on behalf of the WINS server. The resource records that support this functionality—WINS and WINS-R—are found only in Windows DNS servers.

6.4.3.3 Active Directory

If your DNS service does not run on a Windows 2000 server, then you must make sure that the service supports the SRV (service location) resource record in order to support Active Directory. BIND 4.9.6 and later support SRV resource records. According to Microsoft, if you use a third-party server, however, you cannot use the DNS console or Dnscmd.exe, Active Directory integration, secure dynamic update, aging and scavenging of stale records, or remote administration. A complete description of how to integrate non-Windows 2000 DNS servers and Active Directory can be found in the *Microsoft Windows 2000 Server TCPIP Core Networking Guide*, pp. 429–433.[3]

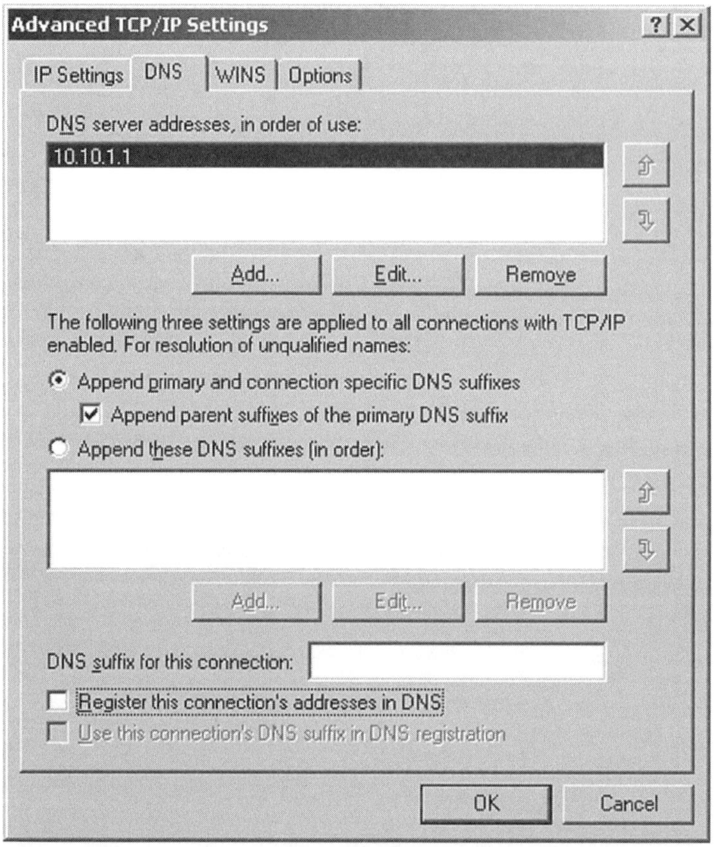

Figure 6–5 Clearing Automatic Client DNS Registration. Get to this screen by right-clicking **My Network Places**, choosing **Properties**, right-clicking **Local Area Connection**, and choosing **Properties→Internet Protocol→Properties→Advanced→DNS**.

6.4.4 DHCP

DHCP was developed to ease the TCP/IP configuration process and to accommodate mobile computing and sites that frequently move their client systems. As DHCP was deployed, it became apparent that there was a new problem to solve: how to keep DNS updated when clients kept changing their IP addresses.

Actually, this problem wasn't so bad for a lot of organizations. Typically, the pattern was that all the UNIX systems used TCP/IP and had their configurations done manually. The PC-based systems, at least initially, ran either NetBEUI or IPX/SPX. As they converted to TCP/IP, their configuration was usually done through a DHCP server because it was so simple to do so. Most sites saw no need for DNS to keep track of PC-based client systems and their IP addresses, since these systems usually did not provide shares or other services. (That's the job of *servers*.)

However, as UNIX systems started becoming DHCP clients, the need to update DNS really became apparent, because things such as file transfers between clients was (and still is, in some places) commonplace in that community.

Windows 2000 DHCP clients can either register their IP information directly with a dynamic DNS server or have the DHCP server do it on their behalf. You can configure Windows 2000 DHCP servers to do this for non-Windows 2000 systems by selecting the **Enable updates for DNS clients that do not support dynamic updates** on the **DNS** tab of the DHCP console. Whether your UNIX DHCP server can do this depends on the vendor. The HP-UX 11 server does not support registering with DNS. The Internet Software Consortium (ISC) DHCP distribution version 3.0, now in beta, will support DNS.

6.5 Conclusion

In this chapter, we looked at how name resolution takes place within Windows 2000 and HP-UX. Windows 2000 computer names are based on DNS domain names. You can set both primary and connection-oriented DNS suffixes in Windows 2000. For compatibility with other Windows systems, Windows 2000 systems still have NetBIOS computer names. In an all-Windows 2000 network, name resolution is done with DNS. In a mixed network with both Windows 2000 and non-Windows 2000 systems, DNS is tried first, then NetBIOS. NetBIOS name resolution is the same on Windows 2000 as it is on pre-Windows 2000 systems. Windows 2000 continues to support WINS for mixed environments.

HP-UX host names are set using the *hostname* command or the *set_parms* script. They do not use NetBIOS computer names unless you install something like Advanced Server/9000. HP-UX systems use the */etc/hosts* file, NIS, DNS, or some combination of the three to resolve computer names. To configure which of these methods to use, and in what order, you configure the name service switch. The BIND resolver has a lookup process similar to the one on Windows 2000, involving a number of system variables and the */etc/resolv.conf* file.

There are also differences in tools such as *nslookup*, DNS, and DHCP. Windows 2000 DNS is a dynamic DNS, whereas you must have BIND version 8.1.2 or later on UNIX systems to support dynamic updates. The Microsoft DHCP server can update a Microsoft DNS server on behalf of its clients.

References

1. Hewlett-Packard, *Installing and Administering LAN/9000 Software*. (Hewlett-Packard, 1997).
2. Hewlett-Packard, *Installing and Administering Internet Services*. (Hewlett-Packard, 2000).
3. Thomas Lee and Joseph Davies, *Microsoft Windows 2000 TCP/IP Protocols and Services Technical Reference*. (Microsoft Press, 2000).
4. Microsoft Corporation, *Microsoft Windows 2000 Server TCP/IP Core Networking Guide*. (Microsoft Press, 2000).

Endnotes

1.–3. From *Microsoft® Windows® 2000 Server Resource Kit* by Microsoft Corporation. Reproduced by permission of Microsoft Press.

CHAPTER 7

DHCP and DNS

Until recently, Dynamic Host Configuration Protocol (DHCP) and Domain Name System (DNS) have not coexisted very well. The latest incarnations of these services from both Microsoft and other sources move them closer together, even to the point of integration. While we mentioned both services in Chapter 6, "Name Resolution," they bear a closer examination here. Because both Hewlett-Packard and Microsoft provide extensive documentation on both of these services, we will examine only the interaction between DHCP and DNS, not explore them in depth.

7.1 DHCP Clients

7.1.1 Windows 2000

By default, a Windows 2000 DHCP client will update its forward name (**A** resource record) with the Dynamic DNS (DDNS) server after receiving its IP address from the DHCP server. The DHCP server in turn updates the DDNS with the reverse name (**PTR** resource record) of the client.

The Windows 2000 client uses an option in its DHCP messages to convey all or part of its domain name to a DHCP server. This option is called option 81, *Client FQDN* (fully qualified domain name), and its minimum length is four bytes. The format of this option is

Code	Len	Flags	Rcode1	Rcode2	Domain Name

The *Flags* field can be set to one of three values. If it is set to 0, the client indicates that it will do its own **A** resource record registration with DNS and let the DHCP server do the **PTR** registration. This is the default setting. If set to 1, the client requests that the DHCP server update DDNS with both **A** and **PTR** records. If the DHCP server is configured to update both records regardless of the client's request, it sets the *Flags* field to 3 in its DHCPOFFER and DHCPACK messages. The DHCP server uses the *Rcode* fields to indicate to the client the response code from the DDNS server after an **A** resource record update and also indicate whether it attempted the update before sending a DHCPACK message. The *Domain Name* field specifies the FQDN of the client and consists of the host name concatenated with the primary DNS suffix.

You can change the *Flags* and *Domain Name* fields by right-clicking on **My Network Places**, and then selecting **Properties**. Right-click on **Local Area Network** and then **Properties**. Select **Internet Protocol (TCP/IP)→Properties→Advanced**. On the **DNS** tab, you have some options to choose from, as shown in Figure 7–1.

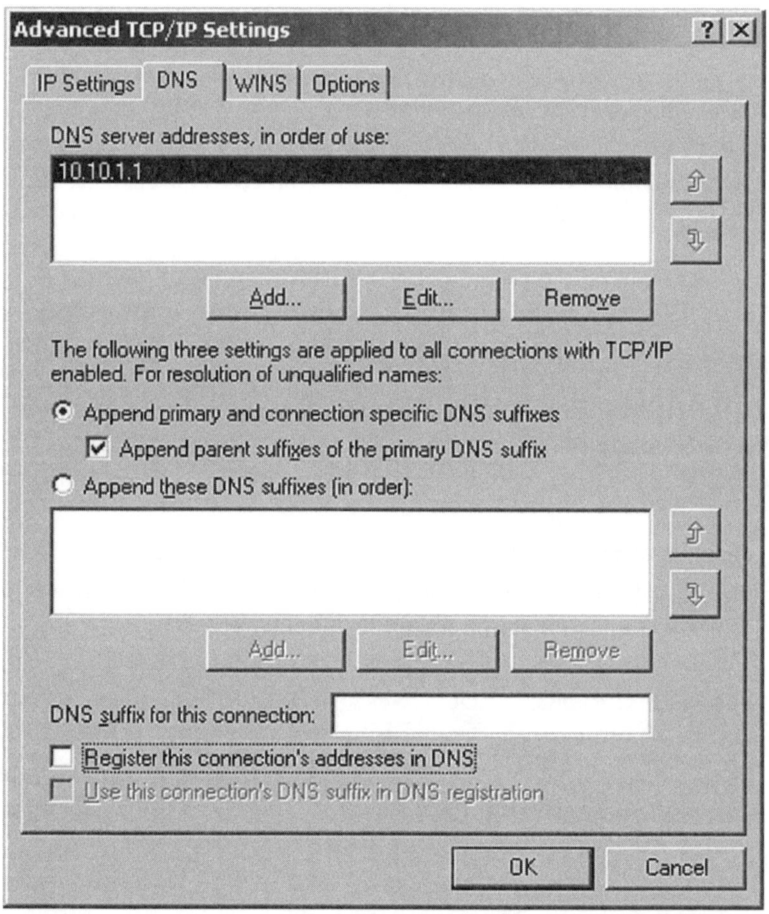

Figure 7–1 The **DNS** Tab of the **Advanced TCP/IP Settings** box.

If the **Register this connection's addresses in DNS** box is selected and the **Use this connection's DNS suffix in DNS registration** box is unselected (the default), the client has the *Flags* field set to 0, and the primary DNS suffix will be used to form the FQDN registered with DNS. If both the former and the latter are selected, the connection-specific DNS suffix will also be registered. To set the *Flags* field to 1, deselect the **Register this connection's addresses in DNS** box.

7.1.2 HP-UX

When you first boot a newly installed HP-UX system, it runs the */etc/auto_parms* script, which handles first-time boot configuration and the management of DHCP leases. This script will ask if you want to configure the system as a DHCP client. Upon subsequent boots, it consults the variable DHCP_ENABLE[*index*] (where *index* indicates the interface number) in */etc/rc.config.d/netconf*. If this variable is set to 1, *auto_parms* will run */usr/lbin/dhcpclient,* which will request a lease on the interface indicated by the index number. Once the system obtains a lease, it will configure networking using the *dhcpdb2conf* utility. Upon system restart, the *auto_parms* script will start *dhcpclient* in maintenance mode (running as a daemon) to handle lease renewal.

You can transform an HP-UX system configured with a static IP address into a DHCP client using System Administration Manager (SAM). Select **Networking and Communications →Network Interface Cards**. Select the card on which you want to enable DHCP and then choose **Actions→Configure** from the pull-down menu. Single-click the **Enable DHCP** button, as shown in Figure 7–2. Statically defined networking values will be overwritten if the system successfully obtains a lease from the DHCP server. If obtaining a lease is unsuccessful, then the original networking values will be retained.

You can also edit the */etc/rc.config.d/netconf* file to set up a DHCP client. Change the value of the DHCP_ENABLE value to 1, and then reboot the system. Whatever method you use will, if obtaining a lease is successful, change the values of the appropriate variables found in */etc/rc.config/netconf*.

7.1.2.1 The HP-UX DHCP Client and DDNS

The current HP-UX DHCP client does *not* support Option 81, the FQDN option, in any of its messages. Therefore, a Windows 2000 DHCP server is unable to register an HP-UX client's FQDN with DNS. Future versions of HP-UX 11, however, will have DHCP clients sending Option 12, the Host Name option, in its messages. Windows 2000 DHCP servers can use Option 12 to register information with DDNS.

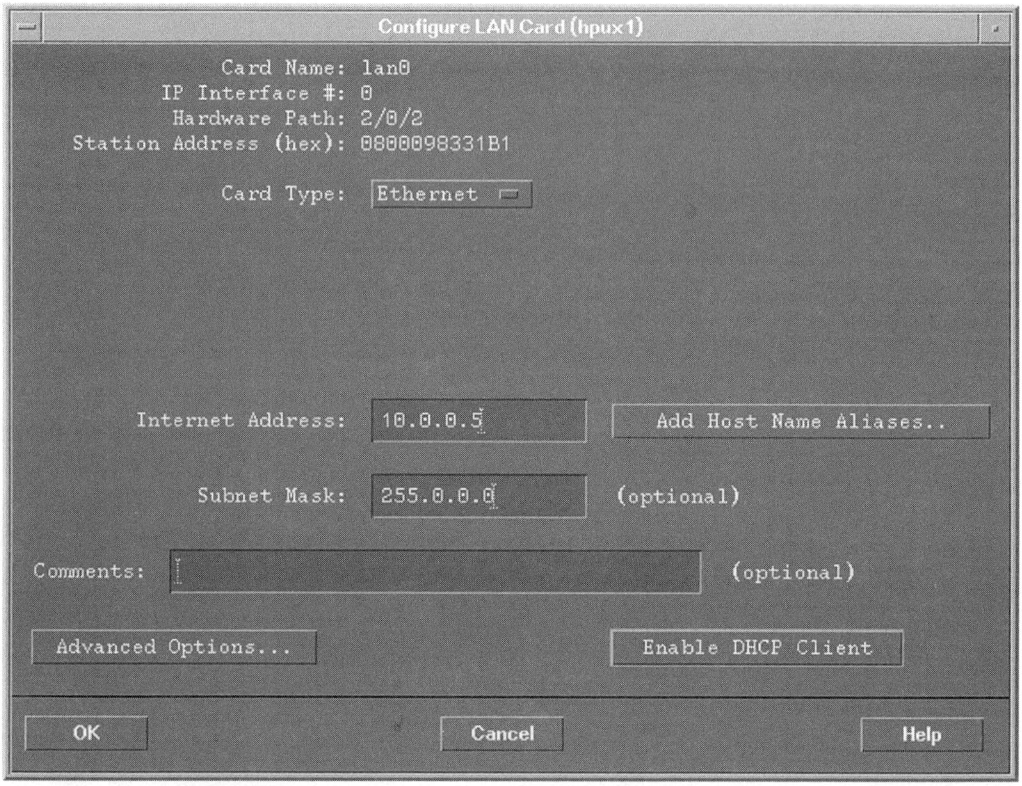

Figure 7–2 Using SAM to enable DHCP.

7.2 Windows 2000 DHCP Server

The Windows 2000 DHCP Server can be configured to update DNS according to client requests or to always update both **A** and **PTR** records. On the DHCP server you run the DHCP manager to configure these options. (See Figure 7–3.) The default configuration is for the **Automatically update DHCP client information in DNS** box to be checked and the **Update DNS only if DHCP client requests** option selected. After dispensing the IP address lease to the client, the server attempts to update the **PTR** record with DNS, while the client attempts to update the **A** record.

If you set the **Always update DNS** option, then the server sets the *Flags* field to 3 and attempts to update DNS regardless of the client request. The client in turn does not attempt any updates. If you deselect the **Automatically update DHCP client information in DNS** box, then the server does no updating, and the client attempts to update both **A** and **PTR** records.

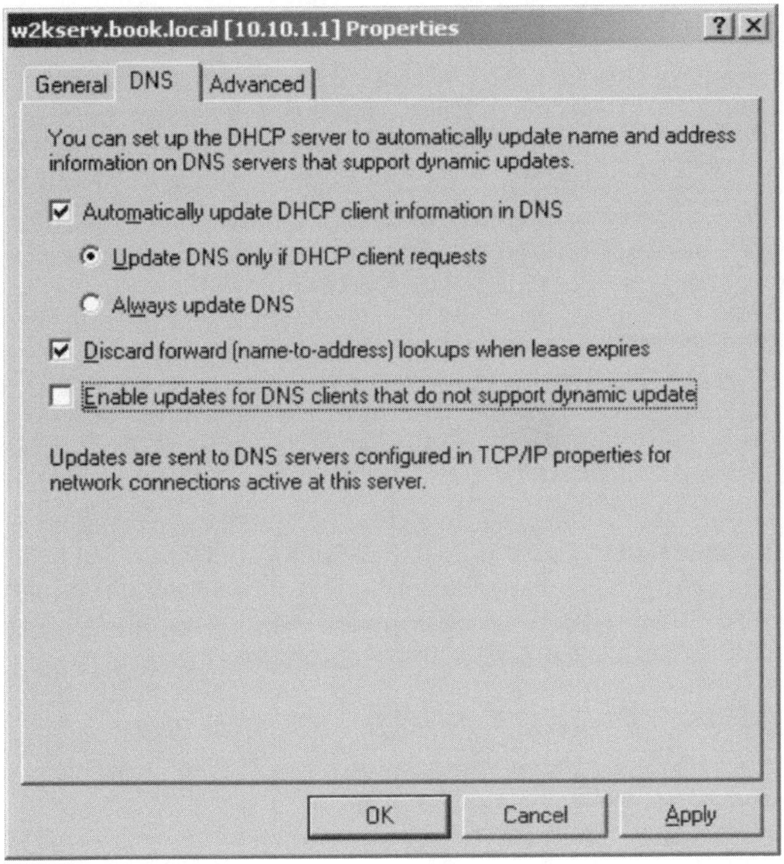

Figure 7–3 The **DNS** tab of the DHCP Manager. Open the **Control Panel** on the DHCP server, double-click on the **DHCP** icon, right-click on the **server** icon choose **Properties**. Then select the **DNS** tab.

7.2.1 DHCP/DNS Interoperability

7.2.1.1 HP-UX DHCP Client and Windows 2000 DHCP Server

On my test HP-UX 11 system, there was no problem making it a DHCP client of a Windows 2000 DHCP server. It received its IP address, domain name, and Network Information Service (NIS) domain successfully. However, the Windows 2000 DHCP server was unable to update the HP-UX client in DDNS (which ran on the same machine), and the client was not DDNS-aware. The HP-UX client supports neither Option 12 nor Option 81 and therefore has no way of informing the DHCP server of its host name.

There is a workaround, however, though it defeats the purpose of DDNS by requiring a manual configuration of the DHCP server. You can create a reservation on the DHCP server for the HP-UX client and then specify Option 12, the host name option, as part of the reservation. Therefore, when the HP-UX client requests a DHCP lease, the server will respond with a lease containing the host name. The DHCP server in turn can use this host name, along with the DNS domain name, to update the DDNS server. While this process works for DDNS, it fails for DHCP, since you have to make reservations for each client that does not support either Option 12 or Option 81 in its DHCP messages. Until HP-UX supports one of these options, having an HP-UX DHCP client of a Windows 2000 server is a bit problematic.

7.2.1.2 Windows 2000 DHCP Client and HP-UX DHCP Server

A Windows 2000 DHCP client can get all the networking configuration it needs from an HP-UX 11 DHCP server. This information includes not only the usual stuff like IP address, DNS server, gateway, and DNS domain name, but also NetBIOS name server (Option 44), NetBIOS node type (Option 46), and NetBIOS Scope (Option 47).

However, the HP-UX DHCP server does *not* perform any update requests to DDNS, be it Windows 2000 DNS or BIND version 8. Therefore, it is up to the Windows 2000 client to perform such an update. To ensure that this happens, you must check the **Register this connection's addresses in DNS** box on the **DNS** tab of the **Advanced TCP/IP Settings** box. (See Figure 7–1.) The Windows 2000 client will then follow the dynamic update process:

1. Query the local name server for the primary name server and the update zone.
2. Using the information in the local name server's response, send a dynamic update request to the authoritative primary server for the zone.

If you want the connection-specific DNS suffix to be registered in DDNS, you must also check the **Use this connection's DNS suffix in DNS registration** box. Otherwise, the client will use the primary DNS suffix.

7.2.1.3 DDNS on HP-UX

You need to upgrade BIND on HP-UX to version 8.1.2 in order to implement DDNS. (As of this writing, this was the latest supported version of BIND on HP-UX.) Once you do so, you enable dynamic updates by editing the */etc/named.conf* file, the BIND configuration file. This file consists of statements ending in semicolons; some statements contain a block of substatements or options. You need to add an *allow-update* option to the *zone* statement. The *zone* statement defines a zone in the configuration file. The *allow-update* option specifies which hosts are allowed to send update requests to DDNS. (The default is to deny updates from all hosts.) For more information, see the "ISC BIND Documentation" page at *www.isc.org/products/BIND/docs/index.html.*

The syntax of this option is *allow-update { address_match_list }*, where *address_match_list* can be an IP address (in dotted-decimal notation), an IP prefix (in the "/" notation), a key ID as defined by the *key* statement, or the name of an address match list previously defined with the *acl* (Access Control List) statement. There are also built-in ACLs: *any* (allows all hosts), *none* (denies all hosts), *localhost* (allows the IP addresses of all interfaces on the system), and *localnets* (allows any host on a network for which the system has an interface).

For my test case, I listed the following in the */etc/named.conf* file:

```
zone "book.local" {
        type master;
        file "db.book";
        allow-update { any; };
};

zone "0.0.10.IN-ADDR.ARPA" {
        type master;
        file "db.10.0.0";
        allow-update { any; };
};
```

I had two *zone* statements: one for the *book.local* domain and one for the *0.0.10.IN-ADDR.ARPA* reverse domain. Both statements contain the *allow-update { any; };* substatement, which essentially opened my BIND server to update requests from any host on the network. (This is not a secure thing to do, but I used it as a proof-of concept tool.) As a result, my Windows 2000 client successfully updated its **RR** and **PTR** records with the server, as shown by the following Network Monitor capture:

```
137     9.546875     LOCAL      HEWLET8331B1     DNS      0x15:Dyn Upd PRE
records to w2kserv.book.local. o W2KSERV       10.0.0.5
+ Frame: Base frame properties
+ ETHERNET: ETYPE = 0x0800 : Protocol = IP:  DOD Internet Protocol
+ IP: ID = 0x6888; Proto = UDP; Len: 102
+ UDP: Src Port: Unknown, (1551); Dst Port: DNS (53); Length = 82 (0x52)
  DNS: 0x15:Dyn Upd PRE records to w2kserv.book.local. of type Canonical name
      DNS: Query Identifier = 21 (0x15)
      DNS: DNS Flags = Query, OpCode - Dyn Upd, RCode - No error
          DNS: 0............... = Request
          DNS: .0101........... = Dynamic Update
          DNS: .....0.......... = Server not authority for domain
          DNS: ......0......... = Message complete
          DNS: .......0........ = Iterative query desired
          DNS: ........0....... = No recursive queries
          DNS: .........000.... = Reserved
          DNS: ............0000 = No error
      DNS: Zone Count = 1 (0x1)
      DNS: Prerequisite Section Entry Count = 2 (0x2)
      DNS: Update Section Entry Count = 0 (0x0)
      DNS: Additional Records Count = 0 (0x0)
      DNS: Update Zone: book.local. of type SOA on class INET addr.
          DNS: Update Zone Name: book.local.
          DNS: Update Zone Type = Start of zone of authority
          DNS: Update Zone Class = Internet address class
      DNS: Prerequisite: w2kserv.book.local. of type Canonical name on class
           Unknown Class(2 records present)
```

```
        DNS: Resource Record: w2kserv.book.local. of type Canonical name on
              class Unknown Class
            DNS: Resource Name: w2kserv.book.local.
            DNS: Resource Type = Canonical name for alias
            DNS: Resource Class = 0x00FE
            DNS: Time To Live = 0 (0x0)
            DNS: Resource Data Length = 0 (0x0)
        DNS: Resource Record: w2kserv.book.local. of type Host Addr on class
              INET addr.
            DNS: Resource Name: w2kserv.book.local.
            DNS: Resource Type = Host Address
            DNS: Resource Class = Internet address class
            DNS: Time To Live = 0 (0x0)
            DNS: Resource Data Length = 4 (0x4)
            DNS: IP address = 10.0.0.6
*************************************************************
138      9.546875     HEWLET8331B1    LOCAL      DNS      0x15:Dyn Upd Resp.
10.0.0.5       W2KSERV       IP

+ Frame: Base frame properties
+ ETHERNET: ETYPE = 0x0800 : Protocol = IP:  DOD Internet Protocol
+ IP: ID = 0xFE5A; Proto = UDP; Len: 40
+ UDP: Src Port: DNS, (53); Dst Port: Unknown (1551); Length = 20 (0x14)
  DNS: 0x15:Dyn Upd Resp.
      DNS: Query Identifier = 21 (0x15)
      DNS: DNS Flags = Response, OpCode - Dyn Upd, RA Bits Set, RCode - No error
          DNS: 1............... = Response
          DNS: .0101........... = Dynamic Update
          DNS: .....0.......... = Server not authority for domain
          DNS: ......0......... = Message complete
          DNS: .......0........ = Iterative query desired
          DNS: ........1....... = Recursive queries supported by server
          DNS: .........000.... = Reserved
          DNS: ............0000 = No error
      DNS: Zone Count = 0 (0x0)
      DNS: Prerequisite Section Entry Count = 0 (0x0)
      DNS: Update Section Entry Count = 0 (0x0)
      DNS: Additional Records Count = 0 (0x0)
      DNS: Query Identifier = 0 (0x0)
      DNS: DNS Flags = Query, OpCode - Std Qry, RCode - No error
          DNS: 0............... = Request
          DNS: .0000........... = Standard Query
          DNS: .....0.......... = Server not authority for domain
          DNS: ......0......... = Message complete
          DNS: .......0........ = Iterative query desired
          DNS: ........0....... = No recursive queries
          DNS: .........000.... = Reserved
          DNS: ............0000 = No error
      DNS: Zone Count = 0 (0x0)
```

Though this output may be hard to decipher, you can probably make out that Frame 137 is a dynamic DNS update request from a system called Local (in this case, a Windows 2000 system) to the HP-UX BIND server (as designated by HEWLET8331B1). The request is to update the *book.local* zone only (for the **A** record). (A later frame requested an update to the *db.10.0.0* zone for the **PTR** record.) Frame 138 contains the BIND server's response, which contains no errors.

This exchange resulted in changes to the *db.book* and *db.10.0.0* files. The HP-UX convention is to name the address resolution data file *db.[domain]*, where *[domain]* is the DNS domain name. The reverse address resolution data file is called *db.[net]*, where *[net]* is the network number of the domain. My *db.book* file looked like the following:

```
;BIND DUMP V8
$ORIGIN local.
book            IN      NS      hpux1.book.local.       ;Cl=2
        600     IN      A       10.0.0.6        ;Cl=2
                IN      SOA     hpux1.book.local. root.hpux1.book.local. (
                26 10800 3600 604800 86400 )    ;Cl=2
$ORIGIN book.local.
w2kserv         IN      MX      10 w2kserv.book.local.  ;Cl=2
                IN      A       10.0.0.6        ;Cl=2
houyhnhnm       1200    IN      A       10.0.0.7        ;Cl=2
localhost       IN      A       127.0.0.1       ;Cl=2
hpux1           IN      MX      10 hpux1.book.local.    ;Cl=2
                IN      A       10.0.0.5        ;Cl=2
aix1            IN      MX      10 aix1.book.local.     ;Cl=2
                IN      A       10.0.0.9        ;Cl=2
$ORIGIN _msdcs.book.local.
09518ccb-d981-4983-bdb2-db496480ddb8    600     IN      CNAME   w2kserv.book.loc
al.     ;Cl=2
$ORIGIN _tcp.dc._msdcs.book.local.
_ldap   600     IN      SRV             0 100 389 w2kserv.book.local.   ;Cl=2
_kerberos       600     IN      SRV             0 100 88 w2kserv.book.local.
;Cl=2
$ORIGIN _tcp.Default-First-Site._sites.dc._msdcs.book.local.
_ldap   600     IN      SRV             0 100 389 w2kserv.book.local.   ;Cl=2
_kerberos       600     IN      SRV             0 100 88 w2kserv.book.local.
;Cl=2
$ORIGIN _tcp.pdc._msdcs.book.local.
_ldap   600     IN      SRV             0 100 389 w2kserv.book.local.   ;Cl=2
$ORIGIN _tcp.457306ad-d496-421c-98db-57ad6efdc06d.domains._msdcs.book.local.
_ldap   600     IN      SRV             0 100 389 w2kserv.book.local.   ;Cl=2
$ORIGIN _tcp.gc._msdcs.book.local.
_ldap   600     IN      SRV             0 100 3268 w2kserv.book.local.  ;Cl=2
$ORIGIN _tcp.Default-First-Site._sites.gc._msdcs.book.local.
_ldap   600     IN      SRV             0 100 3268 w2kserv.book.local.  ;Cl=2
$ORIGIN _udp.book.local.
_kpasswd        600     IN      SRV             0 100 464 w2kserv.book.local.
;Cl=2
_kerberos       600     IN      SRV             0 100 88 w2kserv.book.local.
;Cl=2
```

```
$ORIGIN _tcp.Default-First-Site._sites.book.local.
_ldap    600      IN       SRV              0 100 389 w2kserv.book.local.    ;Cl=2
_kerberos        600      IN       SRV              0 100 88 w2kserv.book.local.
;Cl=2
_gc      600      IN       SRV              0 100 3268 w2kserv.book.local.  ;Cl=2
$ORIGIN _tcp.book.local.
_ldap    600      IN       SRV              0 100 389 w2kserv.book.local.    ;Cl=2
_kpasswd         600      IN       SRV              0 100 464 w2kserv.book.local.
;Cl=2
_kerberos        600      IN       SRV              0 100 88 w2kserv.book.local.
;Cl=2
_gc      600      IN       SRV              0 100 3268 w2kserv.book.local.  ;Cl=2
```

You can see that the Windows 2000 system, called *w2kserv,* has several resource records: **A**, **MX**, and **SRV**. An **SRV** record (server resource record) is used to register and locate well-known TCP/IP services and is used in Windows 2000 to locate domain controllers. You can see that some of the well-known services included in this file are LDAP and Kerberos.

The *db.10.0.0* file looked like

```
;BIND DUMP V8
$ORIGIN 0.10.IN-ADDR.ARPA.
0                 IN       NS       hpux1.book.local.         ;Cl=5
                  IN       SOA      hpux1.book.local. root.hpux1.book.local. (
                  16 10800 3600 604800 86400 )      ;Cl=5
$ORIGIN 0.0.10.IN-ADDR.ARPA.
4                 IN       PTR      aix.book.local. ;Cl=5
6        1200     IN       PTR      w2kserv.book.local.       ;Cl=5
7        1200     IN       PTR      houyhnhnm.book.local.     ;Cl=5
         1200     IN       PTR      houyhnhnm.isus.emc.com.   ;Cl=5
5                 IN       PTR      hpux1.book.local.         ;Cl=5
```

7.2.1.4 HP-UX DNS Server and Windows 2000 DHCP Server

If you run BIND version 8.1.2 or higher on HP-UX 11, you can also have a Windows 2000 DHCP server perform dynamic update requests on behalf of Windows 2000 clients successfully. Remember that on Windows 2000 clients, you must deselect the **Register this connection's addresses in DNS** box on the **Advanced TCP/IP Settings** window. (See Figure 7–1.) Also, you must select the **Automatically update DHCP client information in DNS** and the **Always update DNS** options in the DHCP management console, as shown in Figure 7–4. Finally, for non-Windows 2000 DHCP clients, you need to select **Enable updates for DNS clients that do not support dynamic update**. In my test environment, I managed to get the Windows 2000 DHCP server to update the records of an AIX system.

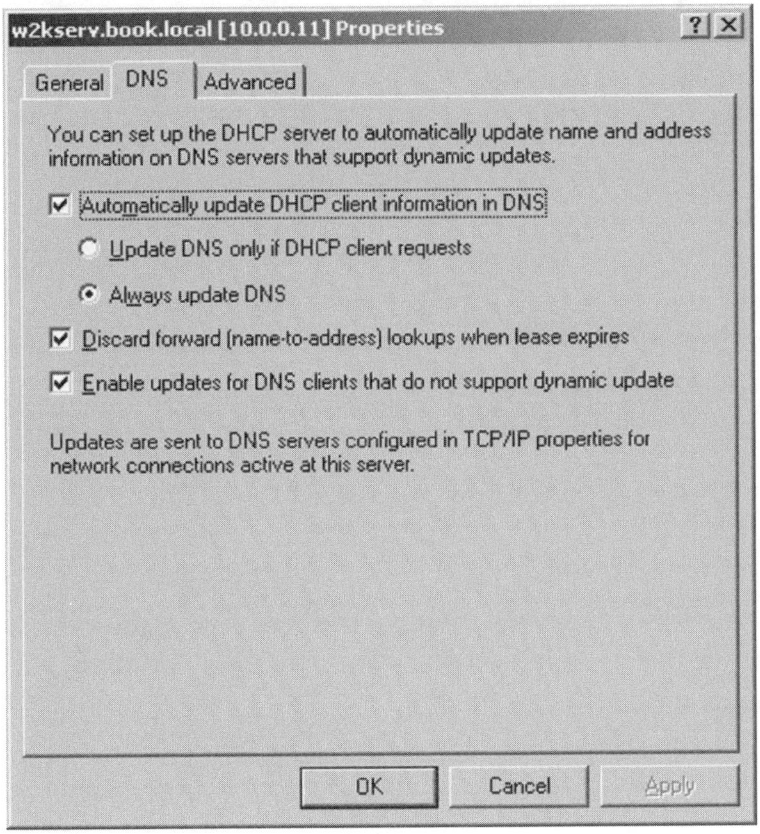

Figure 7–4 Configuring the DHCP server to update DNS. Open the DHCP MMC, select your server, and then choose **Properties**.

The following Network Monitor output shows how (in frame 57) the Windows DHCP server, called *W2KSERV*, requested the HP-UX DNS server, designated by HEWLET8331B1, to update the **A** record for the Windows 2000 DHCP client *houyhnhnm.book.local*. The very last line of this frame indicates that *houyhnhnm's* IP address is 10.0.0.2

```
57 41.687500 LOCAL HEWLET8331B1 DNS 0xF:Dyn Upd PRE/UPD records to
houyhnhnm.book.loc W2KSERV         10.0.0.5
  Frame: Base frame properties
      Frame: Time of capture = 8/21/2000 15:48:7.390
      Frame: Time delta from previous physical frame: 0 microseconds
      Frame: Frame number: 57
      Frame: Total frame length: 130 bytes
      Frame: Capture frame length: 130 bytes
      Frame: Frame data: Number of data bytes remaining = 130 (0x0082)
  ETHERNET: ETYPE = 0x0800 : Protocol = IP:  DOD Internet Protocol
      ETHERNET: Destination address : 0800098331B1
          ETHERNET: .......0 = Individual address
          ETHERNET: ......0. = Universally administered address
```

```
    ETHERNET: Source address : 0060B06A8E9C
        ETHERNET: .......0 = No routing information present
        ETHERNET: ......0. = Universally administered address
    ETHERNET: Frame Length : 130 (0x0082)
    ETHERNET: Ethernet Type : 0x0800 (IP:  DOD Internet Protocol)
    ETHERNET: Ethernet Data: Number of data bytes remaining = 116 (0x0074)
IP: ID = 0x2760; Proto = UDP; Len: 116
    IP: Version = 4 (0x4)
    IP: Header Length = 20 (0x14)
    IP: Precedence = Routine
    IP: Type of Service = Normal Service
    IP: Total Length = 116 (0x74)
    IP: Identification = 10080 (0x2760)
    IP: Flags Summary = 0 (0x0)
        IP: .......0 = Last fragment in datagram
        IP: ......0. = May fragment datagram if necessary
    IP: Fragment Offset = 0 (0x0) bytes
    IP: Time to Live = 128 (0x80)
    IP: Protocol = UDP - User Datagram
    IP: Checksum = 0xFF09
    IP: Source Address = 10.0.0.11
    IP: Destination Address = 10.0.0.5
    IP: Data: Number of data bytes remaining = 96 (0x0060)
UDP: Src Port: Unknown, (1807); Dst Port: DNS (53); Length = 96 (0x60)
    UDP: Source Port = 0x070F
    UDP: Destination Port = DNS
    UDP: Total length = 96 (0x60) bytes
    UDP: UDP Checksum = 0x278C
    UDP: Data: Number of data bytes remaining = 88 (0x0058)
DNS: 0xF:Dyn Upd PRE/UPD records to houyhnhnm.book.local. of type Canonical name
    DNS: Query Identifier = 15 (0xF)
    DNS: DNS Flags = Query, OpCode - Dyn Upd, RCode - No error
        DNS: 0............... = Request
        DNS: .0101........... = Dynamic Update
        DNS: .....0.......... = Server not authority for domain
        DNS: ......0......... = Message complete
        DNS: .......0........ = Iterative query desired
        DNS: ........0....... = No recursive queries
        DNS: .........000.... = Reserved
        DNS: ............0000 = No error
    DNS: Zone Count = 1 (0x1)
    DNS: Prerequisite Section Entry Count = 1 (0x1)
    DNS: Update Section Entry Count = 2 (0x2)
    DNS: Additional Records Count = 0 (0x0)
    DNS: Update Zone: book.local. of type SOA on class INET addr.
        DNS: Update Zone Name: book.local.
        DNS: Update Zone Type = Start of zone of authority
        DNS: Update Zone Class = Internet address class
    DNS: Prerequisite: houyhnhnm.book.local. of type Canonical name on class
         Unknown Class
        DNS: Resource Name: houyhnhnm.book.local.
        DNS: Resource Type = Canonical name for alias
        DNS: Resource Class = 0x00FE
        DNS: Time To Live = 0 (0x0)
```

```
        DNS: Resource Data Length = 0 (0x0)
    DNS: Update: houyhnhnm.book.local. of type Host Addr on class Req. for
        any(2 records present)
        DNS: Resource Record: houyhnhnm.book.local. of type Host Addr on class
            Req. for any
            DNS: Resource Name: houyhnhnm.book.local.
            DNS: Resource Type = Host Address
            DNS: Resource Class = Request for any class
            DNS: Time To Live = 0 (0x0)
            DNS: Resource Data Length = 0 (0x0)
        DNS: Resource Record: houyhnhnm.book.local. of type Host Addr on class
            INET addr.
            DNS: Resource Name: houyhnhnm.book.local.
            DNS: Resource Type = Host Address
            DNS: Resource Class = Internet address class
            DNS: Time To Live = 900 (0x384)
            DNS: Resource Data Length = 4 (0x4)
            DNS: IP address = 10.0.0.2
```

Frame 58 shows the HP-UX server's response to the update request. The destination address of this frame is 10.0.0.11, which is the IP address of *W2KSERV*, not that of *Houyhnhnm*.

```
58 41.765625 HEWLET8331B1 LOCAL DNS 0xF:Dyn Upd Resp. 10.0.0.5 W2KSERV   IP
  Frame: Base frame properties
      Frame: Time of capture = 8/21/2000 15:48:7.468
      Frame: Time delta from previous physical frame: 78125 microseconds
      Frame: Frame number: 58
      Frame: Total frame length: 60 bytes
      Frame: Capture frame length: 60 bytes
      Frame: Frame data: Number of data bytes remaining = 60 (0x003C)
  ETHERNET: ETYPE = 0x0800 : Protocol = IP:  DOD Internet Protocol
      ETHERNET: Destination address : 0060B06A8E9C
          ETHERNET: .......0 = Individual address
          ETHERNET: ......0. = Universally administered address
      ETHERNET: Source address : 0800098331B1
          ETHERNET: .......0 = No routing information present
          ETHERNET: ......0. = Universally administered address
      ETHERNET: Frame Length : 60 (0x003C)
      ETHERNET: Ethernet Type : 0x0800 (IP:  DOD Internet Protocol)
      ETHERNET: Ethernet Data: Number of data bytes remaining = 46 (0x002E)
  IP: ID = 0xC493; Proto = UDP; Len: 40
      IP: Version = 4 (0x4)
      IP: Header Length = 20 (0x14)
      IP: Precedence = Routine
      IP: Type of Service = Normal Service
      IP: Total Length = 40 (0x28)
      IP: Identification = 50323 (0xC493)
      IP: Flags Summary = 0 (0x0)
          IP: .......0 = Last fragment in datagram
          IP: ......0. = May fragment datagram if necessary
      IP: Fragment Offset = 0 (0x0) bytes
      IP: Time to Live = 64 (0x40)
      IP: Protocol = UDP - User Datagram
```

```
        IP: Checksum = 0xA222
        IP: Source Address = 10.0.0.5
        IP: Destination Address = 10.0.0.11
        IP: Data: Number of data bytes remaining = 20 (0x0014)
        IP: Padding: Number of data bytes remaining = 6 (0x0006)
    UDP: Src Port: DNS, (53); Dst Port: Unknown (1807); Length = 20 (0x14)
        UDP: Source Port = DNS
        UDP: Destination Port = 0x070F
        UDP: Total length = 20 (0x14) bytes
        UDP: UDP Checksum = 0x3BE3
        UDP: Data: Number of data bytes remaining = 12 (0x000C)
    DNS: 0xF:Dyn Upd Resp.
        DNS: Query Identifier = 15 (0xF)
        DNS: DNS Flags = Response, OpCode-Dyn Upd, RA Bits Set, RCode-No error
            DNS: 1............... = Response
            DNS: .0101........... = Dynamic Update
            DNS: .....0.......... = Server not authority for domain
            DNS: ......0......... = Message complete
            DNS: .......0........ = Iterative query desired
            DNS: ........1....... = Recursive queries supported by server
            DNS: .........000.... = Reserved
            DNS: ............0000 = No error
        DNS: Zone Count = 0 (0x0)
        DNS: Prerequisite Section Entry Count = 0 (0x0)
        DNS: Update Section Entry Count = 0 (0x0)
        DNS: Additional Records Count = 0 (0x0)
        DNS: Query Identifier = 0 (0x0)
        DNS: DNS Flags = Query, OpCode - Std Qry, RCode - No error
            DNS: 0............... = Request
            DNS: .0000........... = Standard Query
            DNS: .....0.......... = Server not authority for domain
            DNS: ......0......... = Message complete
            DNS: .......0........ = Iterative query desired
            DNS: ........0....... = No recursive queries
            DNS: .........000.... = Reserved
            DNS: ............0000 = No error
        DNS: Zone Count = 0 (0x0)
```

7.2.2 Security Problems

The ability of BIND 8.1.2 running on HP-UX 11 to handle dynamic updates is great, but there is a caveat. As of this writing, the Internet Software Consortium (ISC) has announced at least two serious security bugs involving BIND version 8.1.2: the "solinger" bug and the "fdmax" bug. (See *www.isc.org/products/BIND/bin8.html.*) For this reason, the ISC recommends that you upgrade to at least BIND 8.2.2 patch level 5, though Hewlett-Packard does not support it at this time. By the time this book is published, HP may very well do so. Windows 2000 implements secure dynamic updates, but to do so, you must integrate DNS with Active Directory.

According to Microsoft's *Microsoft Windows 2000 Server TCP/IP Core Networking Guide*, p. 406, "Windows 2000 supports secure dynamic updates through the Generic Security Service Application Program Interface (GSS-API, specified in RFC 2078) rather than Domain

Name System Security Extensions (RFC 2535) or Secure Domain Name System Dynamic Update (RFC 2137)."[1] This means that in any event Windows 2000 secure dynamic updates is incompatible with BIND's DNSSEC (DNS Security Extensions). BIND version 8.2 supports, though incompletely, DNSSEC. Complete DNSSEC will be available with BIND version 9.

7.2.3 Active Directory and DNS

Windows 2000 can store a primary DNS zone in Active Directory, making the data therein Active Directory objects. Therefore, in addition to normal DNS zone transfers, you can have zone information replicated through the Active Directory replication process. The advantage of integrating DNS with Active Directory is that you can have *multimaster replication*, with multiple domain controllers updating the zone. (See *Microsoft Windows 2000 Server TCP/IP Core Networking Guide*, p. 376.)[2] With traditional DNS, only a zone's primary server can update the database.

According to the *Microsoft Windows 2000 Server TCP/IP Core Networking Guide*, p. 429, for the domain controller locator to work properly, the primary DNS server that is authoritative for the names that are to be registered by the Netlogon service on the domain controller, must support the service location resource record (**SRV RR**).[3] Fortunately, as we have already seen, BIND 8.1.2 on HP-UX does indeed support **SRV** records. Because you would have to manually update the primary zone when you configure Active Directory if you use an older version of BIND, Microsoft also recommends that your DNS support dynamic updates. Again, BIND 8.1.2 does so.

The ISC has published on its Web site, *www.nominum.com/resources/bind-faq.html*, the following statement regarding BIND and Active Directory.

> **Microsoft Windows 2000 and BIND**
>
> BIND, by default, checks all records to ensure that only host names are used where host names are expected to prevent accidental interoperability problems.
>
> Microsoft Windows 2000 uses a subzone called "_msdcs" to hold the Active Directory data. While this subzone cannot clash with any legal host name, it also makes it impossible to put hosts within this subzone without using an illegal name. The use of such host names will be rejected, by default, by BIND.
>
> The Active Directory wants to have its "global catalog" server within *msdcs (e.g., gc.*_msdcs.example.com), which will be rejected by default. To work around this issue we recommend that the Active Directory be a separate zone (e.g., "_msdcs.example.com) configured to not check for illegal host names. This should be reasonable as the Windows 2000 servers create this data and should not have interoperability problems with other Windows 2000 machines wanting to access this data. For example,
>
> ```
> zone "_mscds.example.com" {
>     type master;
>     file "_mscdcs.example.db";
>     check-names ignore;
>     allow-update { localnets; };
> };
> ```

7.3 Conclusion

I have demonstrated that it is possible to integrate DHCP and DNS with both HP-UX and Windows 2000. However, much of what was presented was a proof-in-concept. Whether you choose to implement dynamic updates depends on how secure you want your environment to be. If you want to implement secure updates immediately, Windows 2000 now offers this capability, which means you might have to convert from BIND to Windows 2000 DNS in your environment, something that may be expensive and time consuming. If you choose to keep BIND, you can still avoid using dynamic updates and maintain your IP addresses manually. Something to keep in mind is that traditionally it is mobile clients, such as laptops, that really need DHCP. Such systems should never be servers of any kind, so why should they need their IP addresses registered in DNS? Besides, all clients, regardless of whether they are laptops or workstations, should not require IP address registration because they should be *dataless*. For a more complete discussion of dataless clients, consult Robert W. Lucke's book, *Designing and Implementing Computer Workgroups* (Prentice Hall PTR, 1999). In other words, evaluate carefully your need to implement dynamic updates until the security incompatibilities between Windows 2000 DDNS and BIND are resolved.

References

1. The Internet Software Consortium's BIND Web site at *www.isc.org/products/BIND/*.
2. Paul Albitz and Cricket Liu, *DNS and BIND, 3rd Ed.* (O'Reilly, 1998).
3. Thomas Lee and Joseph Davies, *Microsoft Windows 2000 TCP/IP Protocols and Services Technical Reference.* (Microsoft Press, 2000).
4. Robert W. Lucke, *Designing and Implementing Computer Workgroups.* (Prentice Hall PTR, 1999).
5. Microsoft Corporation, *Microsoft Windows 2000 Server TCP/IP Core Networking Guide.* (Microsoft Press, 2000).

Endnotes

1.–3. From *Microsoft® Windows® 2000 Server Resource Kit* by Microsoft Corporation. Reproduced by permission of Microsoft Press.

CHAPTER 8

User Authentication

Before we look at the interoperability of applications, we need to look at the issue of user authentication. We do so because most, if not all, of these applications require some kind of verification that the users are who they say they are. For example, if you use the Telnet application on a Windows 2000 computer to connect to a UNIX system, you are asked to provide a user name and password. You are already authenticated by Windows 2000, but you need authentication from the UNIX system. If you install a Telnet server on a Windows 2000 system and wish to connect to it via Telnet, you will go through an authentication process there as well. So it is a good idea to examine how authentication takes place in both Windows 2000 and UNIX (again using HP-UX as our example), so that we have some idea of what's going on when you issue a user name and password.

This chapter examines *authentication* only, not *authorization*. Authentication is the process of verifying the identity of a user to the system. From the system's standpoint, authentication answers the question, "Do I know you?" If it does, then you have access to the system. If not, then you do not have access. Authorization is the process of determining what an authenticated user can or cannot do. The system may know who you are and grant you access, but exactly what you can perform on the system is a matter of authorization.

8.1 Windows 2000

In Windows 2000, the Security Accounts Manager (SAM) stores local user accounts in the local registry. Domain accounts are stored in Active Directory, though a SAM for these accounts continues to exist for backward compatibility. Local accounts are just that: They exist only for the local computer. Domain accounts extend to all the computers that are members of the domain. A Windows 2000 domain controller thus has two user databases: Active Directory for domain accounts and SAM for backward compatibility. You can start a domain controller in Directory Services Restore Mode, in which case the controller uses SAM instead of Active Directory for its user database. Workstations, member servers, and standalone servers still maintain a SAM database.

8.1.1 Interactive Logon

Interactive logon is getting access to your local system. It begins with the Secure Attention Sequence (pressing the CTRL+ALT+DEL keys). Executing this sequence signals the Winlogon process (winlogon.exe), which has been running since system startup, to call the Graphical Identification and Authentication (GINA) DLL. GINA displays the **Log On to Windows** dialog box, collects the user information necessary for log on, and sends it to the Local Security Authority (LSA). This dialog box provides you with the opportunity to log on to the local computer or to a domain. The LSA is responsible for verifying a user's credentials, which include the user name and password. (See Figure 8–1 for a depiction of the LSA.) Upon receipt of these credentials, LSA runs a module (or "package") based on which authentication protocol is in use. Windows 2000 supports two authentication protocols for network logons: NT LAN Manager and Kerberos v5. These protocols also support remote logons as well, but for now we will concentrate on how they handle interactive logons.

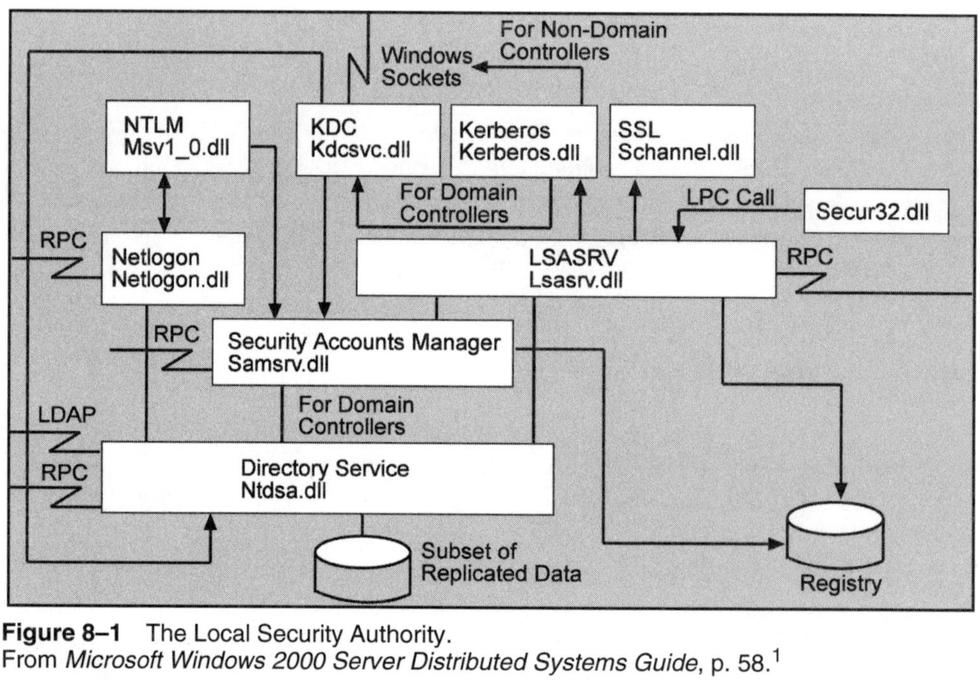

Figure 8–1 The Local Security Authority.
From *Microsoft Windows 2000 Server Distributed Systems Guide*, p. 58.[1]

8.1.1.1 NTLM

NTLM was the default for pre-Windows 2000 systems and is still supported for mixed environments and for logging on using local accounts. It uses the MSV1_0 authentication package and the Net Logon service.

MSV1_0 takes the clear text password issued by the user, encrypts it, and then converts it into a LAN Manager password and a Windows NT password. If the account is local, MSV1_0 queries the local SAM to validate the password. If the account is a domain account, MSV1_0 passes the password to the local Net Logon service. Net Logon then sets up a secure communications channel with the authenticating server's Net Logon service. The authenticating server then takes over the task of validating the user against *its* SAM (which is also the domain's SAM.) The domain's SAM sends a Security Identifier (SID) for the user to the LSA, together with SIDs for the user's groups, which then creates the access token based on this information for the logon session. The access token also contains the user's privileges and is attached to every process the user creates.

8.1.1.2 Kerberos

For authenticating domain users, Windows 2000 uses the Kerberos v5 authentication protocol by default. However, users running pre-Windows 2000 systems will continue to be authenticated using NTLM.

MIT developed the Kerberos authentication system, and its Web site is still one of the best sources on the protocol. Since we will describe Kerberos only in its most basic form in this chapter, it is best to consult *web.mit.edu/kerberos/www* for more information. MIT Kerberos is available for free download. Kerberos on Windows 2000 is an integral part of the operating system.

The name Kerberos comes from Greek mythology: It was the name of the three-headed watchdog of Hades. In keeping with this heritage, the Kerberos authentication system consists of three main parts: the application client (e.g., ftp), the application server (e.g., ftpd), and a key distribution service running on a separate, physically secure server that acts as an intermediary between the application client and the application server. The key distribution service, as the name implies, dispenses keys to both clients and servers. These keys are used to encrypt and decrypt messages that verify the identity of the parties involved. The key distribution service runs on the Key Distribution Center (KDC). The KDC also provides clients with *tickets,* which give them access to services.

The KDC maintains a database of *security principals.* A security principal is anything that has an account in this database: a user, a group, a computer, or a service. The database of security principals maintained by the KDC constitutes its *realm,* more or less the equivalent of a Windows 2000 domain. It should be no surprise, therefore, that the KDC runs as a Windows 2000 domain service on each domain controller, using Active Directory (not SAM) as its account database. The account database contains, among other things, an encryption key for all users, derived from their logon passwords. This encryption key is often referred to as the *long-term key.*

All Windows 2000 domain controllers are peers; therefore more than one KDC can exist in a domain. According to the *Microsoft Windows 2000 Server Distributed Systems Guide,* p. 659, "Windows 2000 does not, however, implement the Kerberos replication protocol. Instead, it replicates the information store for Active Directory by using a proprietary multimaster replication protocol over a secure channel between replication masters."[2]

The Authentication Service Exchange The Authentication Service (AS) Exchange is where the KDC provides the client a logon session key and a Ticket-Granting Ticket (TGT) for use with other services. When a user logs onto a Windows 2000 domain from a Windows 2000 workstation (thus defaulting to Kerberos authentication), the workstation's LSA converts the user's password to an encryption key and saves the result in the credentials cache, a protected area of volatile memory. The LSA (via the Kerberos client) then sends an authentication request (KRB_AS_REQ) to the KDC containing the user's name and pre-authentication data encrypted with the long-term key.

The KDC looks up the user in the security principal database, fetches the long-term key associated with that user, decrypts the pre-authentication data, and checks the request's timestamp. If all checks out, the KDC creates a logon session key and encrypts a copy with the user's long-term key. It also embeds another copy of the logon session key along with authorization data for the user in a TGT. Authorization data include the user's SID and SIDs for the user's groups. The TGT is also encrypted, this time with the KDC's own long-term key, and is sent to the client in an authentication service reply (KRB_AS_REP). The client then uses the locally cached encryption key to decrypt the logon session key and stores it in the credentials cache. It then extracts the TGT and stores in it the credentials cache as well.

At this point, the client has a TGT that it can present when it needs session tickets for services in the domain. The next step is for the client to obtain a session ticket for the current logon session. Once it has done so, then the user has access to his or her workstation.

The Ticket-Granting Service Exchange This process provides the client with a session ticket that provides the user with access to the local workstation. The client requests credentials for the ticket-granting service (TGS) from the KDC. This request (KRB_TGS_REQ) contains the user's name, an authenticator encrypted with the logon session key, the TGT, and the name of the user's computer. The KDC decrypts the TGT, extracts the logon session key, and uses it to decrypt the authenticator. If all is well, the KDC extracts the user's authorization data from the TGT and creates a session key to enable the user to use the workstation.

Once the client receives this session key, the LSA decrypts it with the locally cached encryption key and extracts her authorization data. The LSA also checks the local SAM to see if the user belongs to any local groups. If so, it adds those SIDs to the list of SIDs contained in the authorization data. The LSA then builds an access token for the user and passes it to Winlogon, which completes the logon process.

The Bare Essentials Paraphrasing a section from the *Microsoft Windows 2000 Server Distributed Systems Guide*, p. 671, can sum up this complicated logon process.[3] To authenticate a user and set up his logon session on the computer, the LSA must obtain the following:

1. A TGT that is good for admission to the TGS.
2. A session ticket that is good for admission to the computer.

Additional authentication requests, for example, when connecting to network shares, involves another exchange known as the client/server (CS) exchange. These requests do not require reentering your user password and are known as *remote logins*.

8.1.2 Remote Logon

Remote logon is also known as network authentication. In other words, you have already gained access to your workstation; you now want to access resources on the network. With share-level security, you have to enter a password at a dialog box to access the share, even though you have already logged on. With user-level security, you perform interactive logon only once. Thereafter, a behind-the-scenes mechanism takes place to authenticate the service, acting on your behalf. After all, that is what takes place with network services. A network client runs *on your behalf* and somehow has to prove it to the network server. Exactly how this takes place depends on the protocol.

8.1.2.1 NTLM

NTLM uses a challenge-response protocol at connection time, for example, when a user attempts to map a network drive. When a server receives a connection request, the server authenticates the user by issuing a *challenge* (bytes chosen at random) to the client. The client encrypts this challenge with a hash of the user's password and returns the whole thing to the server. The server takes this information and contacts the domain controller to verify the user's identity. If verification is successful, the domain controller sends the server the user's SIDs, and the LSA on the server in turns builds a security access token based on those SIDs. The server can then use the access token to determine whether to grant the user's request to access one of its shares.

The key point to remember in this process is that user authentication in a remote logon is the responsibility of the server, not the client. The server must contact the domain controller to verify the identity of the user.

8.1.2.2 Kerberos

In order for a user to access a network share from a computer using Kerberos, the client must initiate a TGS exchange with the KDC requesting service from the server. Remember that in a TGS exchange, the client sends a TGS request to the KDC, which includes the user's name, an authenticator, the TGT, and the name of the service for which the user wants a ticket. The KDC verifies the information and creates two copies of a session key. One copy is encrypted with the user's logon session key. The other is embedded in a ticket, along with the user's authorization data, all of which is encrypted with the *server's* long-term key.

The client stores both the session key and the ticket to the service in its credentials cache (after decryption, of course). It then requests a connection on the server by sending the server an application request (KRB_AP_REQ) containing an authenticator encrypted with the session key for the service, the ticket for the service, and an indication as to whether mutual authentication is required. The server decrypts this message and extracts the user's authorization data and session key.

The KDC provides the user's authorization data, including SID information, when the user requests a TGT. It also provides authorization when it grants a session ticket. After verifying the client's credentials, the Kerberos package on the server passes the authorization data on to the LSA. The LSA in turn builds an access token to determine authorization.

Remember that with the NTLM protocol, the server must contact the domain controller to authenticate a user. With Kerberos, the server does not do this. Instead, the client obtains a ticket for the service from the KDC, and the server determines the validity of the ticket without having to consult a domain controller. The process that makes all this possible can be quite complex, but such is the basic difference between NTLM and Kerberos authentication.

8.2 HP-UX

Traditional HP-UX user authentication follows that of nearly all UNIX-based systems. In the early days of UNIX, you had a single user database contained in the */etc/passwd* file. Users accessed this single database from text-based terminals. When the system started, it started a *getty* (get terminal type) process, which displayed a simple login screen. This is as good a place as any to mention a little but irritating divergence between UNIX systems and Windows 2000 systems, namely the terminology referring to gaining access to the system. UNIX systems have a process called login, which is actually a program; Windows 2000 calls it the logon process, which is a procedure, not a program. The user would login, and the system would provide a command-line interface (a shell) and a user environment. As long as you had a single system with multiple terminals, you had an easy-to-manage multiuser system.

However, around the mid-1980s, things began to change with the introduction of the UNIX workstation. Each workstation had its own */etc/passwd* file—its own user database. As long as all applications were local, and as long as each user had her own workstation with no need to access any other system, things were still fine. All you had to do was set up one user account per system. But that's not how most people used these systems. Users wanted to transfer files from one system to another; administrators wanted to share applications over the network. As a result, you had to ensure each user had an account on each system, something that became increasingly difficult as the number of systems multiplied. The most popular mechanism to manage user accounts from a single source has been Network Information Services (NIS).

8.2.1 Basic Authentication

The file */etc/passwd* is a list of users known to the system. Each line of this file contains, among other things, a user's login name, encrypted password, user identifier (UID), and default group identifier (GID). Each UID is simply an integer and must be unique so that the operating system can distinguish between users. If your system is part of a network (and most are these days), you must ensure that all UIDs are unique across the network. The */etc/passwd* file does not contain passwords; instead, it contains *encrypted* passwords created using a one-way hashing function called *crypt( )* and user passwords as keys. *Crypt( )* uses an algorithm based on the Data Encryption Standard (DES) of the National Institute of Standards and Technology. More common these days is for a UNIX system to store the encrypted passwords in a separate file, usually called /etc/shadow (as in "shadow password file"). Only the root user can read this file. Otherwise, ordinary users can obtain a list of the encrypted passwords and, using special programs, possibly determine the actual passwords themselves.

If you are logging into a text-based terminal, you interact with the *getty* process. This process prompts you for a user name. When you provide this name, *getty* calls the *login* process, which prompts you for a password, takes the password you type, encrypts it using the same process described previously, and then compares the result with your encrypted password in */etc/passwd.* If there is indeed a match, you are then authenticated and have access to your local system.

If you are logging into a workstation running the Common Desktop Environment (CDE, the default for HP-UX), the *dtlogin* and *dtgreet* processes handle logins. Yet the essential process is the same: the password you type while logging in is encrypted, the result of which is compared to the entry for your user name in */etc/passwd.*

8.2.2 Network Authentication

In the UNIX world, network authentication is simply the act of making the */etc/passwd* file information on one machine available to other machines on the network. The technology that makes this possible is NIS. With this technology, the system consults its local */etc/passwd* file to verify a user. If the user is not found, then the system consults the "networked version" of */etc/passwd*, usually called a *map*.

The exact process of how this works varies according to vendor and is documented in countless numbers of books and manuals. However, the key point here is that even though a networked version of */etc/passwd* exists, *authentication still takes place on the local system, not on a server.* So, though the master copy of */etc/passwd* exists on the NIS master server, the local *login* or *dtlogin* process does the actual authentication. Therefore, once a local system authenticates a user, using either the local */etc/passwd* file or the networked map, the user has access to the system. If a user wants to access, say, a networked file system, then the client simply says, "I am this user because my local system says so." The file server simply accepts this assertion and does not try to find out on its own if the information is correct.

8.2.3 Pluggable Authentication Modules

HP-UX 11 supports Pluggable Authentication Modules (PAM). These modules make it possible to use mechanisms other than */etc/passwd* or NIS to authenticate users. Other authentication methods include NTLM, Kerberos, and the Distributed Computing Environment (DCE). You configure PAM by editing the */etc/pam.conf* file for one or more of four possible authentication services:

- Authentication—Used to verify the identity of a user and to set the user-specific credentials.
- Account management—Used to determine whether the current user's *account* (not password) is valid. This includes checking for password and account expiration, as well as verifying access hour restrictions.
- Session management—To set up and terminate login sessions.
- Password management—To change a user's authentication token or password.

In */etc/pam.conf* you specify what happens when you invoke a particular application for each of these services. As an example, *pam.conf* may look like the following:

```
#
# PAM Configuration
#
# Account Management
#
dtaction  account  required  /usr/lib/security/libpam_unix.1
dtlogin  account  required  /usr/lib/security/libpam_unix.1
ftp  account  required  /usr/lib/security/libpam_unix.1
login  account  required  /usr/lib/security/libpam_unix.1
su  account  required  /usr/lib/security/libpam_unix.1
OTHER  account  required  /usr/lib/security/libpam_unix.1
#
# Authentication Management
#
dtaction  auth  required  /usr/lib/security/libpam_unix.1
dtlogin  auth  required  /usr/lib/security/libpam_unix.1
ftp  auth  required  /usr/lib/security/libpam_unix.1
login  auth  required  /usr/lib/security/libpam_unix.1
su  auth  required  /usr/lib/security/libpam_unix.1
OTHER  auth  required  /usr/lib/security/libpam_unix.1
#
# Password Management
#
dtaction  password  required  /usr/lib/security/libpam_unix.1
dtlogin  password  required  /usr/lib/security/libpam_unix.1
login  password  required  /usr/lib/security/libpam_unix.1
passwd  password  required  /usr/lib/security/libpam_unix.1
OTHER  password  required  /usr/lib/security/libpam_unix.1
```

```
#
# Session Management
#
dtaction   session   required   /usr/lib/security/libpam_unix.1
dtlogin   session   required   /usr/lib/security/libpam_unix.1
login   session   required   /usr/lib/security/libpam_unix.1
OTHER   session   required   /usr/lib/security/libpam_unix.1
```

The first field in this file indicates the name that the application uses to identify itself to PAM, such as *login*. This name is usually the name of the command invoked by the user. The second field is the keyword for the type of authentication service, *account* for account management, *auth* for user authentication, *password* for password management, and *session* for session management. The third field is a keyword specifying how to handle multiple definitions for the same application. If this keyword is *required*, as in this example, then the test for this module must succeed before moving on to successive tests. If *optional*, the test for the module can fail. If *sufficient*, then no further tests are performed if the first test succeeds.

The "pluggable" portion of PAM is specified in the fourth field, the dynamically loadable object invoked to provide a particular type of user authentication. In the example above, each application under each service calls */usr/lib/security/libpam_unix1*, the standard HP-UX module, to handle authentication. For PAM NTLM, this object is */usr/lib/security/libpam_ntlm.1*. For PAM Kerberos, it is */usr/lib/security/libpam_krb5.1*. For more information, see the following *man* pages: *pam*(3), *pam.conf*(4), *pam_upde*(5), and *pam_user.conf*(4).

8.2.4 PAM NTLM

Using PAM NTLM, anyone logging into an HP-UX 11 system can be authenticated by a Windows NT or Windows 2000 server. PAM NTLM is part of HP's CIFS/9000 Client product. This product enables HP-UX users to mount shares from Windows servers using the Common Internet File System (CIFS) protocol, an alternative to installing NFS on Windows servers. To access these shares, you must either run the *cifslogin* utility or use PAM NTLM for authentication. PAM NTLM authenticates users using encrypted passwords and supports the ability to change passwords on Windows 2000 using the HP-UX *passwd* command.

The PAM NTLM configuration file is */etc/opt/cifsclient/pam/smb.conf*. Before you configure PAM, you must set the *workgroup* and *password server* parameters in this file to reflect your Windows 2000 domain name and domain controller name. For example, if your domain is called BOOK and your domain controller is W2KSERV, then your configuration file will look like the following:

```
#
# Any line which starts with a ; (semi-colon) or a # (hash)
# is a comment and is ignored. In this example we will use a #
# for commentry and a ; for parts of the config file that you
# may wish to enable
#
#
```

```
#================== Global Settings ========================
[global]

# workgroup = NT-Domain-Name or Workgroup-Name, eg: REDHAT4
   workgroup = BOOK

# Use password server option only with security = server or domain
   password server = w2kserv
```

Once you have configured */etc/opt/cifsclient/pam/smb.conf,* you then change parameters in */etc/pam.conf*. For each application, you must specify the */usr/lib/security/libpam_ntlm.1* authentication module. On one of my test systems, for example, I configured PAM to use NTLM for CDE login (*dtlogin*), CDE actions (*dtaction*), and password management. Therefore, my */etc/pam.conf* looks like the following:

```
#
# PAM Configuration
#
# Account Management
#
dtaction  account  required  /usr/lib/security/libpam_ntlm.1
dtlogin  account  required  /usr/lib/security/libpam_ntlm.1
ftp  account  required  /usr/lib/security/libpam_unix.1
login  account  required  /usr/lib/security/libpam_unix.1
su  account  required  /usr/lib/security/libpam_unix.1
OTHER  account  required  /usr/lib/security/libpam_unix.1
#
# Authentication Management
#
dtaction  auth  required  /usr/lib/security/libpam_ntlm.1
dtlogin  auth  required  /usr/lib/security/libpam_ntlm.1
ftp  auth  required  /usr/lib/security/libpam_unix.1
login  auth  required  /usr/lib/security/libpam_unix.1
su  auth  required  /usr/lib/security/libpam_unix.1
OTHER  auth  required  /usr/lib/security/libpam_unix.1
#
# Password Management
#
dtaction  password  required /usr/lib/security/libpam_ntlm.1
dtlogin  password  required  /usr/lib/security/libpam_ntlm.1
login  password  required  /usr/lib/security/libpam_unix.1
passwd  password  required  /usr/lib/security/libpam_ntlm.1
OTHER  password  required  /usr/lib/security/libpam_unix.1
#
# Session Management
#
dtaction  session  required  /usr/lib/security/libpam_ntlm.1
dtlogin  session  required  /usr/lib/security/libpam_ntlm.1
login  session  required  /usr/lib/security/libpam_unix.1
OTHER  session  required  /usr/lib/security/libpam_unix.1
```

As you can see, the *dtaction* and *dtlogin* applications specify *libpam_ntlm.1*. This permits me to log into CDE. (See Figure 8–2.) Once I have logged in, I can run the *passwd* command. If I do so, *passwd* will change my password on the Windows 2000 domain controller. If I want to access a share on a Windows 2000 server, I do not have to run the *cifslogin* utility first because I will have already been authenticated via NTLM. In other words, my *interactive login* takes place at the CDE login screen; my *network login (remote login)* takes place behind the scenes, as described in the Windows 2000 section of this chapter.

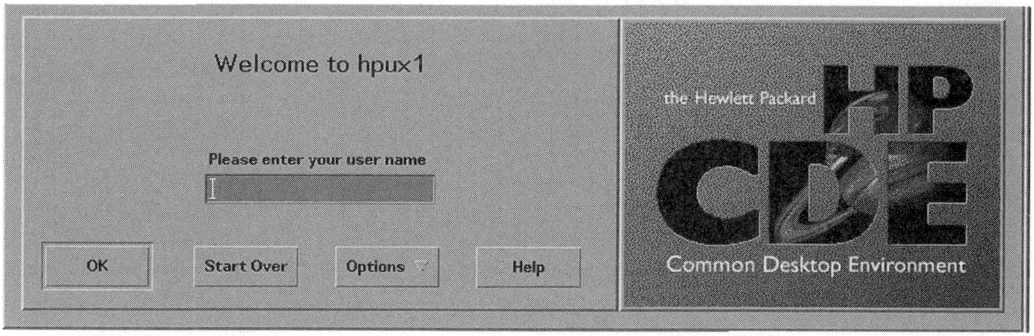

Figure 8–2 The CDE login screen. This screen is managed by the *dtlogin* process, not *login.*

Using NTLM in this manner provides a single sign-on capability in that a single Windows 2000 domain controller maintains login and password management. However, it would be incorrect to think that you have a unified user account management system. In order for you to do anything on your HP-UX system (run commands, utilities, applications), you have to have a user account on that system. To log in you have to have another account on your Windows 2000 domain controller. In other words, you have to have *two* accounts. Therefore, if you have a new user to your network, you will have to create an HP-UX account *and* a Windows 2000 domain account. To make this form of interoperability easier, you should keep the user names the same on both systems. Otherwise, you have to maintain a user map file. This file maps HP-UX user names to Windows 2000 domain user names so that when you log in to HP-UX, PAM NTLM knows what Windows 2000 user name to use when authenticating. You will probably need to have this file regardless of whether user names match because in at least one case—the administrative account—you will have two different names: root for HP-UX and administrator for Windows 2000.

For more detailed information on PAM NTLM, consult *Installing and Administering the CIFS/9000 Client*, available at *docs.hp.com*.

8.3 PAM Kerberos

HP-UX 11 supports Kerberos, based on Kerberos Authentication System v5, developed by MIT, in the form of a PAM module. This PAM integrates HP-UX login with any Kerberos 5 Server, including a Windows 2000 KDC and an MIT-based KDC. Documentation of PAM Kerberos is limited to the release note, found at */usr/share/doc/PAMKerberosRelNotes.pdf* after you install the package. What follows is essentially a summary of that release note.

8.3.1 Configuring an HP-UX KDC and Application Server

You need to install MIT Kerberos version 1.x to make an HP-UX system either a KDC or an application server. Doing so will provide you with important documentation and tools (such as *kadmin* and *ktutil*). You can get MIT's distribution at *web.mit.edu/kerberos/www/*. You need to configure the following files for KDCs and application servers:

- /usr/local/var/krb5kdc/kdc.conf
- /etc/pam.conf
- /etc/krb5.conf
- /etc/services

8.3.1.1 /usr/local/var/krb5kdc/kdc.conf

This file contains KDC configuration parameters and is for KDCs only. The following is a sample *kdc.conf* file found in the release note. Modify it to suit your environment.

```
[kdcdefaults]
     kdc_ports = 88,750

[realms]
  REALM.HP.COM = {
   database_name = /usr/local/var/krb5kdc/principal
   admin_keytab = /usr/local/var/krb5kdc/kadm5.keytab
   acl_file = /usr/local/var/krb5kdc/kadm5.acl
   dict_file = /usr/local/var/krb5kdc/kadm5.dict
   key_stash_file = /usr/local/var/krb5kdc/.k5.REALM.HP.COM
   kadmind_port = 749
   max_life = 10h 0m 0s
   max_renewable_life = 7d 0h 0s
   master_key_type = des-cbc-crc
   supported_enctypes = des-cbc-crc:normal
  }
```

There are additional steps to making an HP-UX system a KDC. For more information, see both the Installation Guide that comes with the MIT distribution and HP's PAM Kerberos Release Note (available at *docs.hp.com*). However, it is probably best to use a Windows 2000 domain controller as a KDC, since Kerberos is installed and a realm configured by default.

8.3.1.2 /etc/pam.conf

Your HP-UX application server is the host running the server version of Telnet (*telnetd*), Ftp (*ftpd*), or similar program. Therefore, for example, if you want to connect to another system via Telnet, you must make sure that system is configured to use Kerberos authentication. If you want

Kerberos to do your authenticating when you log in to your local workstation using CDE, then you must also configure *dtlogin* to use Kerberos. You configure these services by editing */etc/pam.conf* and specifying the PAM Kerberos authentication module (*/usr/lib/security/libpam_krb5.1*) for each. The following is an example for *login* and *ftp*:

```
login    auth    required   /usr/lib/security/libpam_krb5.1
ftp      auth    required   /usr/lib/security/libpam_krb5.1
```

8.3.1.3 /etc/krb5.conf

This file specifies the defaults for the realm and for Kerberos applications, mappings of host names onto Kerberos realms, and the location of KDCs for Kerberos realms. A sample */etc/krb5.conf* is as follows:

```
[libdefaults]
     default_realm = REALM.HP.COM
     default_tkt_enctypes = DES-CBC-CRC
     default_tgs_enctypes = DES-CBC-CRC
     ccache_type = 2

[realms}
     REALM.HP.COM = {
     kdc = hostname.hp.com:88
     admin_server = hostname.hp.com
     }

[domain_realm]
.cup.hp.com = REALM.HP.COM

[logging]
     kdc = FILE:/var/adm/krb5kdc.log
     admin_server = FILE:/var/adm/kadmin.log
     default = FILE:/var/adm/krb5lib.log
```

In your environment, of course, you would specify your own realm instead of REALM.HP.COM. In the *[libdefaults]* section, you must include "ccache_type = 2" for PAM Kerberos configuration. In the *[realms]* section, you specify the KDC and administrative server for each realm. You specify the location of log files issued by the KDC and administrative server in the *[logging]* section.

8.3.1.4 /etc/services

When you install PAM Kerberos, the following entries are automatically placed in your */etc/services* file:

```
#
# Kerberos (Project Athena/MIT) services
#
kerberos5     88/udp    kdc          # Kerberos 5 kdc
klogin        543/tcp                # Kerberos rlogin -kfall
kshell        544/tcp   krcmd        # Kerberos remote shell -kfall
```

```
ekshell         545/tcp  krcmd          # Kerberos encrypted remote shell -kfall
kerberos        750/udp  kdc            # Kerberos (server) udp -kfall
kerberos        750/tcp  kdc            # Kerberos (server) tcp -kfall
kerberos_master 751/tcp kadmin          # Kerberos kadmin
krbupdate       760/tcp  kreg           # Kerberos registration -kfall
kpasswd         761/tcp  kpwd           # Kerberos "passwd" -kfall
eklogin        2105/tcp                 # Kerberos encrypted rlogin ñkfall
```

You don't need to change these entries in any way.

8.3.2 Employing a Windows 2000 KDC with HP-UX Application Servers and Clients

The following is derived mostly from a Microsoft white paper entitled *Step-by-Step Guide to Kerberos 5 (krb5 1.0) Interoperability.* Be sure that the MIT Kerberos distribution is installed on the HP-UX system and that the Support Tools are installed on the Windows 2000 KDC. The Support Tools, which are stored on the Advanced Server Installation CD, include the *ktpass* utility.

1. Using the Active Directory Users and Computers management tool on the KDC, create a *user* account for the HP-UX *host*. (That's right, a *user* account for a *computer.*)
2. On the KDC, use *ktpass* to create the keytab file and set up the account for the HP-UX host. The syntax is

   ```
   C:> ktpass -princ host/hostname@REALM-NAME -mapuser account -out -pass
   password keytabfile.out
   ```

   where *hostname* is the host FQDN, *REALM-NAME* is the uppercase name of the Windows 2000 domain, *account* is the user account for the computer, *password* is a complex password for the account, and *keytabfile.out* is the name of the output file. Microsoft's documentation used *unixmachine.keytab*, but you can use a different name. For example,

   ```
   C:> ktpass -princ host/hpux1.book.local@BOOK.LOCAL -mapuser hpux1
   -pass password -out unixmachine.keytab

   Successfully mapped host/hpux1.book.local to hpux1.
   Key created.
   Output keytab to unixmachine.keytab:

   Keytab version: 0x502
   keysize 59 host/hpux1.book.local@BOOK.LOCAL ptype 1
   (KRB5_NT_PRINCIPAL) vno 1 et
   ype 0x1 (DES-CBC-CRC) keylength 8 (0x754f3e5ed67601c8)
   Account has been set for DES-only encryption.
   ```

3. Copy the keytab file to the HP-UX system. The documentation says to *securely* copy the keytab file, but I used FTP anyway (even though it sends passwords over the wire unencrypted).

4. On the HP-UX system, merge the imported keytab file with the default keytab file */etc/krb5.keytab* using the *ktutil* utility. My installation put this utility in */opt/krb5-1.2/src/kadmin/ktutil*. For example,

```
# cd /opt/krb5-1.2/src/kadmin/ktutil
# ./ktutil
ktutil:  rkt unixmachine.keytab
ktutil:  list

slot KVNO Principal
---- ---- ---------
   1    1 host/hpux1.book.local@BOOK.LOCAL

ktutil:  wkt /etc/krb5.keytab
ktutil:  q
```

   In this example, the user runs *ktutil* to read *(rkt)* the imported keytab file (*unixmachine.keytab*), list its contents, and then to write (*wkt*) the contents to */etc/krb5.keytab.*
5. On the HP-UX system, edit */etc/krb5.conf* to refer to the Windows 2000 domain controller as the KDC. You can use the sample */etc/krb5.conf* file shown previously, but you won't need the *[logging]* stanza, since your KDC is a Windows 2000 system. If your HP-UX system's DNS name is the same as the realm name, then you won't need the *[domain_realm]* stanza. Otherwise, use that stanza to map your DNS domain name to your Kerberos realm name. For example,

```
[libdefaults]
        default_realm = BOOK.LOCAL
        default_tkt_enctypes = DES-CBC-CRC
        default_tgs_enctypes = DES-CBC-CRC
      ccache_type = 2
[realms]
        BOOK.LOCAL = {
        kdc = w2kserv.book.local:88
        adm_server = w2kserv.book.local
        }
```

6. Synchronize your system clocks to within two minutes of the KDC's clock to prevent authentication errors due to clock skews.
7. Create corresponding user accounts on both the Windows 2000 domain controller and HP-UX system. The HP-UX user account does not need a password, since authentication goes to the Windows 2000 KDC. However, do include the UID, shell, and home directory information so that the user actually has access to the workstation once authenticated.

The examples above came from my small lab used in writing this book. The system called W2KSERV, a Windows 2000 domain controller, was my KDC, and BOOK.LOCAL was my realm name. I created a user account for my HP-UX system, *hpux1*, on the KDC and then used *ktpass* to create a keytab file. I copied this keytab file to *hpux1* and then ran *ktutil* to merge it with */etc/krb5.keytab*. I then edited */etc/krb5.conf* as in the example in step 6, synchronized the clocks, and then created two users on the KDC: *root* and *dylan*.

After some experimentation, I came up with a basic */etc/pam.conf* file to suit my needs. The contents of this file were

```
#
# PAM Configuration
#
# Account Management
#
dtaction  account  required  /usr/lib/security/libpam_krb5.1
dtlogin  account  required  /usr/lib/security/libpam_krb5.1
ftp  account  required  /usr/lib/security/libpam_krb5.1
login  account  required  /usr/lib/security/libpam_krb5.1
su  account  required  /usr/lib/security/libpam_unix.1
OTHER  account  required  /usr/lib/security/libpam_krb5.1
#
# Authentication Management
#
dtaction  auth  required  /usr/lib/security/libpam_krb5.1
dtlogin  auth  required  /usr/lib/security/libpam_krb5.1
ftp  account  required  /usr/lib/security/libpam_krb5.1
login  auth  required  /usr/lib/security/libpam_krb5.1
su  auth  required  /usr/lib/security/libpam_unix.1
OTHER  auth  required  /usr/lib/security/libpam_krb5.1
#
# Password Management
#
dtaction  password  required  usr/lib/security/libpam_krb5.1
dtlogin  password  required  /usr/lib/security/libpam_krb5.1
login  password  required  /usr/lib/security/libpam_krb5.1
passwd  password  required  /usr/lib/security/libpam_unix.1
OTHER  password  required  /usr/lib/security/libpam_krb5.1
#
# Session Management
#
dtaction  session  required  /usr/lib/security/libpam_krb5.1
dtlogin  session  required  /usr/lib/security/libpam_krb5.1
login  account  required  /usr/lib/security/libpam_krb5.1
OTHER  session  required  /usr/lib/security/libpam_krb5.1
```

In my */etc/passwd* file on *hpux1,* the user *dylan* had a disabled password. The user *dylan* on the KDC did have a password. Logging into *hpux1*, whether using CDE, Telnet, or FTP, worked. However, I found that *su* did not work properly if configured to use Kerberos. Therefore, I reverted to UNIX authentication for that utility. That enabled me to delete the Windows 2000 user called *root*. Thereafter I logged into HP-UX as *dylan* and then ran *su* to become root. However, to change passwords as the *root* user, I discovered that it was also good to have *passwd* configured to use UNIX authentication. This file is highly configurable, and you can have a version of this file pertain to specific users. See the *man* pages for more information. If you find that you can't log in as *root*, go back to you Windows 2000 KDC and create a user called *root* there, and try again.

8.4 Conclusion

We've looked at authentication basics in this chapter, yet there is a lot more involved. For example, what if you have more than one Windows 2000 domain? For more information regarding this and other issues, the best source is Part 2 of the *Microsoft Windows 2000 Server Distributed Systems Guide.* Now that we've laid this foundation, we can examine common applications that interoperate between HP-UX and Windows 2000.

References

1. Hewlett-Packard, *Installing and Administering the CIFS/9000 Client.* (Hewlett-Packard, 2000).
2. Hewlett-Packard, *PAM Kerberos Release Note, Edition 1.* (Hewlett-Packard, 2000).
3. *Microsoft Windows 2000 Server Distributed Systems Guide.* (Microsoft Press, 2000).
4. MIT's Kerberos Web Site at *web.mit.edut/kerberos/www/.*

Endnotes

1.–3. From *Microsoft® Windows® 2000 Server Resource Kit* by Microsoft Corporation. Reproduced by permission of Microsoft Press.

CHAPTER 9

Basic TCP/IP Utilities

Bundled with Windows 2000 are a number of TCP/IP utilities that experienced UNIX users have known about for quite some time. With the advent of the Internet, more Windows-oriented users have come to know about at least two of them: Telnet and FTP. We will look at those and other utilities, how they differ between the two platforms, and how to use them between platforms.

9.1 General Observations

In this chapter, we will examine the following utilities:

- Finger
- FTP
- Tftp
- Rsh
- Rcp
- Rexec
- Telnet

On Windows 2000, these utilities are clients only. In other words, they enable access to remote systems running server versions of these utilities, but they do not enable remote systems to access Windows 2000. Even the server versions of Windows 2000 run these utilities only as clients, *with the exception of FTP, the server version of which can be installed with Internet Information Services*. Otherwise, you must install additional software, such as Microsoft's Services for UNIX or Hummingbird's Exceed, to run these utilities as services on Windows 2000.

On UNIX systems, all of these utilities come in both the client and the server varieties. The names of the server versions all end in the letter *d* to indicate that they are *daemons*. In the UNIX world, daemons run as background processes, ready to serve requests. Some daemons run continually; others, including those below, run only when needed. On HP-UX 11, the server versions of the utilities mentioned above are:

- */usr/lbin/fingerd*
- */usr/lbin/ftpd*
- */usr/lbin/remshd*
- */usr/lbin/rexecd*
- */usr/lbin/telnetd*
- */usr/lbin/tftpd*

The clients are:

- */usr/bin/finger*
- */usr/bin/ftp*
- */usr/bin/rcp*
- */usr/bin/rexec*
- */usr/bin/remsh*
- */usr/bin/telnet*
- */usr/bin/tftp*

If you are new to UNIX, it is probably confusing to think that both server and client components of key utilities can be found on a single system, including one that can be considered a "client" system. But such is the case that a system administrator logged on to a UNIX server (a server because it is big and probably runs something big, like a database) can use the Telnet client on that server to connect to the Telnet server running on a client *system* in order to run commands on the client. It happens all the time, even in the Windows world. If you are logged in as an administrator of a Windows 2000 Advanced Server system, you can use your FTP client to connect to the FTP server on a remote UNIX client system. Once you do so, you can issue commands via your FTP client (on Windows 2000 Advanced Server) to the FTP server (on the UNIX workstation) to transfer files. So, in both the UNIX and Windows 2000 arenas, utilities can exist in either client or server form despite the "official" role of the system.

Now, back to how the server versions of the basic TCP/IP utilities work. Because the number of daemons on a given system can grow quite large, and because some daemons, though necessary, are used infrequently, UNIX systems employ an intermediate daemon to manage network requests. This daemon is *inetd*, short for Internet daemon. The daemons discussed in this chapter do not run continually in the background. Instead, */usr/sbin/inetd* runs continually, ready to awaken other daemons as needed to fulfill client requests. Once the daemon's work is done, it dies, to be resurrected again when needed.

The */etc/inetd.conf* file is *inetd's* configuration file. This file lists the services that *inetd* can start. In addition to *inetd.conf*, HP-UX supplies an optional security file called */var/adm/inetd.sec* to provide a layer of security in addition to that provided by the services themselves. See the *inetd.sec man* page for more information.

The University of California at Berkeley created the utilities covered in this chapter, and although the Windows 2000 versions are complete rewrites, they retain their UNIX heritage in that all options (or flags, or switches) are indicated by hyphens (-), not slashes (/). For example, the command to run FTP with interactive prompting turned off looks the same on both systems: *ftp –i*.

9.2 Finger

The *finger* utility provides information about users on a remote system. Among other things, this utility provides you the login name, full name, login time, user's home directory, and login shell. Exactly what you get depends on the implementation of *fingerd* on the remote system. The Windows 2000 version of *finger* has the following syntax:

```
finger [-l] [user]@hostname
```

The *@hostname* parameter is either the target system's host name or IP address and is required. If you do not specify a user, you will get information only about logged in users. If you use the optional *user* parameter, you can get information about that user, regardless of whether he or she is logged in. The *–l* option provides you with complete information about a user. Otherwise, you will get something like the following:

```
C:\>finger @hpux1

[hpux1.book.local]
Login   Name           TTY  Idle  When       Bldg.       Phone
dylan   Dylan Roberts  con  37d Mon 13:36   DT4T        434-1434
```

This is mostly information derived from the *gecos* field in the */etc/passwd* file. The output above shows the user *dylan* having logged in at 1:36 p.m. Monday, after having not logged in for 37 days.

By default, *fingerd* is disabled in HP-UX 11. For example, if you run *finger* on Windows 2000, specifying an HP-UX system as the target, you will get a *Connection refused* message. To enable *fingerd*, edit the */etc/inetd.conf* file and remove the # symbol from the following line:

```
#finger  stream tcp nowait bin /usr/lbin/fingerd  fingerd
```

In the */etc/inetd.conf* file, as in many UNIX configuration files, any line beginning with the pound sign (#), is ignored by the system. (In UNIX verbiage, having a # at the beginning of a line in a configuration file means that that line is "commented out.") Removing that symbol will enable that line; *however,* you must first tell the *inetd* to reread its configuration file by issuing the following command:

```
# /usr/sbin/inetd -c
```

The *finger* command will now work. However, many sites regard this command as a security risk (as does Hewlett-Packard, apparently, since it has chosen to disable *fingerd* by default). Moreover, running this command on an HP-UX system to get information from Windows 2000 systems will fail because *fingerd* does not exist on those machines unless you have installed a version provided by a third party.

9.3 FTP

Because of the omnipresence of the Internet these days, FTP is widely known and used. In all caps, FTP refers to File Transfer Protocol. The user interface to this protocol is spelled Ftp (in Windows documentation) or *ftp* (in UNIX). Using FTP, users copy (not really transfer) files from a server (a server running *ftpd*). On UNIX systems, FTP is available in both client and server versions, while on Windows 2000, you must do one of the following to run *ftpd*: (1) install Internet Information Services, (2) install Services for UNIX, or (3) install a third-party version. For both Windows 2000 and HP-UX, the FTP client supports a number of subcommands, that is, commands available at the *FTP>* prompt. These subcommands are quite similar, yet running the FTP client itself differs.

9.3.1 Windows 2000

The syntax of the FTP command in Windows 2000 is

```
ftp [-v] [-n] [-i] [-d] [-g] [-s:filename] [-a] [-A] [-w:windowsize]
[hostname]
```

where

- *–v* suppresses the display of remote server responses. On HP-UX, this option enables verbose output.
- *–n* suppresses autologon upon initial connection. This is the same on HP-UX.
- *–i* disables interactive prompting by multiple-file commands. This is the same on HP-UX.
- *–d* enables debugging. This option is not available on HP-UX.
- *–g* disables file name globbing (using wildcard characters). This is the same on HP-UX.
- *–s:[filename]* specifies a text file contain FTP commands, run automatically after FTP starts. This option is not available on HP-UX.
- *–a* specifies that any local interface can be used when binding the FTP data connection. Not available on HP-UX.
- *–A* logs in to the FTP server as anonymous. Not available in HP-UX.
- *–w:windowsize* specifies the size of the transfer buffer. The default is 4096 bytes.

The *hostname* parameter is optional. If you specify a host, then FTP starts and immediately opens a connection to the target host. If you do not specify a host, you just get the FTP> prompt. This prompt waits for you to issue subcommands.

9.3.2 HP-UX

The syntax of the FTP client on HP-UX is

```
ftp [-g] [-i] [-n] [-v] [-B size] [server-host]
```

The *–g*, *–i*, and *–n* options are the same as those found in the Windows 2000 version of FTP. The *–B* option sets the buffer size of the data socket to a size in blocks of 1024 bytes. The number of blocks can be from 1 to 64, with 56 being the default. The default connection type is ASCII, though if you connect to another HP-UX system, FTP switches to binary connections.

9.3.3 A Comparison of FTP Subcommands

The FTP clients on each platform vary in the subcommands they support. Table 9–1 compares those subcommands. For more information, see the *ftp man* page on HP-UX or the Help utility on Windows 2000.

Table 9–1 FTP Subcommands on Windows 2000 and HP-UX

Command	Windows 2000	HP-UX
!	Yes	Yes
$	No	Yes
?	Yes	Yes
account	No	Yes
append	Yes	Yes
ascii	Yes	Yes
bell	Yes	Yes
binary	Yes	Yes
bye	Yes	Yes
case	No	Yes
cd	Yes	Yes
cdup	No	Yes

(continued)

Table 9–1 FTP Subcommands on Windows 2000 and HP-UX *(continued)*

Command	Windows 2000	HP-UX
chmod	No	Yes
close	Yes	Yes
cr	No	Yes
debug	Yes	No
delete	Yes	Yes
dir	Yes	Yes
disconnect	Yes	Yes
form	No	Yes
get	Yes	Yes
glob	Yes	Yes
hash	Yes	Yes
help	No	Yes
idle	No	Yes
lcd	Yes	Yes
literal	Yes	No
ls	Yes	Yes
macdef	No	Yes
mdelete	Yes	Yes
mdir	Yes	Yes
mget	Yes	Yes

(continued)

Table 9–1 FTP Subcommands on Windows 2000 and HP-UX *(continued)*

Command	Windows 2000	HP-UX
mkdir	Yes	Yes
mls	Yes	Yes
mode	No	Yes
modtime	No	Yes
mput	Yes	Yes
nlist	No	Yes
nmap	No	Yes
ntrans	No	Yes
open	Yes	Yes
passive	No	Yes
prompt	Yes	Yes
proxy	No	Yes
put	Yes	Yes
pwd	Yes	Yes
quit	Yes	Yes
quote	Yes	Yes
recv	Yes	Yes
reget	No	Yes
rhelp	No	Yes
remotehelp	Yes	No

(continued)

Table 9–1 FTP Subcommands on Windows 2000 and HP-UX *(continued)*

Command	Windows 2000	HP-UX
rename	Yes	Yes
reset	No	Yes
restart	No	Yes
rmdir	Yes	Yes
rstatus	No	Yes
runique	No	Yes
send	Yes	Yes
sendport	No	Yes
site	No	Yes
size	No	Yes
status	Yes	Yes
sunique	No	Yes
system	No	Yes
tenex	No	Yes
trace	Yes	No
type	Yes	Yes
umask	No	Yes
user	Yes	Yes
verbose	Yes	Yes

9.3.4 The HP-UX ftpd

HP-UX 11 has an *ftpd* different from that of previous releases of the operating system. The new *ftpd* supports logging of transfers, logging of commands, on-the-fly compression and archiving, classification of users on type and location, per-directory upload permissions, restricted guest accounts, systemwide and per-directory messages, directory aliases, cdpath, virtual host support, and per-class limits. One of the more significant changes, as we will see later, is a new option, *-K*, which enforces Kerberos Authentication. For complete information on configuring *ftpd* on HP-UX 11, see the release notes at */usr/share/doc/RelNotes_newftp.txt*.

Unlike the Windows 2000 FTP Server, HP-UX by default does not allow anonymous logins. The easiest way to set up anonymous FTP on HP-UX is to use SAM. From the main SAM screen, select **Networking and Communications→Network Services**. Select **Anonymous FTP** and then choose **Actions→Enable** from the menu bar, as shown in Figure 9–1.

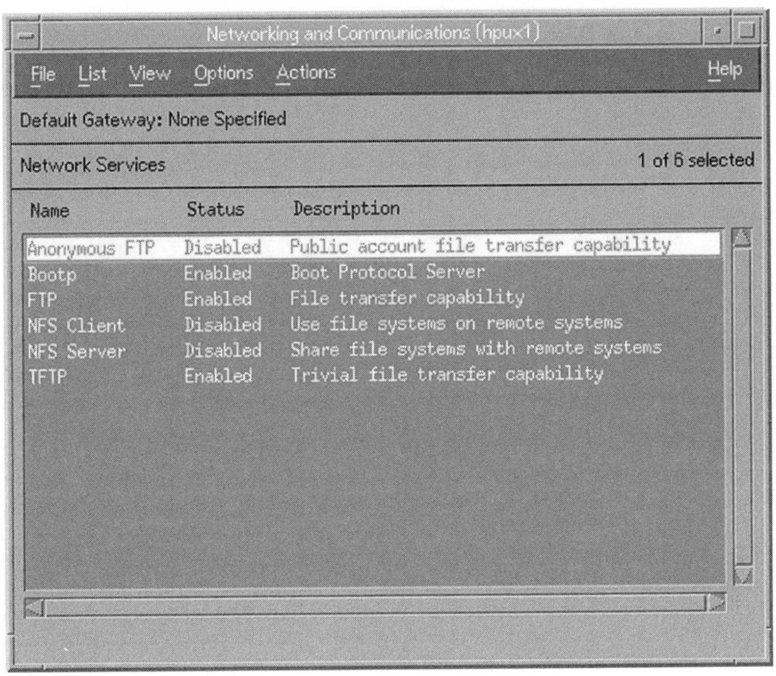

Figure 9–1 Configuring anonymous FTP on HP-UX using SAM.

This process will place anonymous FTP files in the */home/ftp* directory. If you log in as *anonymous* or *ftp*, you will be placed in this directory and will see the following subdirectories: *dist*, *etc*, *pub*, and *usr*.

9.3.5 The Windows 2000 FTP Server

Even though the Windows 2000 installation process installs Internet Information Services by default, you must ensure that the FTP Server is installed as well. If you run **Start→Settings→ Control Panel→Add/Remove Programs** and then select **Add/Remove Windows Components→Internet Information Services,** make sure your window has the **File Transfer Protocol (FTP) Server** box checked, as in Figure 9–2.

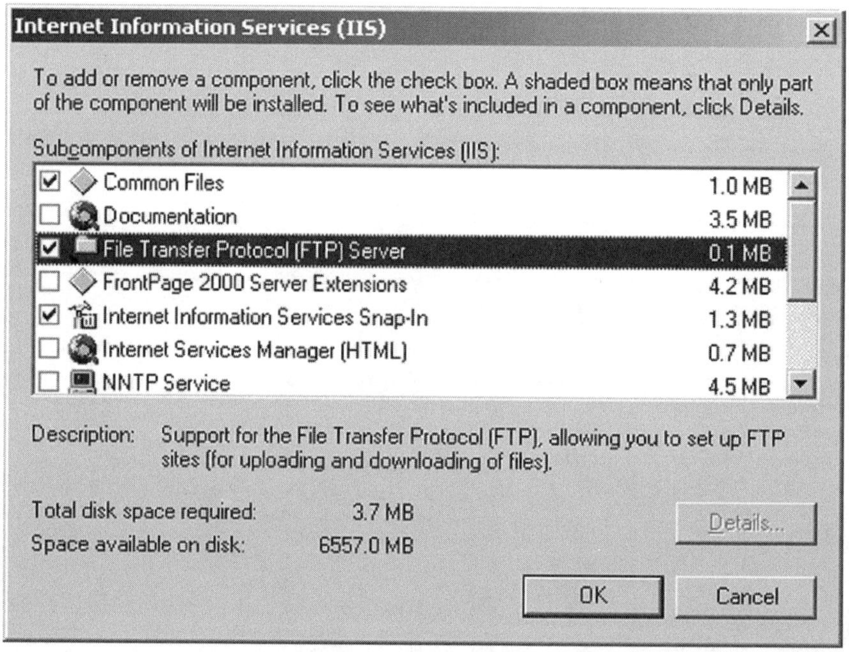

Figure 9–2 Installing the FTP Server on Windows 2000. If you want only the FTP Server, check Common Files, File Transfer Protocol (FTP) Server, and Internet Information Services Snap-In.

By default, the Windows 2000 FTP Server stores files for distribution in the *C:\Inetpub\ftproot* directory and allows anonymous logins. If you log in as a "real" user (not *anonymous*), you are still placed in the *ftproot* directory. The FTP Server is also highly configurable. You configure it by running the Internet Services Manager, found in the Administrative Tools folder.

9.3.6 Transferring Files

The general rule for transferring files is, if you transfer between systems with identical operating systems, use BINARY mode transfer. It's more efficient. If your operating systems differ, use BINARY mode for binary files, ASCII mode for text files.

9.3.7 Windows 2000 FTP Client

If you run the FTP client at a Windows 2000 command prompt and connect to a Windows 2000 FTP Server, you can login as *anonymous* (or *ftp*) or as a user that exists in the domain (if the server is a domain controller) or as a user that exists locally (if the server is a member server). The default transfer mode is ASCII. If you connect to an HP-UX system, you can login as *anonymous* only if anonymous FTP has been configured on that system. Otherwise you login as either a local user or as a user in an NIS domain. Again, the default transfer mode is ASCII.

If you run the FTP client from Internet Explorer by typing a URL, such as *ftp://w2kserv* or *ftp://hpux1*, then the FTP client will by default try to log in as *anonymous*. If anonymous FTP is set up on the HP-UX system, then you will get a window that looks like Figure 9–3.

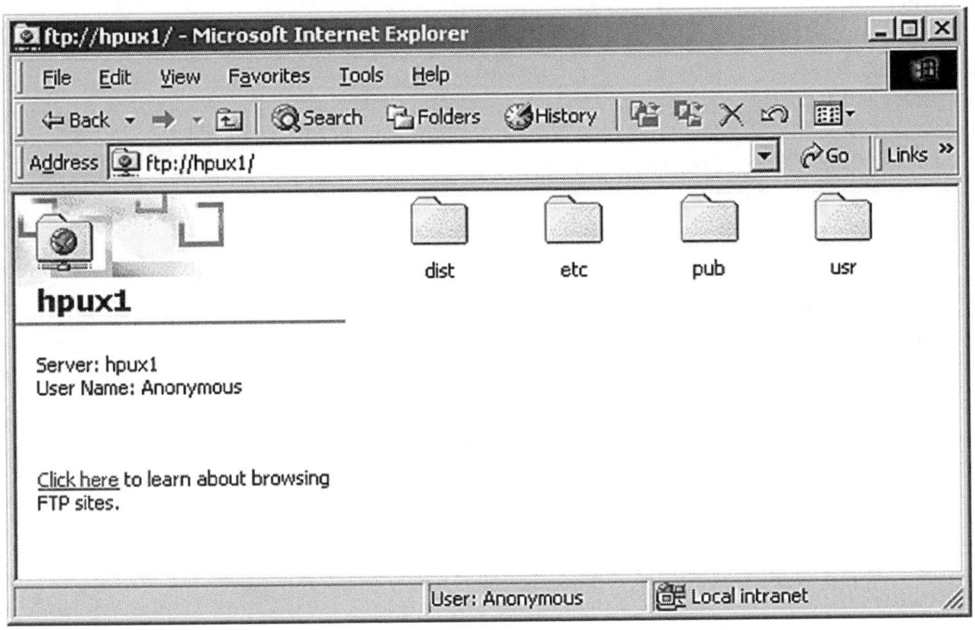

Figure 9–3 Running FTP from Internet Explorer. Here the user is logged in as *anonymous*. Notice the HP-UX anonymous FTP subdirectories.

You can drag-and-drop icons to transfer files. In this case, however, the default transfer mode is BINARY. If you want to log in as a different user, type in the FTP URL in the **Address** box (e.g., ftp://hpux1), and then select **File→Login As...** and fill in the box, as in Figure 9–4.

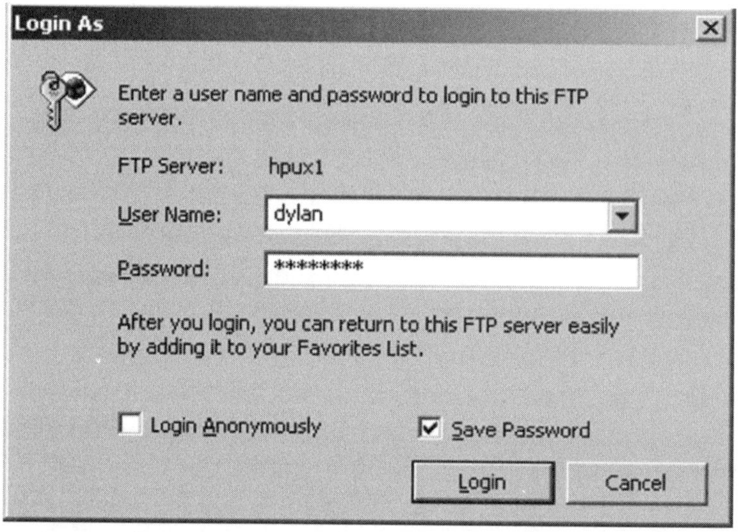

Figure 9–4 Logging in as a User Other Than Anonymous. In this example, the user is logging in as *dylan* on an HP-UX FTP server.

In the window in Figure 9–4, if you check the **Save Password** box, then you can log in without typing a password. For example, if you log in successfully as the *dylan* account on an HP-UX system and save your password, then you can go directly to the home directory (*/home/dylan*) by simply typing the following in the **Address** box in Internet Explorer: *ftp://dylan@hpux1/*. Then you would see something like the window in Figure 9–5.

You can automate this process even further by adding the page displayed by the URL to your Favorites or Links folder.

Remember that if you use Windows 2000 Internet Explorer to connect to a UNIX FTP server, you will have trouble reading text files you copy to your system. For example, in Figure 9-5 there is an icon called *boot.txt*. This file resides on *hpux1*, a UNIX system. You can copy it to your Windows 2000 box by dragging and dropping the icon to your Desktop. However, if you open the file with Notepad, you will see something like Figure 9–6. Notepad does not know what to do with the NL (new line) character that UNIX systems put at the end of a line. Windows-based systems denote the end of a line with the CR-LF (carriage return-line feed) characters. However, if you open the file with either Wordpad or Word, these programs interpret UNIX-created text files with no problem.

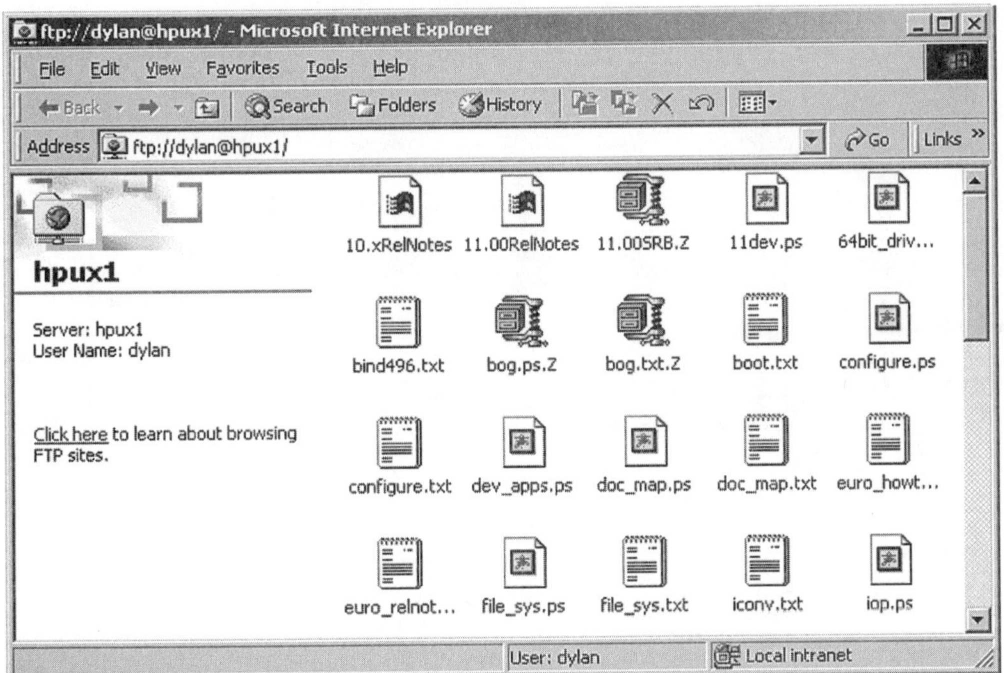

Figure 9–5 Logging in with FTP as a "real" user. In this example, the user *dylan* has logged in. The Address window shows the *ftp://dylan@hpux1* URL. The main window shows the home directory of *dylan*.

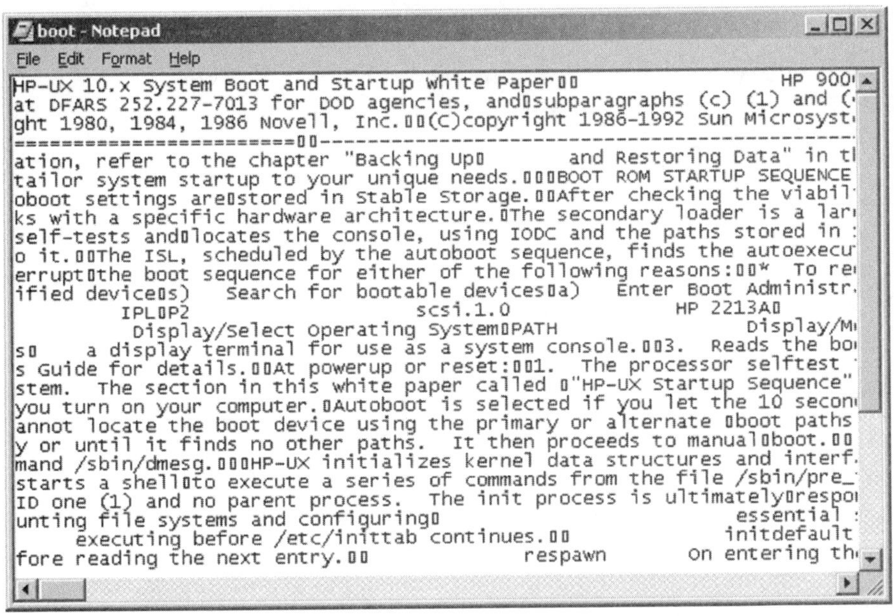

Figure 9–6 Opening a text file with Notepad after a binary transfer. The *boot.txt* file was transferred as a binary file from an HP-UX system to Windows 2000.

You can also just double-click a text file within Internet Explorer before trying to copy it. For example, if you double-click on the *boot.txt* icon as shown in Figure 9–5, Internet Explorer takes care of the end-of-line issue and displays the text as shown in Figure 9–7. You can then execute **File→Save As...** in Internet Explorer to save the display as a text file. NotePad can then read this file with no problem.

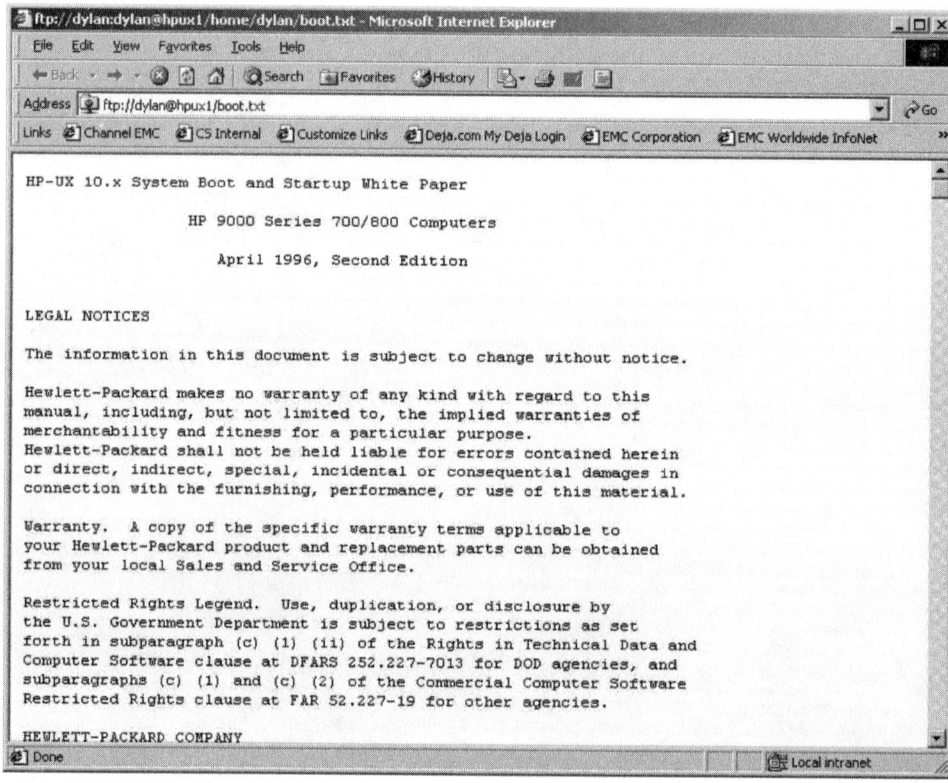

Figure 9–7 Viewing a UNIX text file from Internet Explorer. In this example, the file *boot.txt* displays properly. You can then save this to your Windows 2000 Desktop by executing **File→Save As...** on the menu bar.

9.3.8 HP-UX FTP Client

If you run the FTP client on HP-UX and connect to a Windows 2000 system, then your default transfer mode is ASCII. The following output illustrates this fact:

```
# ftp w2kserv
Connected to w2kserv.book.local.
220 w2kserv Microsoft FTP Service (Version 5.0).
Name (w2kserv:root): ftp
```

```
331 Anonymous access allowed, send identity (e-mail name) as password.
Password:
230 Anonymous user logged in.
Remote system type is Windows_NT.
ftp> get boot.txt
200 PORT command successful.
150 Opening ASCII mode data connection for boot.txt(37064 bytes).
226 Transfer complete.
37064 bytes received in 0.03 seconds (1431.72 Kbytes/s)
ftp>
```

If, however, you connect to another UNIX system from HP-UX, then your default transfer mode is BINARY. Again, the following output verifies this:

```
# ftp hpux1
Connected to hpux1.book.local.
220 hpux1.book.local FTP server (Version 1.1.214.5 Tue Nov 16 09:39:15
GMT 1999) ready.
Name (hpux1:root): root
331 Password required for root.
Password:
230 User root logged in.
Remote system type is UNIX.
Using binary mode to transfer files.
ftp>
```

9.4 Tftp

Trivial File Transfer Protocol (Tftp) provides a way to configure a system as an FTP server that does not require user authentication. For this to work, the user needs to know the name of the Tftp server and the names of the files to retrieve (there is no listing of a Tftp directory), and that's it. The Tftp server is configured with a user called *tftp* whose home directory is the repository for files to be placed or retrieved. Windows 2000 does not have a Tftp server; it only has a client.

9.4.1 Configuring the HP-UX Tftp Server

The easiest way to configure Tftp on HP-UX is to use SAM. Run SAM, select **Networking and Communications→Network Services** (see Figure 9–8). If Tftp is disabled, select **Actions** from the menu bar and choose **Enable.**

Configuring Tftp in this manner does the following:

- Creates a user called *tftp* with a disabled password and a home directory of */home/tftpdir.* This directory has the correct ownership and permissions assigned to it. See the *man* page on *tftpd* for more information.
- Ensures that Tftp is enabled in */etc/inetd.conf.*

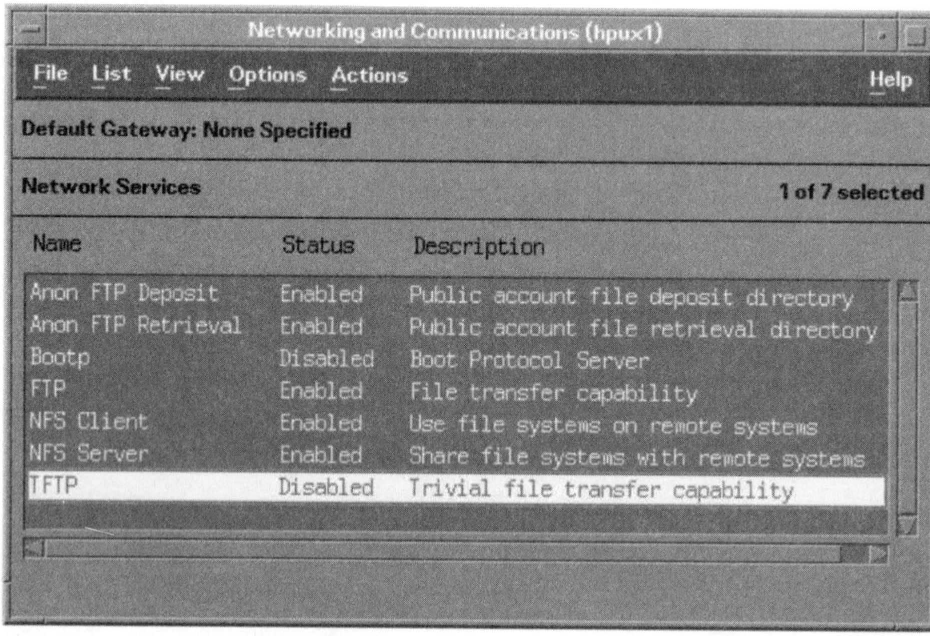

Figure 9–8 Enabling Tftp using SAM.

If you want to give remote systems permissions to retrieve a file through Tftp, the file must be readable by the *tftp* user. If you want to give remote systems permissions to transmit a file to your system through Tftp, the file must already exist and must be writeable by the *tftp* user.

9.4.2 Running Tftp

The syntax of the Windows 2000 Tftp client is

```
tftp [-i] host [get | put] source [destination]
```

This client does not have an interactive mode. Therefore, you must specify whether you are performing a *get* or *put* operation and the file you want to transfer. (The *get* or *put* parameters are required, not optional.) The *destination* parameter is required if there is a subdirectory of the *tftp* directory on the server involved. The `-i` option specifies binary image transfer. The default is ASCII mode, which takes care of end-of-line character transformations on text files.

9.5 Rsh and Rcp

The Windows 2000 utilities Rsh and Rcp execute commands on remote systems running either *rshd* or *remshd.* On HP-UX, *rsh* is not the same command as that found on other UNIX systems and Windows 2000; it runs a *restricted* shell. *Remsh* is the same service as *rsh* on BSD systems. The name was changed due to a conflict with the existing System V command *rsh* (restricted

The name was changed due to a conflict with the existing System V command *rsh* (restricted shell). Therefore, rather than running *rshd*, HP-UX runs *remshd*. To enable *remshd* on HP-UX, the following line should be present in the */etc/inetd.conf* file:

```
shell  stream  tcp  nowait  root /usr/lbin/remshd  remshd
```

If there is a pound sign (#) at the beginning of this line, remove it and run the *inetd –c* command. Because there is no equivalent to *rshd* or *remshd* on Windows 2000, we will confine our discussion to Windows 2000 Rsh and Rcp.

Unlike their UNIX equivalents, Rsh and Rcp do not prompt you for a password if you do not specify a user name when running those commands. If you do not specify a user name when issuing either command, both commands assume that the user name is the same as the one you are currently logged on as. To avoid using passwords, the *remshd* on HP-UX must know if the user running an Rsh or Rcp command on a Windows 2000 system is "equivalent" to a user on the local system or NIS domain. HP-UX determines this user equivalency by means of two files: */etc/hosts.equiv* and *.rhosts*.

For a user to be granted access, the supplied user name must match an entry in one of these files. Also, the HP-UX system must have the user name you specify stored in the local */etc/passwd* file or NIS map. The */etc/hosts.equiv* file defines system-wide equivalency and is searched first. The *.rhosts* file defines equivalency between the HP-UX user and the Windows 2000 user, resides in the HP-UX user's home directory, and is searched second. According to the *man* page on *hosts.equiv*, matches can be literal or can be obtained through the use of wildcards. For example,

- You can specify a particular user from any machine by placing + *user_name* in */etc/hosts.equiv*. This won't work for the *root* user.
- You can specify any user from a particular machine by placing *machine_name* + in your *hosts.equiv* file. The exception to this entry is the *root* user.
- You can specify any user from any system by using + + in your *hosts.equiv* file. Again, the exception is the *root* user.
- The *root* user can grant access only in his or her *.rhosts* file in the *root's* directory, with both the machine name and the user name (or plus signs) specified.

For more details, type *man hosts.equiv* at an HP-UX command-line prompt.

We will now look at running the commands in depth. To simplify matters, I placed a "+ +" entry in */etc/hosts.equiv* on my HP-UX system, which granted all equivalent systems and users access to run Rsh or Rcp. The user *dylan* was the only equivalent user name on both the Windows 2000 and HP-UX systems.

9.5.1 Running Rsh

The syntax of the Rsh command on Windows 2000 is

```
rsh host {-l user_name] [-n] command
```

The *host* parameter is the system actually running the command you specify. I hope it is obvious that the command needs to be an HP-UX command in my examples. The `-l` option specifies the user name to be used on the remote host. If you omit this parameter, the logged-on user's name is used. However, in my tests I've found that you must be very careful here. *You must ensure that both the HP-UX and Windows 2000 account names are the same case.* Yes, it is true that you can log on to Windows 2000 without being case-specific. However, if you create a Windows 2000 account called *Dylan*, you must have an equivalent account called *Dylan* (not *dylan*) on the HP-UX system, *even though you can log on to Windows 2000 with* dylan *as a user name.* The reason is that Windows Rsh will pass the mixed-case user name to the *remshd* on HP-UX. Being an HP-UX program, *remshd* will interpret that name as *Dylan*, not *dylan*. The Rsh command will not work unless either the account names match case or you supply the properly cased name with the `-l` option.

By default, Rsh reads its standard input and sends it to the remote command. The `-n` option redirects the input of Rsh to NUL (never-never land), useful when running a shell script containing the Rsh command, since otherwise Rsh may use input not intended for it. If you use redirection symbols (>, >>) you must quote them if you want redirection to occur on the remote computer. Otherwise, redirection will take place locally.

9.5.2 Examples

Find out when the last system boot took place on *hpux1*.

```
D:\>rsh hpux1 -l dylan who -b
    .          system boot  Oct 24 18:39
```

Notice that I'm specifying the user *dylan* here. You must specify a user that the remote HP-UX system recognizes. If you don't specify a user, then your Windows 2000 user name must match an HP-UX account name *exactly.* Since my HP-UX system does not know anything about a user named *bob*, the following command does not work:

```
D:\>rsh hpux1 -l bob who -b
hpux1.book.local: remshd: Login incorrect.
rsh: can't establish connection
```

Find out the name of all files that end in *.log* on the HP-UX system:

```
D:\>rsh hpux1 -l dylan find / -name "*.log"
find: cannot open /etc/sam/custom
find: cannot open /etc/lvmconf
find: cannot search /etc/ftpd
find: cannot open /var/opt/dce/security/preauth
find: cannot open /var/adm/sw/queue
find: cannot open /var/adm/sw/products
```

```
find: cannot open /var/adm/sw/save
find: cannot open /var/adm/sw/save_custom
find: cannot open /var/spool/uucp/.Corrupt
find: cannot open /var/spool/uucp/.Sequence
find: cannot open /var/spool/uucp/.Workspace
find: cannot open /var/spool/uucp/.Xqtdir
find: cannot open /tmp/.AgentSockets
find: cannot open /usr/newconfig/etc/sam/custom
find: cannot open /.dt/Desktop
/etc/rc.log
/etc/auto_parms.log
/var/opt/ignite/local/install.log
/var/opt/dce/config/dce_config.log
. . .
```

The ". . ." in the above output indicates that there is more output than I wanted to display.

In this command, I specified the user *dylan*, a non-privileged user. Therefore, I got error messages with my *find* command when this user tried to view directories whose permissions forbade users other than *root* to do so. To get rid of these error messages, I can redirect standard error (designated on UNIX systems as file descriptor 2) to */dev/null*, the wastebasket. But remember, I must quote the redirect symbol because there is no */dev/null* on Windows 2000:

```
D:\>rsh hpux1 -l dylan find / -name "*.log" 2">" /dev/null
/etc/rc.log
/etc/auto_parms.log
/var/opt/ignite/local/install.log
/var/opt/dce/config/dce_config.log
/var/opt/dce/dced/dced.log
/var/opt/dce/svc/fatal.log
/var/opt/dce/svc/error.log
. . .
```

If I want to copy this list of files to a Windows 2000 file, then the command would look like

```
D:\>rsh hpux1 -l dylan find / -name "*.log" 2">" /dev/null >
c:\windows\temp\hpux1_log_files.txt
```

The command is actually one line, but is split for display purposes only.

9.5.3 Running Rcp

Rcp lets you copy remote files to either the local Windows 2000 system or to another system running *rshd* or *remshd*. You can also copy a complete directory structure from one system to another. The *help* switch of Windows 2000 Rcp displays the following:

```
rcp [-a | -b] [-h] [-r] [host][.user:]source [host][.user:]
path\destination
```

`-a`	Specifies ASCII transfer mode. This mode converts the EOL characters to a carriage return for UNIX and a carriage return/line feed for personal computers. This is the default transfer mode.
`-b`	Specifies binary image transfer mode.
`-h`	Transfers hidden files.
`-r`	Copies the contents of all subdirectories; destination must be a directory
`host`	Specifies the local or remote host. If host is specified as an IP address OR if host name contains dots, you must specify the user.
`.user`	Specifies a user name to use, rather than the current user name.
`source`	Specifies the files to copy.
`path\destination`	Specifies the path relative to the logon directory on the remote host. Use the escape characters (\ , , ", or ') in the remote paths to use wildcard characters on the remote host.

Let's use some examples to clarify.

I am logged on to Windows 2000 as the user *dylan*. My home directory is *C:\Documents and Settings\dylan*. On my HP-UX system, I have a *dylan* account with a home directory of */home/dylan*. Under these conditions, to copy a file called *CHAPTER.DOC* from my Windows 2000 home directory to my HP-UX home directory, I would type:

```
C:\Documents and Settings\dylan>rcp CHAPTER.DOC hpux1.dylan:
```

The Microsoft documentation suggests that simply typing *rcp CHAPTER.DOC hpux1* would have been sufficient. However, my tests showed that doing so simply copies *CHAPTER.DOC* to a local file called *hpux1*. Thus, all my examples specify *hpux1:dylan* as the destination host and user name.

To copy all files in the Windows 2000 home directory, which is also the current directory, to the HP-UX home directory,

```
C:\Documents and Settings\dylan>rcp * hpux1.dylan:
rcp: .\ntuser.dat is hidden.
rcp: .\ntuser.dat.LOG is hidden.
rcp: .\ntuser.dat.ref.LOG is hidden.
rcp: .\Local Settings is hidden.
rcp: .\Templates is hidden.
rcp: .\Start Menu: not a plain file
rcp: .\SendTo is hidden.
rcp: .\Recent is hidden.
rcp: .\PrintHood is hidden.
rcp: .\My Documents: not a plain file
```

```
rcp: .\NetHood is hidden.
rcp: .\Favorites: not a plain file
rcp: .\Desktop: not a plain file
rcp: .\Cookies: not a plain file
rcp: .\Application Data is hidden.
rcp: .\ntuser.ini is hidden.
```

Notice that hidden files and directories were not copied. To copy the My Documents folder and all its subfolders and hidden files to the *dylan* home directory,

```
C:\Documents and Settings\dylan>rcp -hr "My Documents" hpux1.dylan:
```

This command created a *My Documents* directory, which did not exist, in *dylan's* home directory and copied all that directory's contents to the HP-UX system.

You can do remote copies going in the other direction: from HP-UX to Windows 2000. For example, to copy recursively the subdirectory *test* in *dylan's* home directory on HP-UX to the current directory on Windows 2000, type

```
C:\Documents and Settings\dylan>rcp -r hpux1.dylan:test .
```

Again, this command created the *test* directory in *C:\Documents and Settings\dylan* before copying the rest of the files over.

9.5.4 Things to Remember about Rsh and Rcp

At the risk of repeating myself,

- You must set up either */etc/hosts.equiv* for your remote system or *.rhosts* for individual users on your HP-UX system for these commands to work. This makes for very poor security, however. You just need to know the name of a user on HP-UX, and if */etc/hosts.equiv* has the + + entry, you simply assert any user name (except for *root*) when issuing one of these commands. *For this reason, never set up a .rhosts file for the root user!*
- You must specify legitimate HP-UX users in your Windows 2000 Rsh and Rcp commands. If you don't, your Windows 2000 user name must match the HP-UX user name letter-by-letter, case-by-case.
- Watch your recursive copies. The default transfer mode is ASCII. If you have binary files in your directory structure, those files will not transfer properly.

9.6 Rexec

Rexec is more secure than Rsh and Rcp because it will prompt you for a user name and password for executing the requested command. No configuration of */etc/hosts.equiv* or *.rhosts* is necessary here. Windows 2000 does not have an Rexec server, while HP-UX does. Therefore, we will confine our Rexec client discussion to Windows 2000.

On HP-UX, *rexecd* is the server for Rexec. The *inetd* calls rexecd when a service request is received. To run *rexecd*, the following line should be present in */etc/inetd.conf*:

```
exec  stream  tcp  nowait  root  /usr/lbin/rexecd  rexecd
```

If there is a pound sign (#) at the beginning of this line, remove it and run the *inetd –c* command.

On Windows 2000, the syntax for the Rexec command is the same as that for Rsh:

```
rexec host [-l user_name] [-n] command
```

If you do not specify a user name when issuing this command, the HP-UX system will assume that your user name will be the same as your Windows 2000 user name. If it is, then you can simply press Enter and then type your password. As in the case of Rsh and Rcp, it is important to verify that if you do not specify a user name with the *-l* option, your logged-on Windows 2000 user name must match your HP-UX user name, letter-by-letter, case-by-case.

The *-n* option, as it does with Rsh, redirects the input of Rexec to NUL. See the syntax description of Rsh for more information.

9.6.1 Examples

If you are logged on Windows 2000 as user *dylan* and your HP-UX system account is called *dylan*, then you can execute an Rexec command without the `-l user_name` parameter:

```
C:\>rexec hpux1 date
Name (hpux1.book.local:dylan):
Password (hpux1.book.local:dylan):
Wed Oct 25 20:44:01 PDT 2000
```

If you are logged on Windows 2000 with an account that does not exist on HP-UX (such as *Administrator*), you must supply a different user name (such as *root*). For example,

```
C:\>rexec hpux1 date
Name (hpux1.book.local:Administrator):  root
Password (hpux1.book.local:Administrator):
Wed Oct 25 20:53:05 PDT 2000
```

If you supply a user name, then you are not prompted for a user name:

```
C:\>rexec hpux1 -l dylan date
Password (hpux1.book.local:):
Wed Oct 25 20:55:09 PDT 2000
```

As with Rsh, if you use any command redirection using the > or >> symbols, you must quote them if you want redirection to take place on the remote system. For example,

```
C:\>rexec hpux1 -l root cat /.profile ">" /tmp/root_profile
Password (hpux1.book.local:):
```

This command, issued on a Windows 2000 system, instructs the HP-UX system to concatenate (using the HP-UX *cat* command) the contents of the */.profile* file to a file called */tmp/root_profile* on the HP-UX system. (In the UNIX world, the *cat* command is equivalent to the Windows *type* command.) If you don't see any error messages, you can assume your redirection command worked.

Without the quotes on the redirection symbol, we have the following example:

```
C:\>rexec hpux1 -l root cat /.profile > \windows\temp\root_profile
Password (hpux1.book.local:):
```

Here we get a copy of the HP-UX file */.profile* in the *C:>\windows\temp* directory called *root_profile*. By the way, text files seem to copy just fine using this method, with no end-of-line problems.

9.7 Telnet

According to *Microsoft Windows 2000 Server TCP/IP Core Networking Guide*, p. 828, "This connectivity tool starts terminal emulation with a remote host running a telnet server service. Telnet provides DEC VT 100, DEC VT 52, or ANSI emulation, using the connection-based services of TCP." Yet, what does this mean?

9.7.1 A Word About Terminals and Emulation

Telnet originated in the UNIX world. The first terminals in the UNIX world were *teletypes*, essentially typewriters/printers, which connected to computers via serial ports. In time, CRTs replaced these teletypes. These, too, were serial devices that at first emulated teletypes and then had their own features. Many versions of these terminals exist, each with its own set of capabilities.

For each terminal you configure on a UNIX system, you must have a *getty* process running on each terminal port. This process sets the port's initial characteristics and prompts for a login session. On HP-UX systems, the *getty* process uses the file */etc/gettydefs* to set up speed and terminal settings. The command *tset* sets up the terminal when logging into an HP-UX system. It does terminal-dependent processing, such as setting erase and kill characters, setting or resetting delays, and sending any sequences needed to properly initialize the terminal. It first determines the type of terminal involved, and then does the necessary initializations and mode settings. The type of terminal attached to each HP-UX port is specified in the */etc/ttytype* database. Type names for terminals can be found in the files under the */usr/share/lib/terminfo* directory. Programs such as *vi* and the text version of SAM need to know what terminal you are working on in order to behave properly. They consult the value of the TERM variable, set by the *tset* program upon login, to determine your terminal.

All this processing is necessary for logging into and using physically attached terminals. Telnet is a method whereby you can log into and work on a remote system *as if* you were working on a physically attached system. It achieves this through a process called *terminal emulation*, whereby software produces a screen that pretends to be a terminal. You type commands in this screen, the commands are sent to the remote system, and the output of those commands are sent back to your screen. Widely emulated terminal types include VT52, VT100, and ANSI. With Telnet, you open a terminal emulator and then use it to connect to a remote system over the network.

9.7.2 The Windows 2000 Telnet Client

Microsoft provides a Telnet server with its optional Services for UNIX product; the client is automatically installed. If you run **Start→Run...** and then type *telnet* in the **Open** box, you get a command prompt running the Telnet client, as shown in Figure 9–9.

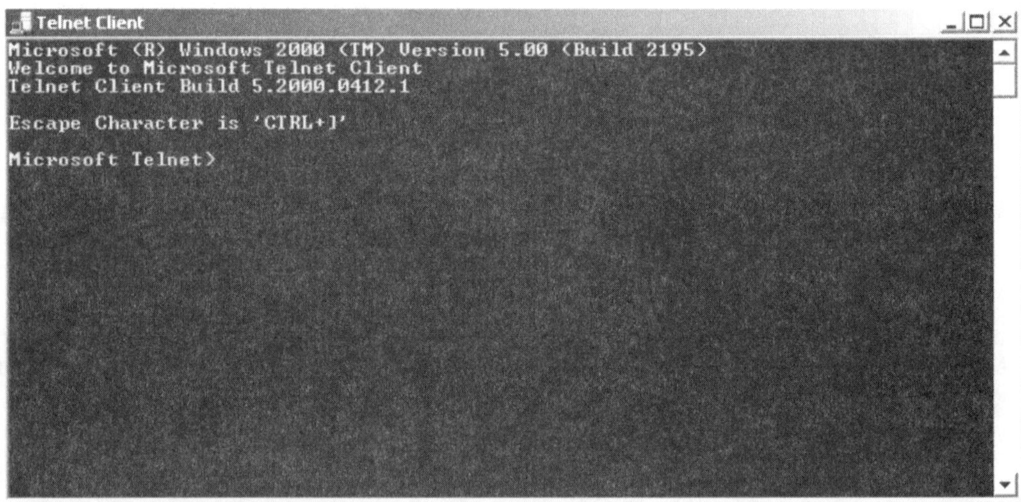

Figure 9–9 The Windows 2000 Telnet client. This client runs in a command prompt window.

The Windows 2000 Telnet client is pretty basic, providing VT100, VT52, and ANSI (based on VT100) emulation and supporting only a few subcommands and options. The syntax of Windows 2000 Telnet is *telnet [host [port]]*, where the optional *host* parameter is the host name of the destination system and the optional *port* parameter is the destination port if the default port of 23 is not used. Typing *telnet* starts the Telnet client, which prompts you for a subcommand. To connect to a remote computer, type the *open* command at the *Microsoft Telnet>* prompt. For example,

```
Microsoft Telnet> open hpux1
```

To view current Telnet client settings, use the *display* command. For example,

```
Microsoft Telnet> display
Escape Character is 'CTRL+]'
WILL AUTH (NTLM Authentication)
LOCAL_ECHO off
Sending both CR & LF
WILL TERM TYPE
Preferred Term Type is ANSI
```

These indicate the options that the Windows 2000 Telnet client will negotiate with the Telnet server. Upon connection, the Telnet clients and servers negotiate options. Here the Telnet client has two options it wants to enable: NTLM Authentication and TERM TYPE, both indicated by the WILL request. Unless you set up PAM NTLM on HP-UX to support Telnet logins, HP-UX will not recognize this option. The Windows 2000 client also wants to set the TERM TYPE, which by default is an ANSI terminal. Also, the client here will turn off local echoing of characters; that is, it will send commands to the remote system a character at a time. Finally, the client will send end-of-line sequences as an ASCII carriage return and line feed pair.

By and large, these settings work fine for HP-UX, with one notable exception: SAM. When you connect to an HP-UX system from a Windows 2000 Telnet client, HP-UX will easily recognize the ANSI terminal type and set the HP-UX TERM variable accordingly. Applications such as *vi* and SAM use the value stored in this variable to determine how to behave properly. While HP-UX recognizes the ANSI terminal type, SAM does not work properly with the Windows 2000 Telnet client. SAM does not redraw the screen correctly after leaving some submenus, often making the application unreadable. Setting the TERM type option to VT100 does not help either. About the only solution to this problem I've found is to use either an X Window server for Windows 2000 or a Telnet client that emulates an HP, HPTERM, or VT220 terminal. Other applications, such as *vi* and *man,* seem to work fine with the Microsoft Telnet client.

9.8 Authentication Issues

The Windows 2000 Finger, Rsh, and Rcp utilities do not require user authentication; they require system configuration. Rexec requires user authentication but does not support Kerberos authentication. Therefore, when you type a password when executing Rexec, that password is sent over the wire unencrypted. Traditionally, FTP and Telnet do the same. However, in Chapter 8, "User Authentication," we saw that we can configure HP-UX FTP and Telnet servers to use Kerberos authentication. Doing so avoids the use of plain-text passwords and thus makes the use of these utilities more secure.

9.9 Conclusion

The basic TCP/IP utilities we looked at in this chapter are found on both Windows 2000 and HP-UX systems, though their syntax and behavior differ. Of these utilities, the most widely used are undoubtedly FTP and Telnet. An FTP server and client are included in HP-UX, while on Windows 2000, we have the client only—unless you install the server with Internet Information Services. Both a Telnet server and client are bundled with HP-UX; only the client is bundled with Windows 2000. We look at the Windows 2000 server, available in a separate product, in the next chapter.

References

1. Hewlett-Packard, *Using HP-UX.* (Hewlett-Packard, 1997).
2. Hewlett-Packard, *Using Internet Services.* (Hewlett-Packard, 1997).
3. Microsoft Corporation, *Microsoft Windows 2000 Server TCP/IP Core Networking Guide.* (Microsoft Press, 2000).

CHAPTER 10

Windows Services for UNIX

Microsoft provides an optional product called Windows Services for UNIX (SFU for short) to facilitate the interoperability of Windows and UNIX systems. Although version 2.0 of this product was released to support Windows 2000 systems, it can be installed on Windows NT 4 with Service Pack 4 or higher. SFU can work with Solaris 2.6 and above, HP-UX 10.20 and above, Tru64 UNIX 5.0 and above, and Red Hat Linux 5.1 and above. SFU includes the following default components:

- **Telnet Client and Server.** The Server provides access to Windows 2000 systems via Telnet. The Telnet client provided with SFU has a bit more functionality than that bundled with the operating system.
- **Server for NIS.** NIS (Network Information Services) has been widely used in the UNIX world to provide commonly used information over the network. Server for NIS turns a Windows 2000 Server into an Active Directory-enabled NIS server.
- **Password Synchronization.** Passoword Synchronization provides users with the ability to change account passwords from one platform and have a corresponding change take place on the other.
- **Korn Shell and UNIX Utilities.** The Korn Shell is a command-line interpreter available on all UNIX systems and is now available for Windows 2000. It contains a number of built-in commands and is supplemented by commonly used UNIX utilities, such as *grep* and *vi*.
- **Server for NFS.** Server for NFS (Network File System) enables a Windows 2000 system to share its files with UNIX systems.
- **Client for NFS.** Client for NFS lets a Windows 2000 system access files on a UNIX system.
- **Gateway for NFS.** Gateway for NFS lets a Windows 2000 system mount UNIX file systems and then share them as if they were Windows shares.

- **User Name Mapping.** This component maps Windows-based network user names to UNIX-based network user names. Server for NFS, Client for NFS, and Gateway for NFS use User Name Mapping for NFS authentication and access.

There is a lot of stuff in SFU, so let's look at only some of what it has to offer, beginning with Telnet and Server for NIS. Since NFS concerns file sharing issues, we will defer that discussion to the next chapter.

SFU comes on a compact disc; inserting it into your CD-ROM drive starts the Windows Installer program. If your system is installed with Windows 2000 Professional, the following standard products are installed: Telnet Client, Telnet Server, Client for NFS, Korn Shell, and Utilities. Standard installation on Windows 2000 Servers also includes Server for NFS. The Custom Install of SFU allows you install other components. You cannot install Client for NFS and Gateway for NFS on the same computer. If you want to synchronize the passwords of domain accounts, you must install Password Synchronization on a domain controller. Also, you must install Server for NIS on a domain controller. By default, the installer will place SFU in the *\SFU* directory and create an environment variable called SFUDIR. If you choose a different directory, be sure that directory does *not* contain a space (like Program Files). The space can cause problems with shortcuts and the functioning of NFS.

SFU is administered through a Microsoft Management Console (MMC). Once you install your components, run **Start→Programs→Windows Services for UNIX→Services for UNIX Administration** to get the MMC shown in Figure 10–1.

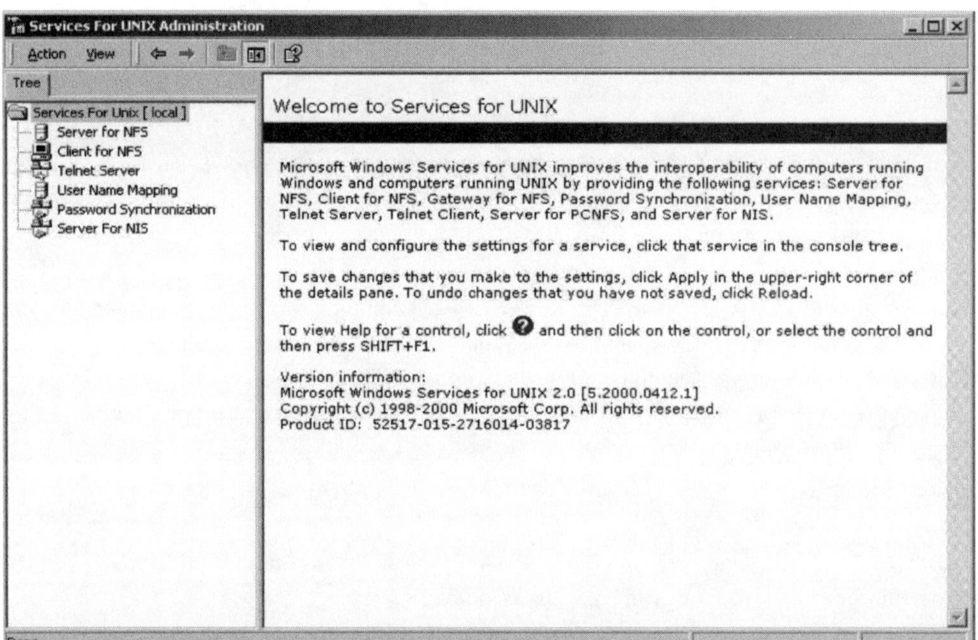

Figure 10–1 Services for UNIX Administration. The installed components you can administer here are Server for NFS, Client for NFS, Telnet Server, Password Synchronization, and Server for NIS.

10.1 Telnet Client

The SFU Telnet Client's command has options the bundled client does not have. The syntax of the former is

```
telnet [-a] [-e escapeChar] [-f logfile] [-l user] [-t term] [host [port]]
```

The *–a* and *–l* options attempt an automatic logon, which works only when the Telnet server supports the ENVIRON option. In my attempts to connect to either HP-UX 11 or Solaris 8 using those options, I found that the Telnet servers on both systems did not recognize the ENVIRON option. You can set the escape character (the keyboard sequence that takes you to the *Microsoft Telnet>* prompt while connected) to something other than the default CTRL+] with the *–e* option. You can set up a connection log file with the *–f* option. The log file you specify records the input and output of your Telnet session. The default terminal type for this Telnet client is VT100. If you want to specify a different one, use the *–t* option with VT52, ANSI, or VTNT as the terminal type. You can specify either a host name or an IP address to connect to the remote system, as well as a port number if you do not use the default port of 23.

Telnet subcommands are also a bit different from the standard Telnet client. Listed in Table 10–1 are the subcommands documented by Microsoft. I've also indicated the command abbreviations in parentheses.

Table 10–1 SFU Telnet Client Subcommands

open (*o*)	Establishes a Telnet connection to a host.
close (*c*)	Closes an existing Telnet connection.
display (d)	Produces a list of current settings for the Telnet client.
quit (q)	Exits from Telnet.
set	Sets the terminal type for the connection, turns on local echo, sets authentication to NTLM, sets the escape character, and sets up logging.
unset (u)	Turns off local echo or NTLM authentication.
status	Determines whether the Telnet client is connected.

The *display* subcommand of the SFU Telnet Client provides the following output:

```
Microsoft Telnet> d
Escape Character is 'CTRL+]'
Will auth(ntlm Authentication)
```

```
Local echo off
Line feed mode - Causes return key to send 0x0D
Current mode: Console
Will term type
Preferred term type is VT100
```

These parameters are similar to those of the standard Telnet client. If you type *SET NTLM* at the Telnet prompt, you will be authenticated via NTLM. If you are connecting to a Windows 2000 Telnet Server, then you will not be prompted for a password. *Even if you are using PAM NTLM on HP-UX, however, you will still be prompted for a user name and password because the HP-UX Telnet Server does not recognize the* WILL NTLM *option.* Your default terminal type with this client is VT100, usually just fine for connecting to UNIX systems. If you will be connecting to Windows 2000 Telnet Servers and plan to use applications such as EDIT, then you should set your terminal type to VTNT. In my tests using this Telnet client with HP-UX or Solaris Telnet servers, there was no need to change the line feed mode.

10.2 Telnet Server

When you install the SFU Telnet Server, you can configure it using the MMC snap-in, as shown in Figure 10–2.

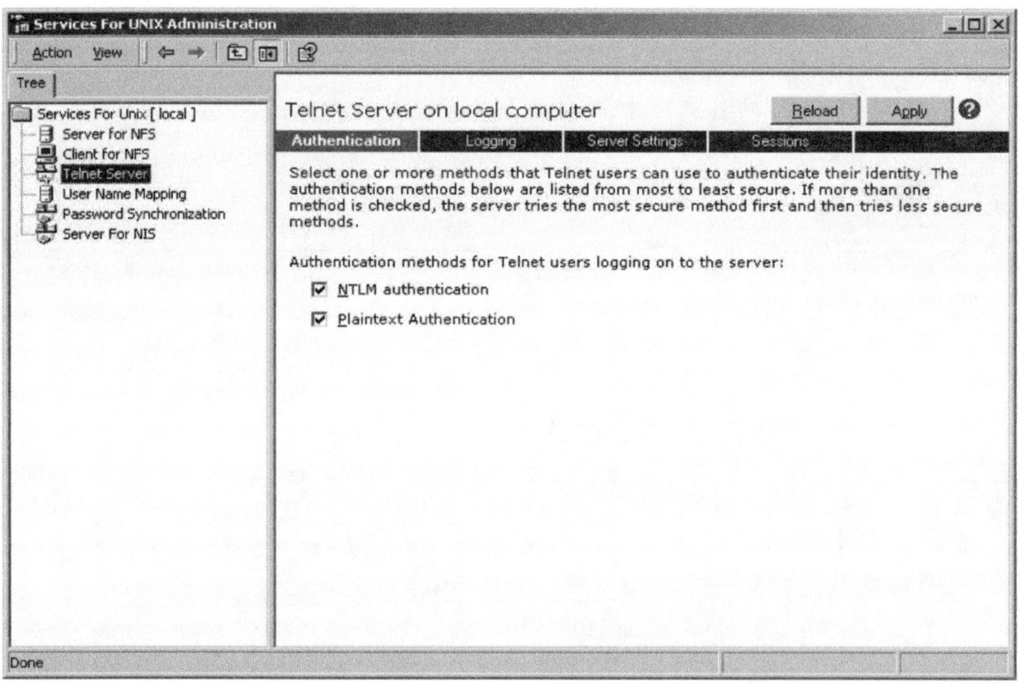

Figure 10–2 The Telnet Server MMC snap-in. This snap-in automatically opens on to the Authentication screen.

There are four areas you can configure: Authentication, Logging, Server Settings, and Sessions, each of which has its own configuration page. When you make changes to these pages, you must stop and then restart the Telnet service by either right-clicking on the Telnet Server icon on the snap-in or by entering the following commands at a command-line prompt:

```
tnadmin stop
tnadmin start
```

You can administer remote systems with this snap-in by right-clicking on the **Services For Unix** folder and selecting **Connect to Another Computer**. To configure the remote system, you should be logged on to the local system as a user with administrative rights and that user must be recognized by the remote system. Otherwise, you must start Windows Services for UNIX Administration using the *runas* command. For example,

```
runas /profile /user:RemoteComputer\AdminiUser "mmc %SFUDIR%\sfumgmt.msc"
```

For more information on *runas*, see the Help utility. You can also administer a remote system by using the Telnet client and running *tnadmin*. The *tnadmin* command provides a command-line interface to all the functions available via the MMC. More information on this command can be found in **Help for Services for UNIX**. (Run **Start→Windows Services for UNIX→Help for Services for UNIX**).

10.2.1 Authentication

The Telnet Server supports both NTLM and plain text authentication. NTLM authentication works quite well with Windows Telnet clients; it avoids having the user enter a user name and password and thereby keeps unencrypted passwords off the network. With HP-UX Telnet clients, however, the SFU Telnet server will prompt for a user name and password, *even if you use PAM NTLM to authenticate you with HP-UX.* The reason for this is that the Telnet client and server negotiate which options they will employ at session startup. Windows 2000 Telnet clients and servers support option 37, the Authentication Option, to enable NTLM authentication. HP-UX clients and servers do not. Therefore, even if PAM NTLM authenticated you when you logged on to your HP-UX workstation, the Windows 2000 Telnet server will still ask for a user name and password because the HP-UX Telnet client does not support option 37.

Once authenticated, Windows 2000 runs the %SYSTEMROOT%\system32\login.cmd script, which by default looks like the following:

```
@echo off
rem
rem  Default global login script for the Telnet Server
rem
rem  In the default setup, this command script is executed when the
rem  initial command shell is invoked.  It, in turn, will try to
rem  invoke the individual user's login script.
rem
```

```
echo *===============================================================
echo Welcome to Microsoft Telnet Server.
echo *===============================================================

cd /d %HOMEDRIVE%\%HOMEPATH%
```

10.2.2 Logging

The Logging screen of the Telnet Server MMC snap-in (see Figure 10–3) makes it possible for you to log events in either the application log or a file (or both).

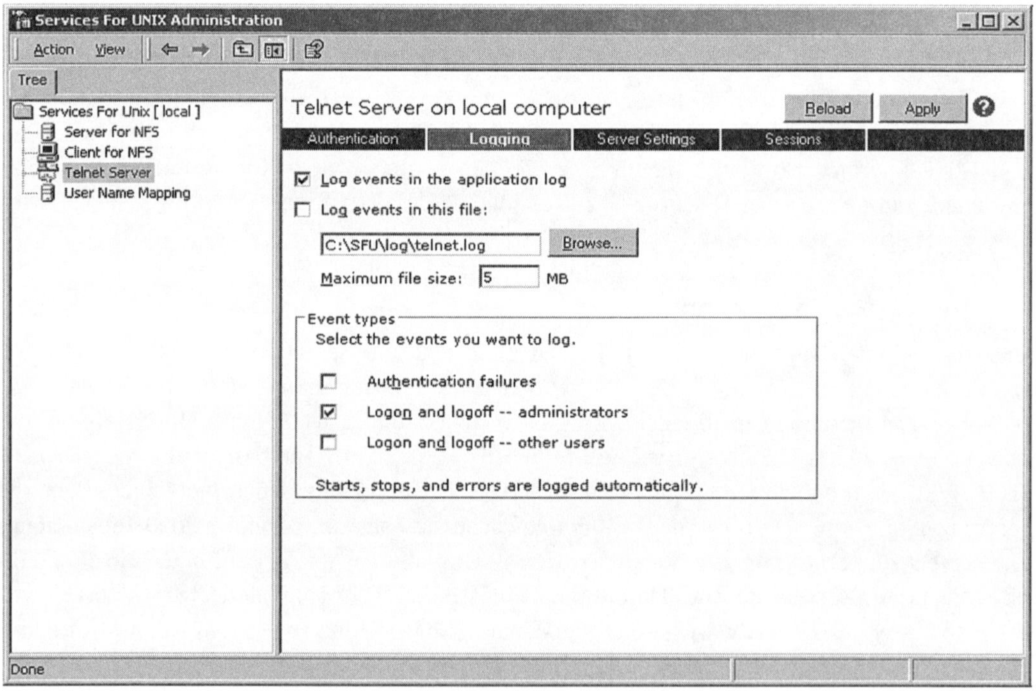

Figure 10–3 The Logging Screen of the Telnet Server MMC snap-in.

10.2.3 Server Settings

On the Server Settings page, you can set a number of parameters, as shown in Figure 10–4. If you need to run an application that might need an ALT key press, you must be sure that the **Interpret CTRL+A as ALT** is checked on this page.

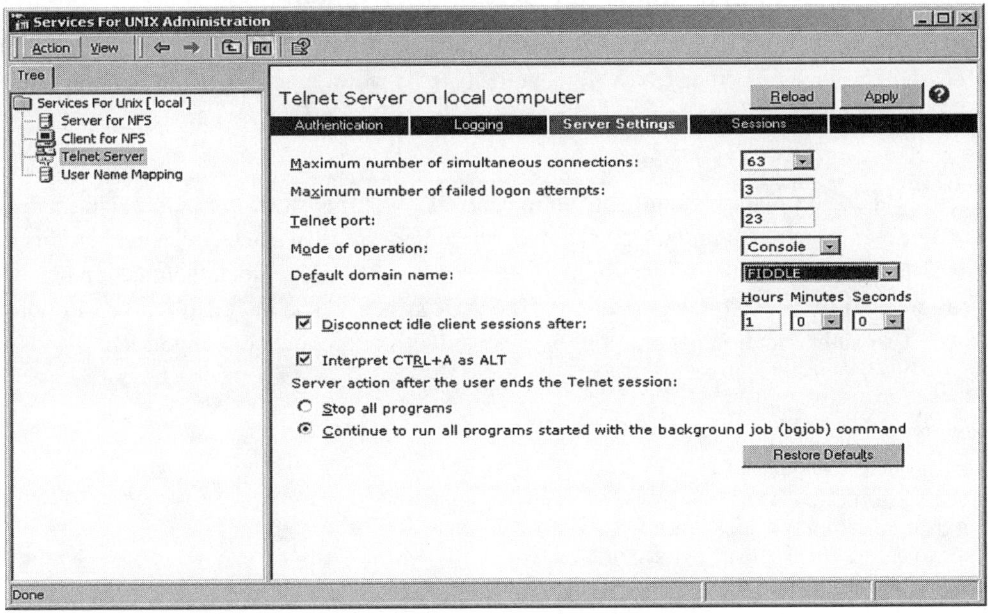

Figure 10–4 The Server Settings Page of the Telnet Server MMC snap-in.

10.2.4 Sessions

The Sessions page lets you see who is logged on and provides you with a means to disconnect users and to send messages to users. Figure 10–5 shows a sample Sessions page.

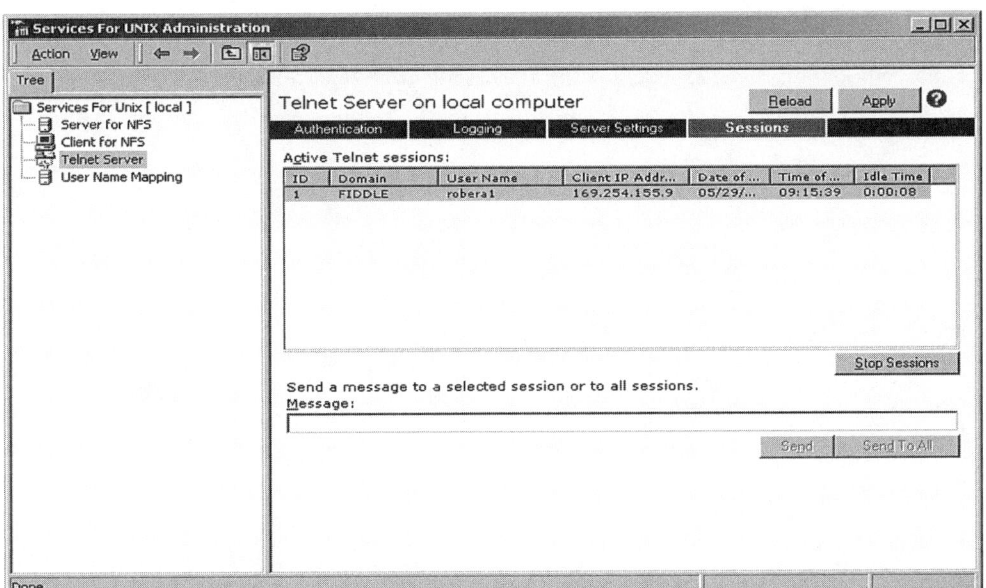

Figure 10–5 Sessions page of the Telnet Server MMC snap-in.

10.2.5 Connecting to Telnet Server with UNIX Telnet Clients

Though I have used an HP-UX system to provide most of the UNIX examples in this book, I have found the behavior of other UNIX Telnet clients to be worth mentioning. To illustrate each process, I've used the *toggle options* subcommand with the UNIX Telnet clients.

10.2.5.1 AIX

With both NTLM and plain text authentication enabled, I got the following output. Notice that the AIX received from the Windows 2000 Telnet server a message of *do 37*. (I've marked this in bold text.) This means that the Windows 2000 server wants the AIX to do authentication negotiation (in order to do NTLM authentication). The AIX system responds (also marked in bold) that it won't do authentication negotiation (because it doesn't recognize or support it).

```
Trying.
Conected to w2kserv.book.local.

Escape character is '^]'.
SEND do ECHO
SEND do SUPRESS GO AHEAD
SEND will TERMINAL TYPE (don't reply)
SEND do SUPORT SAK
SEND will NEGOTIATE WINDOW SIZE (don't reply)
RCVD do 37 (reply)
SEND wont 37 (don't reply)
RCVD will ECHO (reply)
SEND do ECHO (don't reply)
RCVD will SUPRES GO AHEAD (reply)
SEND do SUPRES GO AHEAD (don't reply)
RCVD do 39 (reply)
SEND wont 39 (don't reply)
RCVD do NEGOTIATE WINDOW SIZE (don't reply)
SEND suboption TELOPT_NAWS Width 91, Height 28
RCVD do BINARY (reply)
SEND will BINARY (don't reply)
RCVD will BINARY (reply)
SEND do BINARY (don't reply)
RCVD do TERMINAL TYPE (don't reply)
RCVD wont SUPORT SAK (don't reply)
Microsoft (R) Windows 20 (TM) Version 5.0 (Build 2195)
Welcome to Microsoft Telnet Service
Telnet Server Build 5.20.0412.1
login:
```

The result of this exchange is that the AIX client eventually gets a login prompt. With NTLM authentication disabled, the following exchange takes place:

```
Trying.
Conected to w2kserv.book.local.
Escape character is '^]'.
SEND do ECHO
```

```
SEND do SUPRESS GO AHEAD
SEND will TERMINAL TYPE (don't reply)
SEND do SUPORT SAK
SEND will NEGOTIATE WINDOW SIZE (don't reply)
RCVD will ECHO (reply)
SEND do ECHO (don't reply)
RCVD will SUPRESS GO AHEAD (reply)
SEND do SUPRESS GO AHEAD (don't reply)
RCVD do 39 (reply)
SEND wont 39 (don't reply)
RCVD do NEGOTIATE WINDOW SIZE (don't reply)
SEND suboption TELOPT_NAWS Width 80, Height 24
RCVD do BINARY (reply)
SEND will BINARY (don't reply)
RCVD will BINARY (reply)
SEND do BINARY (don't reply)
RCVD do TERMINAL TYPE (don't reply)
RCVD wont SUPORT SAK (don't reply)
Microsoft (R) Windows 20 (TM) Version 5.0 (Build 2195)
Welcome to Microsoft Telnet Service
Telnet Server Build 5.20.0412.1
```

Notice that the option 37 negotiation does not take place.

10.2.5.2 Solaris 8

With both NTLM and plain text authentication enabled, I got the following output. Note that Solaris recognizes option 37 (thereby calling it by name rather than by number) but does not support it.

```
Trying w2kserv...
Connected to w2kserv.
Escape character is '^]'.
SENT DO SUPPRESS GO AHEAD
SENT WILL TERMINAL TYPE
SENT WILL NAWS
SENT WILL TSPEED
SENT WILL LFLOW
SENT WILL LINEMODE
SENT WILL NEW-ENVIRON
SENT DO STATUS
RCVD WILL ECHO
RCVD WIL SUPRESS GO AHEAD
RCVD DO AUTHENTICATION
SENT WONT AUTHENTICATION
RCVD WILL ECHO
SENT DO ECHO
RCVD WILL SUPPRESS GO AHEAD
RCVD DO NEW-ENVIRON
RCVD DO NAWS
SENT IAC SB NAWS 0 80 (80) 0 25 (25)
```

```
RCVD DO BINARY
SENT WILL BINARY
RCVD WILL BINARY
SENT DO BINARY
RCVD DO TERMINAL TYPE
RCVD DONT TSPEED
RCVD DONT LFLOW
RCVD DONT LINEMODE
RCVD IAC SB NEW-ENVIRON SEND
SENT IAC SB NEW-ENVIRON IS
RCVD IAC SB NEW-ENVIRON SEND USERVAR "SFUTLNTVER" USERVAR
"SFUTLNTMODE"
SENT IAC SB NEW-ENVIRON IS USERVAR "SFUTLNTVER" USERVAR "SFUTLNTMODE"
RCVD WONT STATUS
Microsoft (R) Windows 2000 (TM) Version 5.00 (Build 2195)
Welcome to Microsoft Telnet Service
Telnet Server Build 5.2000.0412.1
login:
```

Connection time was very fast, as was connection time when NTLM authentication was disabled.

10.2.5.3 HP-UX

Connecting to the Windows 2000 Telnet server with the HP-UX Telnet client proved difficult. With both NTLM and plain text authentication enabled, I never got a login prompt! Check out the following output. The portion I've placed in bold text shows that the HP-UX received an authentication negotiation request (*RCVD do 37*). Not only did the HP-UX client not recognize that option, it failed to supply a proper response.

```
Trying...
Connected to w2kserv.book.local.
Escape character is '^]'.
SENT do SUPPRESS GO AHEAD
SENT will TERMINAL TYPE (don't reply)
SENT will TERMSPEED (don't reply)
SENT will LFLOW (don't reply)
SENT will NAWS (don't reply)
RCVD do 37 (reply)
SENT ??? 37 (don't reply)
RCVD will ECHO (reply)
Local flow control off
SENT do ECHO (reply)
RCVD will SUPPRESS GO AHEAD (don't reply)
RCVD do 39 (reply)
SENT wont 39 (don't reply)
RCVD do NAWS (don't reply)
Sent suboption NAWS 0 80 (80) 0 25 (25)
                                        RCVD do BINARY (reply)
SENT will BINARY (don't reply)
```

```
RCVD will BINARY (reply)
SENT do BINARY (reply)
RCVD do TERMINAL TYPE (don't reply)
RCVD dont TERMSPEED (reply)
SENT wont TERMSPEED (don't reply)
RCVD dont LFLOW (reply)
SENT wont LFLOW (don't reply)
Connection closed by foreign host.
#
```

As a result, the Windows 2000 Telnet server never got an answer to its authentication negotiation request, timed out, and closed the connection. After turning off NTLM authentication, I was successful in connecting. Notice that option 37 does not appear in the output.

```
Trying...
Connected to w2kserv.book.local.
Escape character is '^]'.
SENT do SUPPRESS GO AHEAD
SENT will TERMINAL TYPE (don't reply)
SENT will TERMSPEED (don't reply)
SENT will LFLOW (don't reply)
SENT will NAWS (don't reply)
RCVD will ECHO (reply)
Local flow control off
SENT do ECHO (reply)
RCVD will SUPPRESS GO AHEAD (don't reply)
RCVD do 39 (reply)
SENT wont 39 (don't reply)
RCVD do NAWS (don't reply)
Sent suboption NAWS 0 80 (80) 0 25 (25)
                                            RCVD do BINARY (reply)
SENT will BINARY (don't reply)
RCVD will BINARY (reply)
SENT do BINARY (reply)
RCVD do TERMINAL TYPE (don't reply)
RCVD dont TERMSPEED (reply)
SENT wont TERMSPEED (don't reply)
RCVD dont LFLOW (reply)
SENT wont LFLOW (don't reply)
Microsoft (R) Windows 2000 (TM) Version 5.00 (Build 2195)
Welcome to Microsoft Telnet Service
Telnet Server Build 5.2000.0412.1
login:
```

> It seems, therefore, that until HP fixes its Telnet client, it will work only if you turn NTLM authentication off on the Windows 2000 Telnet server.

10.3 Server For NIS

10.3.1 Background

Windows Services for UNIX includes software called NIS Server. So what is NIS? NIS is Network Information Services, developed by Sun Microsystems in the 1980s to centralize commonly used data in UNIX workgroups. As long as UNIX systems worked much like mainframe systems, that is, serving multiple users from terminals, there was no need for something like NIS. But with the advent of the UNIX workstation in the 1980s, you suddenly had multiple users of multiple systems. Each system had its own user database, its own hosts file, its own services file. For a workgroup of such systems to function properly, administrators had to ensure that each machine had identical versions of each of the necessary configuration files. Even a small workgroup of, say, 10 machines, made administration cumbersome. But as workgroups expanded in size, it became ever more likely that at least a few systems would not be "in sync" with the others.

NIS attempts to avoid this problem by providing uniform configuration information to all systems in a particular workgroup, called a *domain*. In this general sense, an NIS domain resembles a Windows NT domain. NIS master servers maintain key information such as user and group accounts in the form of *maps*. NIS client systems obtain such information by consulting either the master server or a slave server. An administrator can modify the master server's maps, and master servers can replicate their maps to slave servers. There is only one master server and any number of slave servers per NIS domain.

Windows NT domains maintain key configuration information in domain controllers. Clients obtain this information from either Primary Domain Controllers (PDCs) or Backup Domain Controllers (BDCs). Administrators can modify network information on PDCs, and PDCs replicate their information to BDCs. There is only one PDC and any number of BDCs per NT domain. As we know, Windows 2000 domains maintain network information in Active Directory, maintained by domain controllers in a peer-to-peer fashion, so the analogy starts to break down here. However, I think you get the idea.

Rather than go into all the ins and outs of NIS, let's use a basic example to illustrate how it works. The most common use of NIS is the centralization of user and group data. Without NIS, a system authenticates a user by consulting the */etc/passwd* and */etc/group* text files. With NIS, a system consults a user and group map made available by an NIS master server on the network. The master server creates these maps using *its* local */etc/passwd* and */etc/group* files. Therefore, the contents of these files on the master server serve as the domain's user and group information. When you configure a master server, the contents of */etc/passwd* and */etc/group* are translated into databases (or maps) with names like *passwd.byname.dir*, *passwd.byname.pag*, and *group.byname.dir*. Therefore, an NIS client will authenticate a user by consulting these maps rather than */etc/passwd* and */etc/group*. (Administrators frequently configure their clients to consult both.)

When an administrator creates an NIS domain account, he or she creates an entry in the NIS master server's */etc/passwd* and */etc/group* files. The administrator then runs the shell script *ypmake* to update the maps. To replicate the changes of these maps to the slave servers, he or she then uses a utility called *yppush*. The exact process can vary according to implementation and can be customized, but the essential elements of this process are the same: Make a change to the configuration file, update the map, "push" the map to the slave servers.

Network Information Service Plus (NIS+), is the next generation of the NIS. Like NIS, it is a distributed database system that allows you to maintain commonly used configuration information on a master server and propagate the information to all the hosts in your network. However, it is not an enhancement to NIS; it is a whole new service. The Windows 2000 Server for NIS does *not* support NIS+. But this should not be a problem, since NIS implementations are far more common.

10.3.2 What Server for NIS Can Do

Server for NIS can make a Windows 2000 domain controller serve as an NIS master server for a domain (or multiple domains) with UNIX slave servers and clients. It can also turn a domain controller into a slave server, as long as the master is also a Windows 2000 system running Server for NIS. The reason for this is that Server for NIS stores maps in Active Directory, the information of which is automatically replicated with Active Directory replication. UNIX slave servers obtain copies of Server for NIS maps via the usual NIS protocols.

Storing NIS maps in Active Directory is a key feature of Server for NIS. In addition to replication, you have strong security mechanisms in place. Perhaps most significant, though, is the unification of Windows and UNIX user accounts in Active Directory. So far we have seen, and will see in later chapters, that interoperability schemes typically require duplicate user accounts: one for UNIX, one for Windows. These accounts must be identical to the letter and case for these schemes to work. Server for NIS will take any NIS object that has a corresponding Windows object, such as a user, and adds UNIX attributes to the Windows object. It does so by creating an auxiliary class for the Active Directory **User** group. In this auxiliary class are attributes corresponding to the fields of */etc/passwd*. There are attributes for the user identifier (UID), the group identifier (GID), password, home directory, login shell, gecos information, as well as others. This effectively unifies the UNIX and Windows 2000 user databases.

Server for NIS stores the user's password in UNIX format in the *msSFUPassword* attribute. When a user sets or changes his or her password while working on a Windows 2000 system, Server for NIS stores the UNIX-style encrypted password in this attribute. As long as the user makes a password change on a Windows 2000 system, the Windows and NIS passwords will be synchronized. However, if a user changes his or her password on a UNIX system using a utility like *yppasswd*, the user's password is changed only in this attribute, with no effect on the Windows password. Thus, we still have a dichotomy in user accounts, which can be resolved only with the separate Password Synchronization feature of SFU.

10.3.3 Migrating an HP-UX NIS Master to Server for NIS

You can migrate the data of an HP-UX NIS master server to Server for NIS and then use the Windows 2000 system as the new master server. You can either use a command-line utility called *nis2ad* to migrate your data, or you can use the Migration wizard. This example will use the Migration wizard.

10.3.3.1 First Step: Check the Name Service Switch

You must be careful with the name service switch, which is configured by the */etc/nsswitch.conf* file. By default, this file has the following contents:

```
passwd:        files nis
group:         files nis
hosts:         dns [NOTFOUND=return] nis [NOTFOUND=return] files
networks:      nis [NOTFOUND=return] files
protocols:     nis [NOTFOUND=return] files
rpc:           nis [NOTFOUND=return] files
publickey:     nis [NOTFOUND=return] files
netgroup:      nis [NOTFOUND=return] files
automount:     files nis
aliases:       files nis
services:      nis [NOTFOUND=return] files
```

If, for example, you have the name service switch consult NIS only for **services**, and the **services** map is empty, then your system cannot communicate with your HP-UX system on the network. (I discovered this the hard way.) My recommendations:

1. Leave the default */etc/nsswitch.conf* file alone; it can accommodate most environments.
2. Migrate only the **passwd**, **group**, and **hosts** maps. These are easily modified on Windows 2000.

10.3.3.2 Second Step: Run the Migration Wizard

To open NIS Server Migration, click **Start**, point to **Programs**, point to **Windows Services for UNIX**, and then click **NIS Server Migration**. You get the screen shown in Figure 10–6.

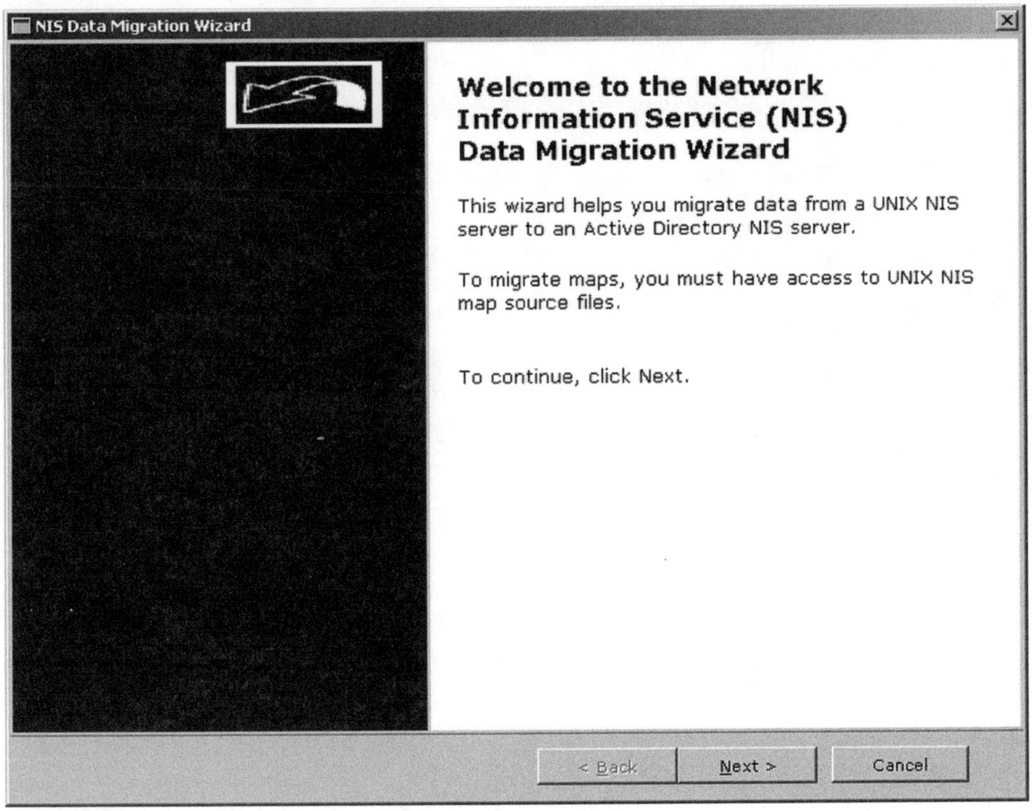

Figure 10–6 The NIS Data Migration Welcome screen.

Note that this screen says that you will have to have access to the NIS map source files. I used FTP to copy */etc/passwd*, */etc/group*, and */etc/hosts* to a local directory called *D:>\NIS*. If you do not put other source files there, such as */etc/services* or */etc/netgroup*, then the maps associated with those source files will be empty. Be sure your */etc/nsswitch.conf* file is configured to consult local files at some point. After clicking **Next**, I got the **Domain and Server Selection** screen. (See Figure 10–7.)

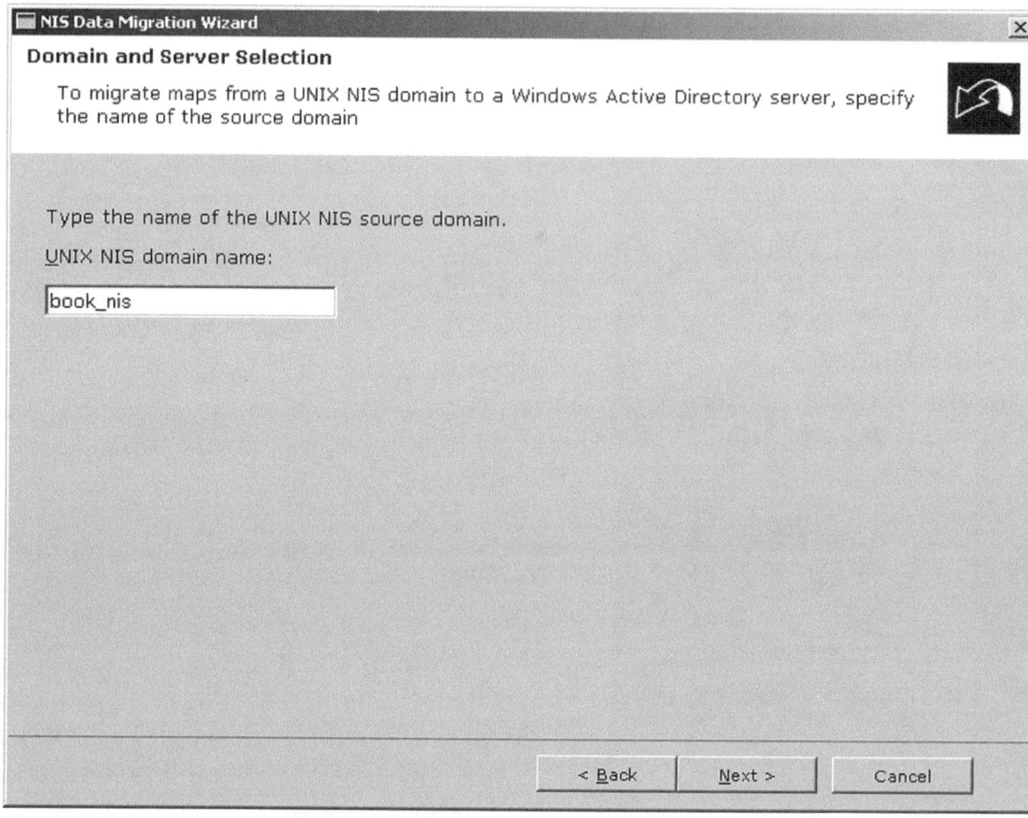

Figure 10–7 The Domain and Server Selection screen.

My HP-UX master server's NIS domain was called *book_nis*. Clicking **Next** brought me to the next screen, the **Administrator Authentication** screen. I was already logged on as Administrator, so there was no need to supply another account name.

The next screen was the **NIS Map Selection** screen. (See Figure 10–8.) I selected only three maps to migrate: **passwd**, **group**, and **hosts**. Later, the Migration Wizard will get the source files for these maps and migrate them; the other maps will be created but will contain nothing.

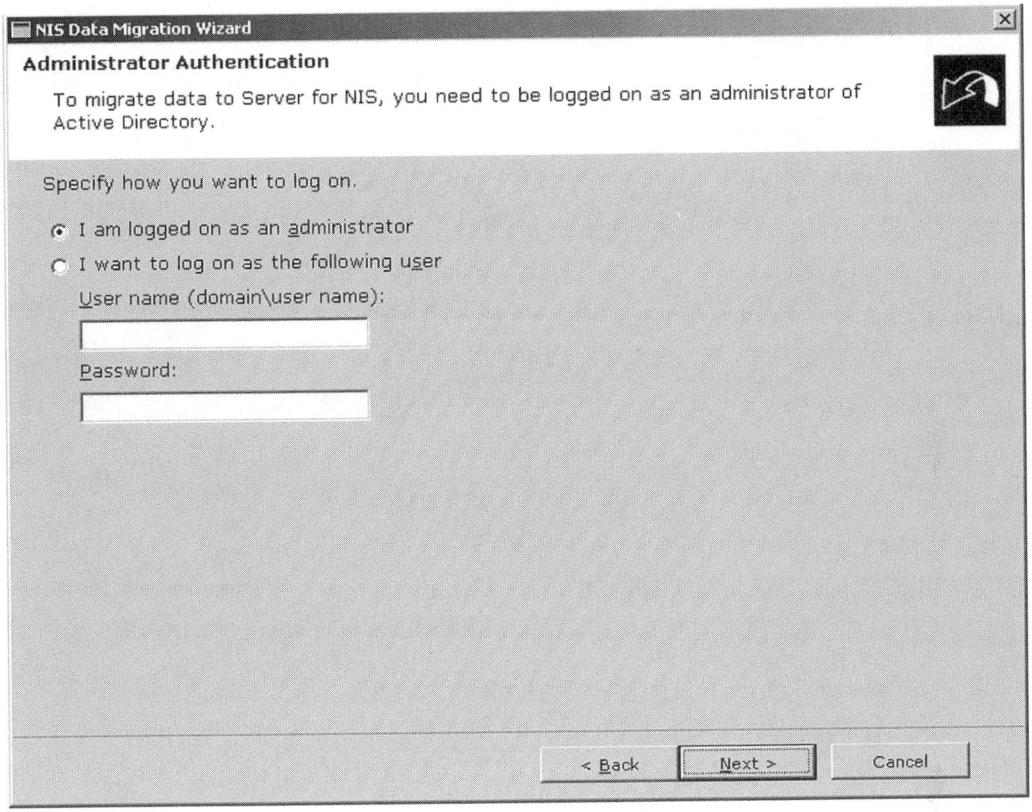

Figure 10–8 The NIS Map Selection screen.

The next screen, the **Location of UNIX NIS Map Source Files** screen, simply asks for the location of the source files to migrate. In my case, I copied them via FTP to a directory called *D:\NIS*. The **Destination Domain for Migration** screen follows (see Figure 10–9). By default, the Migration Wizard will migrate maps to an NIS domain that is the same name as the Windows 2000 domain. Microsoft also recommends that you keep the default Active Directory container for migration. Otherwise, some objects will not appear in the Active Directory Users and Computers MMC.

The Migration Wizard then asks how you will handle conflicts during the migration. Active Directory may already contain objects that exist in the NIS maps being migrated. If, for example, you have a user with accounts in both the Windows 2000 and the UNIX NIS networks, and that account name is the same, then you will have a conflict. Your choices will be to keep the existing entry, replace the existing entry with the new entry, and/or report the conflict. The Migration Wizard will run the migration in "dummy mode" first so that you can view the log files for conflicts you may want to resolve before actually performing the migration.

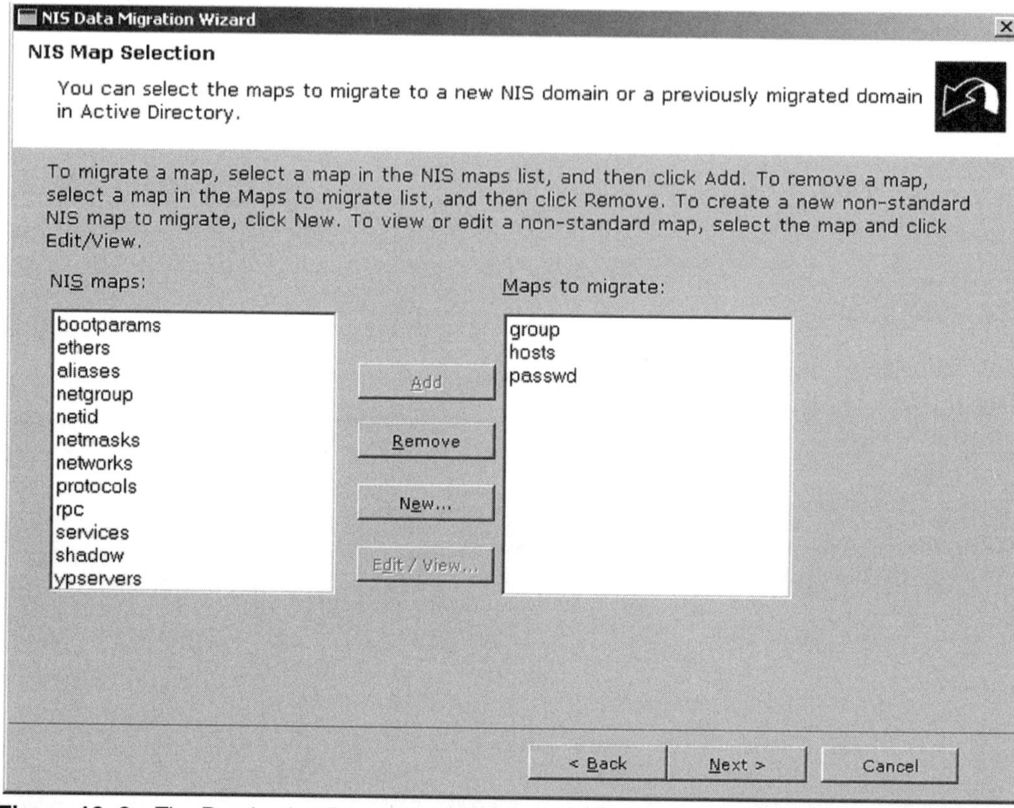

Figure 10–9 The Destination Domain for Migration screen.

In my case, conflicts were logged in *D:\SFU\nis\conflicts*. Following is an excerpt from that file:

```
### Mon Nov 27 12:53:24 2000 : Conflict details of entries from map
file and existing entries in AD. map file = 'passwd'.  ###

conflicts with  CN=dylan,CN=Users,DC=book,DC=local
existing data = A Windows only object (User/Group/Computer). No Unix
attributes found for this object.

new data      = dylan:kIg86vWct3dFg:102:20:Dylan Roberts,DT4T,434-
1434,454-4545:/home/dylan:/usr/bin/sh
```

Essentially, this output tells us that there was already a Windows 2000 user named *dylan* in the *book.local* domain. As a result, the migration added new data, including the password, home directory, and login shell, to the Active Directory entry for *dylan*.

10.3.3.3 Step Three: Disable the Old Master Server

On HP-UX, the easiest way to disable an NIS master is through SAM. Start SAM, select **Networking and Communications**, and then click on the NIS icon. You will get the **NIS Configuration** screen (see Figure 10–10). From the menu bar, choose **Actions→Disable Server**. To turn the system into an NIS client of the new master server (the Windows 2000 system), choose **Actions→Disable Client** and then **Actions→Set Domain Name**. Set the domain name to the new domain created during the migration process. In my case, I set the domain name to *book* instead of *book.local*. Then, run **Actions→Enable Client**.

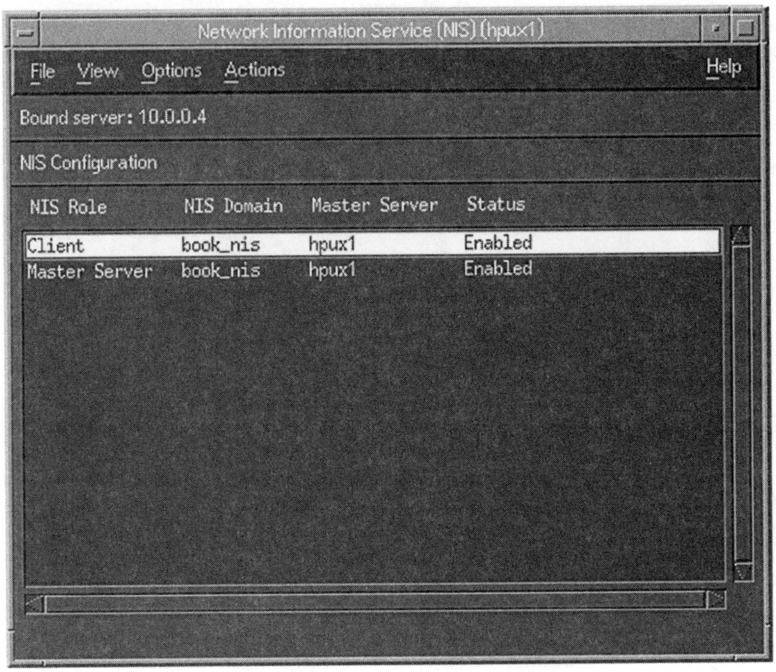

Figure 10–10 The NIS Configuration screen in SAM.

10.3.4 Issues with Migration

10.3.4.1 UIDs

Since my test bed was so small, there was not much for me to be worried about, so I ran the migration without much concern. The only problem I ran into was that the Active Directory account *dylan* did not seem to retain the UNIX UID for that user (which was 102). In Figure 10–11, I show the UNIX Attributes tab of the *dylan* account. Because I chose not to overwrite any data of any Windows object, the UID was set to a different number. The result was that although I could log in as user *dylan* on the HP-UX system (after converting the master server into a client), I had file permission problems. Changing *dylan's* UID in Active Directory to 102, the original value, fixed everything.

Also, in HP-UX the default GID for the **users** group is 20. But Server for NIS reserves GIDs below 100. So, you either have to change the GID to a number over 100 in Server for NIS or leave it alone and ensure the name service switch consults files at some point. If you want to be sure your name service switch works properly, use the *nsquery* utility. For example,

```
# /usr/contrib/bin/nsquery group users

Using "files nis" for the group policy.

Searching /etc/group for users
Group name: users
Group Id: 20
Group membership: root
Switch configuration: Terminates Search
```

Note that *nsquery* found the **users** group with GID 20, because the name service switch consults */etc/group* first.

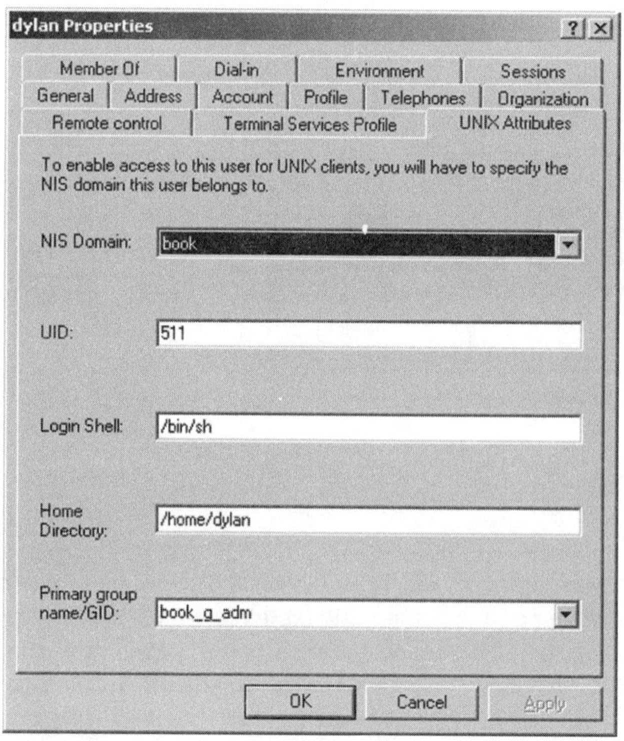

Figure 10–11 The UNIX Attributes tab. Run **Start→Programs→Administrative Tools◊Active Directory Users and Computers**. Then right-click the user and choose **Properties**.

10.3.4.2 Passwords

Because the *dylan* account already existed in Active Directory, the UNIX password for that account was set to be the same as that on the HP-UX system. However, the Windows 2000 password for *dylan* did not change. To synchronize the password, I logged on as *dylan* on my Windows 2000 server and changed the password. (In the default Domain Controller Policy object, I had to grant the users group the right to log on locally in order to do this.) The result was that both passwords were changed, and the NIS **passwd** map was pushed to the HP-UX client.

However, when I logged into *hpux1* as *dylan*, I used *yppasswd* to change my NIS password:

```
$ yppasswd
Changing password for dylan on NIS server
Old NIS password:
New password:
Re-enter new password:
NIS(YP) passwd/attributes changed on w2kserv, the master NIS server.
```

Indeed, the NIS password changed. The Windows 2000 password, however, did not. Two-way synchronization is possible only by installing and configuring the separate Password Synchronization tool in SFU.

10.3.4.3 Creating a New User

If, during migration, the Migration Wizard creates a new Windows user because there was no equivalent user in place at the time of migration, the user's UNIX password in Active Directory will be the same as the existing UNIX password. However, the user will be required to change his or her password upon the next logon to Windows.

Since the Windows 2000 domain controller is now the NIS master server, you can create new users for both Windows and UNIX clients using the Active Directory Users and Computers tool. However, if you do so, only the Windows password will be set; there will be no NIS password. In other words, logging on to Windows will require a password; logging on to a UNIX NIS client will not. As we have seen, logging on to UNIX and using *yppasswd* will set the NIS password on the domain controller, but the only sure way to synchronize the passwords (unless you are using the separate Password Synchronization tool) is to have the user log on to a Windows client system and change passwords there.

10.3.4.4 Home Directories

If you create a new user on the domain controller running Server for NIS, that new user will have a UNIX home directory that defaults to the form of the migrated **passwd** map. So, for example, if your UNIX home directories are in */home*, Active Directory will specify */home/username* in its UNIX Home Directory attribute. So, where are these home directories to be found? Well, unless you centralize their location using either NFS or Common Internet File System (CIFS), then you must make sure they are created on each UNIX system. Centralizing data, including home directories, is what it's all about. So, in coming chapters we will look at methods to make this possible.

10.3.4.5 Map Management

There is good news and bad news when it comes to map management. The good news is that you can edit the **passwd**, **group**, and **hosts** maps using Active Directory Users and Computers. (You can also use the *nisadmin* command.) The bad news is that for all other maps, you have to use the ADSI Edit utility found in the Support Tools folder of the Windows 2000 media.

To edit **passwd**, **group**, and **host** maps using Active Directory, just start Active Directory Users and Computers and select the domain you want to edit. Then, for **passwd** and **group** maps, click **Users**. For the **hosts** map, click **Computers**. Right-click on the user or computer you want to edit, choose **Properties**, and select the **UNIX Attributes** tab to make your changes. See Figure 10–11 for a picture of the **UNIX Attributes** tab. Make sure the **NIS Domain** box contains the name of the correct NIS domain. When creating a new user account or computer entry, this box will specify **<none>** by default. Just click on the arrow to the right of that box to select the NIS domain.

I would suggest not using the other maps. My forays into ADSI Edit were fraught with frustration. Therefore, keep references to other information local until Microsoft comes up with an easier way to edit all other maps on Server for NIS.

10.4 Conclusion

If you are beginning to see potential for some real complexity developing here, you are right. In this and previous chapters we've seen a number of authentication schemes: local UNIX authentication, NIS, NTLM, Kerberos. In the next chapter, we turn to file sharing. File sharing involves authorization in addition to authentication. We can share files from UNIX systems to Windows systems using NFS or CIFS. We can do the same in the other direction. We have share permissions, NFS permissions, UNIX permissions, NTFS permissions. Whew!

Did I say this was going to be easy?

References

1. Hal Stern and Mike Loukides, *Managing NFS and NIS.* (O'Reilly, 1997)
2. The Services for UNIX Help File

CHAPTER 11

NFS File Sharing

In late 1984, Sun Microsystems introduced the Network File System (NFS), a means of sharing files among computers connected to a network. Though it was designed to be operating system-independent, NFS originated in SunOS, a Berkeley-based UNIX operating system, and dominates file sharing in the UNIX world. However, NFS does exist on other systems, including mainframes, minicomputers, and PCs. Windows Services for UNIX version 2 provides both an NFS server and client for Windows 2000 systems.

11.1 Basic Concepts

NFS is designed as a client-server technology. A system running an NFS server can *export* file systems to client systems. The NFS clients running on the client systems *mount* (gain access to) the server's exported file systems. The mount process essentially "attaches" a remote file system to a local directory, making it appear to the local system and the user that the remote file system is actually local. Thus, with the appropriate permissions, a user can change directories to the mounted file system and list, create, and delete files there, with no indication (barring a ridiculously slow network) that he or she is actually working on remote files.

While there are certainly many differences between NFS and CIFS (Common Internet File System, the Windows file sharing system), those familiar with the latter can draw some parallels. Instead of *exporting* file systems, Windows systems make directories available over the network in the form of *shares*. Clients connect to these shares either by *mapping a network drive* or by referring to a Universal Naming Convention, or UNC. The mapping process is somewhat analogous to mounting a file system. Windows users can click on the icons representing network drives, and—depending on the permissions—add, delete, edit, list, or print files.

11.2 NFS and Windows 2000 Issues

These basic concepts, then, are quite similar. The differences, however, are both numerous and substantial, as we shall see in the course of this and the next chapter. In order to share files between UNIX and Windows systems, we have to either modify, or adjust, the NFS protocol to make it compatible with Windows systems or adapt the CIFS protocol to make it compatible with UNIX. In this chapter, we concentrate on NFS, as provided by Windows Services for UNIX, and how to make it work on Windows systems.

11.2.1 Local File Systems and NFS

Between UNIX (including UNIX clones) and Windows 2000, there are a number of different file systems in existence. HP-UX has Hierachical File System (HFS) and JFS. Solaris has UFS. Linux has *ext2*. Windows 2000 has File Allocation Table (FAT), FAT32, and NTFS. Practically all operating systems support CD-ROM File System (CDFS). However, NFS was designed after UNIX file system semantics. All UNIX disk file systems store information about each file, the metadata, in *inodes*. Instead of inodes, NFS manipulates *rnodes*, which contain similar information, such as the UID of the owner of the file, the GID associated with the file, and the permission bits. Other file systems, such as FAT and NTFS, have different structures. Therefore, to accommodate different file systems, NFS employs a file system interface known as the *Virtual File System (VFS)/Virtual File Node (VNODE)*, which separates the file system interface from the specific file system implementation. While the VFS interface works, some NFS operations, such **symlink**(), which creates a symbolic link to a file on a remote host, do not work—for example, if the remote file system is FAT. Also, since NTFS file attributes differ from those in UNIX file systems, there must be some mechanism to map these attributes.

11.2.1.1 NFS, FAT, and CDFS

FAT and CDFS do not provide any security mechanism. CD-ROM file systems are always read-only. To make FAT file systems writable over NFS, you must grant read/write access when mounting the file system. FAT file systems also have no concept of file ownership. Therefore, if you grant read/write access to a FAT file system exported by NFS, all users have full access to the file system. The only way to protect your exported FAT file system is to mount it as read-only.

11.2.1.2 NTFS

File and directory permissions differ between UNIX file systems and NTFS. For example, UNIX does not have the Take Ownership permission. Somehow, NTFS permissions on a Server for NFS resource need to be mapped in such a way that the UNIX client can understand them. Fortunately, Server for NFS handles this transparently.

11.2.2 User Authentication and Authorization

The NFS protocol utilizes the Remote Procedure Call (RPC) mechanism to perform operations. RPC is a means whereby a client application passes a set of arguments to the local RPC library, which packages the arguments and sends them to a server. The server processes the call and returns the results to the client. NFS-RPC procedures can obtain and set file attributes, read and write data from or to files, and create and remove directories. Each RPC request that a client system sends to a server must include UNIX credentials—the UID and GIDs—of the user initiating the request. The NFS server uses these credentials to determine what level of file access, if any, the user has.

The problem here is that Windows 2000 does not use UIDs and GIDs to authenticate and authorize users. It uses SIDs and security descriptors instead. Even if you install Server for NIS, which can incorporate UNIX attributes such as UIDs and GIDs into Active Directory, Windows systems running Server for NFS still need to have some kind of mapping between UIDs/GIDs and security descriptors in order to determine access. To achieve this mapping, you must use the User Name Mapping Service, a component of Windows Services for UNIX (SFU).

Also, keep in mind that with NFS, user authentication actually takes place at the client when a user logs in. The RPC request contains the UID and GID of the user initiating the request. The user can't initiate a request unless he or she has successfully logged in, and after that, the client does the work. The NFS server simply accepts the UID and GID of the RPC request as valid and uses them to determine file access.

11.3 Windows 2000 NFS Client/HP-UX NFS Server

If you want to access NFS files systems from an HP-UX server on a Windows 2000 system, you must configure the HP-UX system as an NFS server and install Client for NFS on Windows 2000. But first you must set up User Name Mapping.

11.3.1 Setting Up User Name Mapping

In order for Server for NFS to validate an RPC request containing a UNIX UID and GID, it needs to find the equivalent user in Active Directory. The only way to accomplish this is to use some form of mapping of UNIX and Windows users. The same is true for Client for NFS. Since this client runs on a Windows 2000 system, there must be a way to provide the UNIX NFS server with a UNIX-style UID and GID if anonymous users are not allowed.

User Name Mapping provides the means for both Server for NFS and Client for NFS to obtain UIDs and GIDs for use in their transactions. This service runs on only one system in the network (on a domain controller if you want to map domain user accounts to UNIX accounts), thus providing a single mapping source for Windows NFS components. When Server for NFS needs to find the equivalent Windows user for a given UID, it consults User Name Mapping before processing the request. When Client for NFS needs to insert a UID/GID combination into its RPC requests for a Windows user, it consults User Name Mapping before sending the request.

If a user has accounts in both a UNIX network and a Windows 2000 domain, and those names are identical, User Name Mapping maps the names automatically with no administrator intervention. This is known as simple mapping. If you have users with accounts in both the UNIX and Windows 2000 worlds and those accounts differ, then you must manually map these users using the User Name Mapping MMC. This is known as advanced mapping. Figure 11–1 shows the page of the User Name Mapping MMC that addresses simple and advanced mapping.

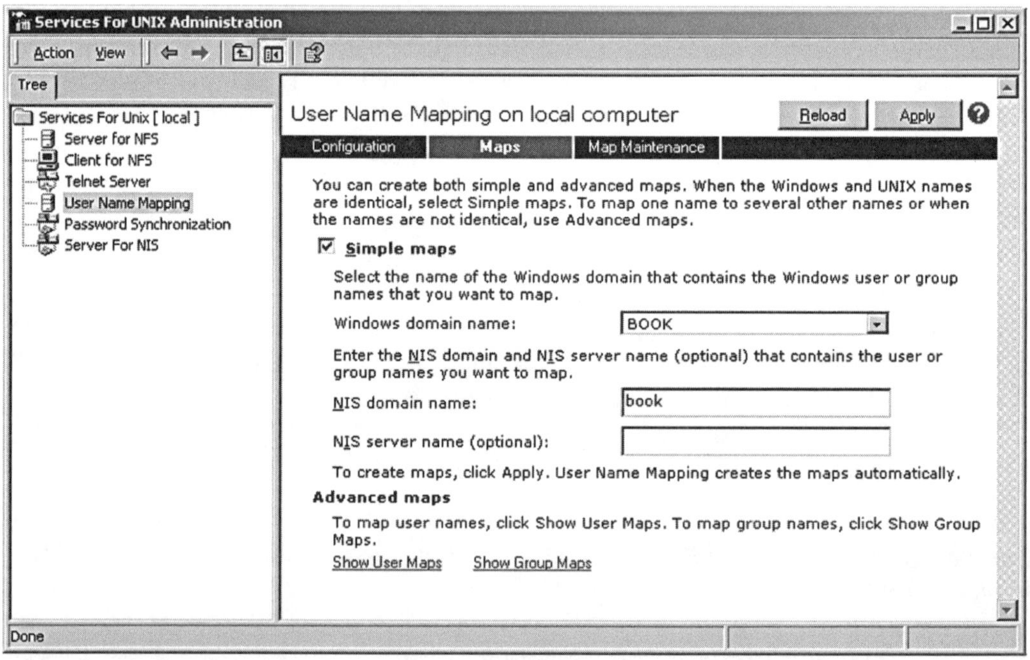

Figure 11–1 The Maps page of the User Name Mapping MMC.

11.3.2 Configuring HP-UX

Again, using SAM is the quick and easy way to configure HP-UX. After running SAM, select **Networking and Communications→Networked File Systems→Exported File Systems**. If you are not already configured as an NFS server, you will get the note shown in Figure 11–2.

Figure 11–2 First-time NFS Server Configuration note.

When you do as the warning suggests (selecting **Add** from the **Actions** menu), you will get another warning, as shown in Figure 11–3.

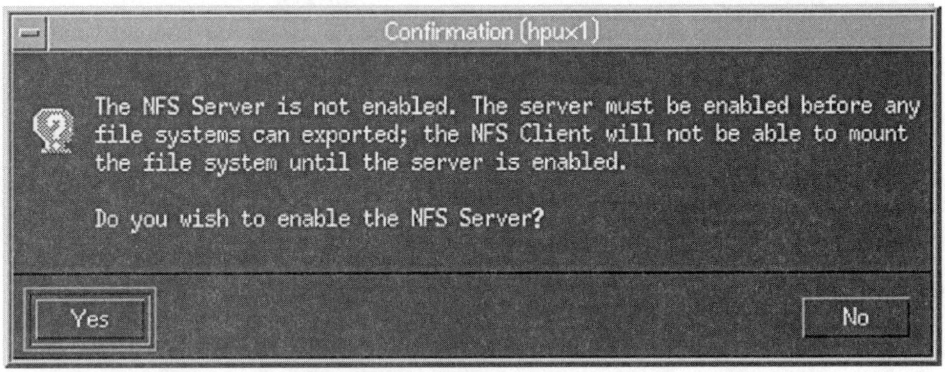

Figure 11–3 NFS Server Confirmation message.

At this point you are provided with a window requesting information about what file system to export and what the options are. A sample is shown in Figure 11–4.

You might want to consult Hewlett-Packard's document *Configuring and Administering NFS* for more detail on export options. The default options include the following:

- **Option for Unknown User ID**. By default, this option will map anonymous users to the user *nobody.* Any NFS request not containing user credentials is considered to be from an anonymous user. The *nobody* user in HP-UX is listed in */etc/passwd* as having a UID of –2, though this value is sometimes represented as 65534 (the 16-bit unsigned representation of –2).
- **Allow Asynchronous Writes**. An asynchronous write occurs when an NFS server returns a write response to a client before writing the data to disk. The default is not to allow such writes.
- **Permission for File Access**. The default is to allow read/write access for all systems. You can specify other kinds of access to different systems, though.
- **Specify Root User Access**. Normally, any NFS request containing *root* user credentials is mapped to the anonymous user, for security reasons. If you want *root* access from your administration system, you need to specify it here. Otherwise, the default is that no systems are granted root access.

If you accept the defaults, you will export the file system you specify with anonymous users given the UID of 65534 (–2).

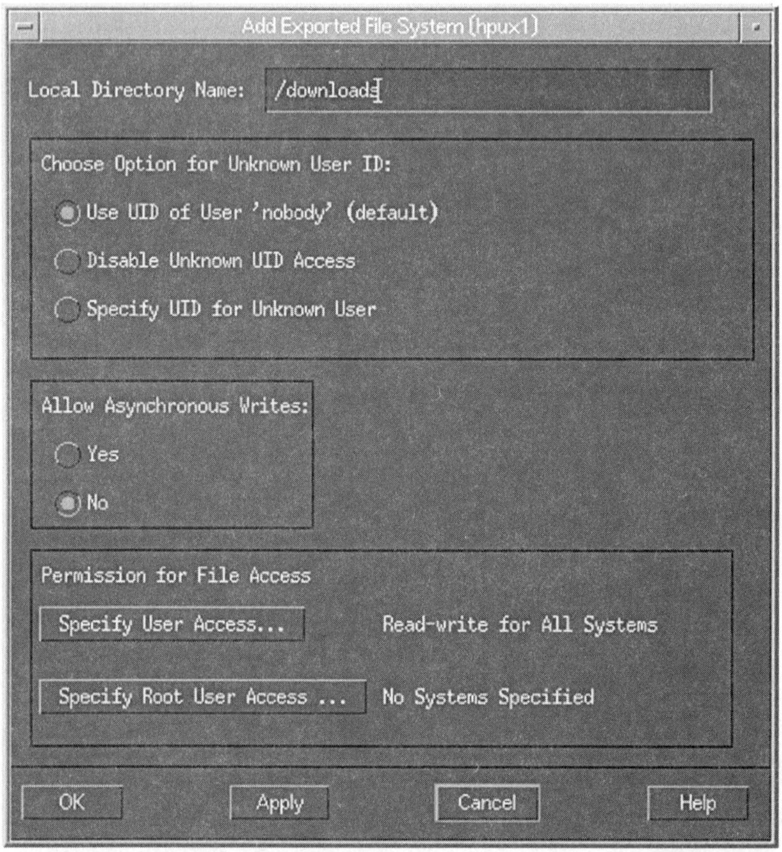

Figure 11–4 Specifying Exported File Systems and Options in SAM.

You cannot export a directory and its parent if they are on the same disk or logical volume. The same goes for a directory and one of its subdirectories. For example, you cannot export the root directory (*/*) and */opt* if both reside on the same disk or logical volume. If two directories reside in the same tree but on different disks or logical volumes, then you can export both as long as you do so explicitly in */etc/exports*.

11.3.2.1 Symbolic Links

Watch for symbolic links when exporting file systems on HP-UX (or any UNIX system, for that matter). A symbolic link is a file name that points to a file located elsewhere. If the link points to a file outside the file system being exported, the Windows 2000 Client NFS client will not be able to access the file, even though an icon for the link appears in Windows Explorer.

11.3.2.2 Permissions

Regular HP-UX file and directory permissions override any export permissions. Therefore, even if you export a file system as read-write, only users with the right HP-UX permissions can actually read or write data on a mounted file system. You can also specify access permissions in the mount operation on the client side. If the mount permissions differ from the export permissions, the more restrictive permissions take precedence.

11.3.3 Using Client for NFS

After you install Client for NFS, you get a new folder in **My Network Places** called **NFS Network**. After you find this folder, double-click on **My Network Places** and then on **Entire Network**. In this folder is an icon called **Default LAN**, which represents all the NFS servers discovered via broadcast on the local segment. There is also an icon called **Favorite LAN**. You can add NFS servers from different segments to this folder, the idea being to add those that you use most frequently.

You can see what a particular NFS server is exporting by right-clicking on the icon representing that server and then selecting **Properties**. You will get a window similar to the one shown in Figure 11–5.

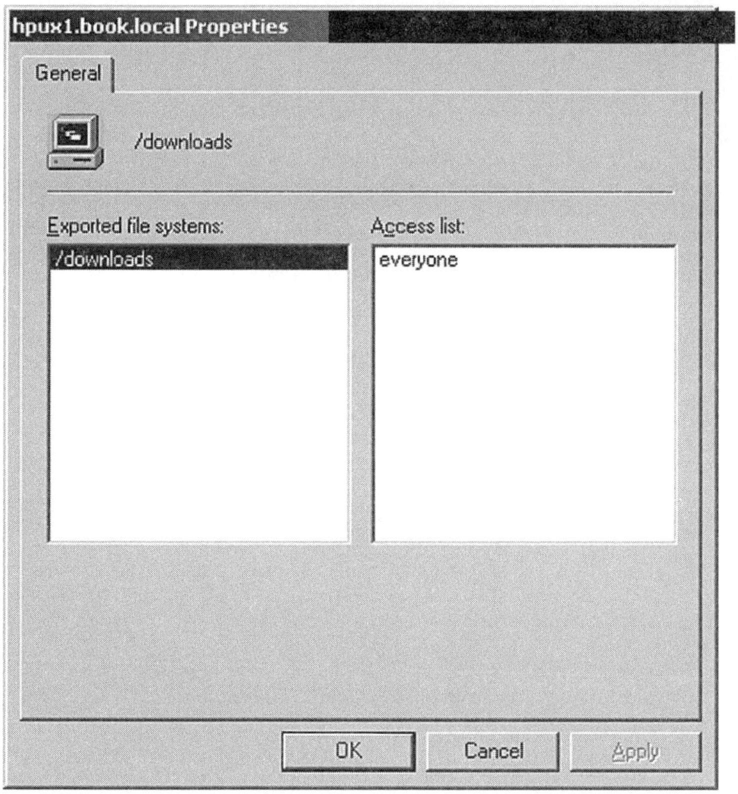

Figure 11–5 NFS server properties.

This screen shot shows the NFS Server *hpux1* exporting the */downloads* directory with everyone having access. I configured this server using the process described in the previous section. This configuration gives users with a recognized UID read/write access to */downloads*. Anonymous users have read-only access. Double-clicking on an NFS Server icon will display icons representing all the exported directories. If you right-click on one of those icons and select **Properties**, you get a window describing that directory's attributes.

11.3.3.1 Mounting a File System

Before a user can mount a file system, you should set up User Name Mapping and then direct Client for NFS to use the name mapping server. To do the latter, open the **Services for UNIX Administration** MMC, and select **Client for NFS**, as shown in Figure 11–6.

On the Authentication page, provide the name of your User Name Mapping server. When a user tries to access an NFS resource, Client for NFS sends his or her Windows user name to the User Name Mapping server. This server checks to see if the user name has been mapped to a UNIX account. If so, the server returns the UID and GID to Client for NFS, which then imbeds them into the NFS request. If there is no mapping for the user account, Client for NFS assigns –2 for the UID and –1 for the GID, thus establishing anonymous access.

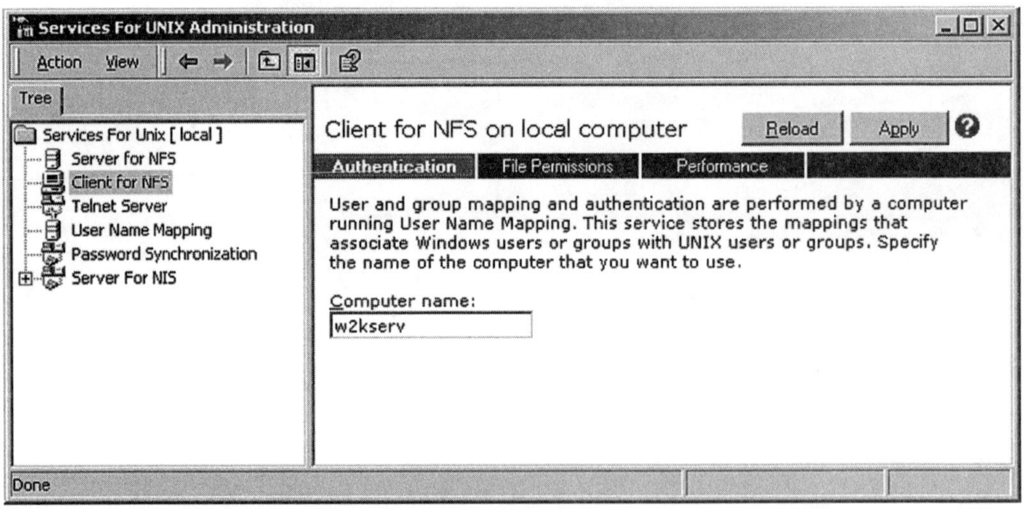

Figure 11–6 Defining the User Name Mapping server.

You mount NFS resources using either the *mount* command or using Map Network Drive. See the Help pages for more information on the *mount* command. The following is the procedure listed in Help for using Map Network Drive:

1. Open Windows Explorer.
2. On the **Tools** menu, click on **Map Network Drive**.
3. In the **Drive** list, click on the drive letter to use.
4. To locate the NFS share, click **Browse**, or, in **Folder**, type the path to the share. You can specify the path as:
   serverName:/path
   (for example: `goldbug:/poe/stories`),
   or as:
   \\serverName\path
   (for example: `\\goldbug\poe\stories`).
5. To connect using a different user name or password, click on **Connect using a different user name**, type the user name and password, and then click on **OK**.

Microsoft recommends that you use the *serverName:/path* syntax when connecting to an NFS resource. The other format searches for Windows NT file systems with this name first, and then searches for NFS resources, thus slowing connection time.

When you attempt to connect, you will get a message similar to that in Figure 11–7.

Figure 11–7 The NFS Login Successful message.

This is confirming the UID and GID supplied by the User Mapping Service. If you do not want these credentials, select **No** in the window and then click on **Connect using a different user name**, type the user name and password, and then click on **OK**.

11.4 Windows 2000 NFS Server/HP-UX NFS Client

SFU provides Server for NFS, which can turn a Windows 2000 system into an NFS server to UNIX NFS clients. Two important components of the Server for NFS package are User Name Mapping, which we have already discussed, and NFS Authentication. If you use User Name Mapping to map local Windows 2000 users, then you must ensure that NFS Authentication is installed on that local system. If you will map domain users, then you must install NFS Authentication on all domain controllers. NFS Authentication works with User Name Mapping to use the UIDs and GIDs provided in NFS requests to find equivalent Windows users and groups and determine access rights.

11.4.1 Configuring Server for NFS

You can configure and administer Server for NFS using either the SFU Administration tool or through various commands. We will concentrate on the administration tool, taking material directly from SFU Help.

11.4.1.1 Setting Up Authentication

After ensuring that User Name Mapping and NFS Authentication are installed, you need to set up authentication. To set up authentication,

1. Open **Windows Services for UNIX Administration**.
2. If necessary, connect to the computer you want to manage.
3. Click **Server for NFS**.
4. Click the **User Mapping** tab.
5. In **Computer Name**, type the name of the computer running User Name Mapping that you want to use for authentication, and then click **Apply**. See Figure 11–8.

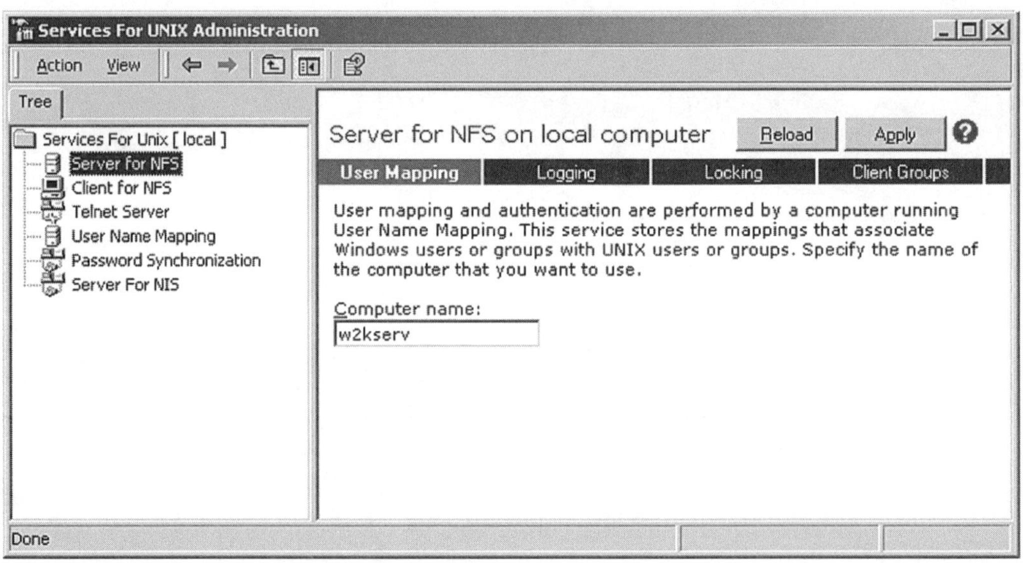

Figure 11–8 Setting up user authentication.

11.4.1.2 Logging, Locking, and Client Groups

The SFU Administration MMC also enables you to configure logging, locking, and client groups. You can easily configure the logging of the following events:

- **Mount.** Users making mount and unmount requests.
- **Locking.** Users locking and unlocking files.
- **Read.** Users making requests to read a file.
- **Write.** Users making requests to write to a file.
- **Create.** Users making requests to create a file.
- **Delete.** Users making requests to delete a file.
- **All.** All of the above.

Just click on the **Logging** tab of the SFU MMC to configure logging. In the Locking tab you set the number of seconds users have to reestablish locks after a server reboot or you can manually release locks on specified clients.

UNIX and Windows 2000 NFS servers differ in how they handle locks. According to SFU Help, "UNIX computers follow advisory locking for all lock requests. This means that the operating system does not enforce lock semantics on a file, and applications that check for the existence of locks can use these locks effectively. However, Server for NFS implements mandatory locks even for those locking requests that are received through NFS. This ensures that locks acquired through NFS are visible through the server message block (SMB) protocol and to applications accessing the files locally. Mandatory locks are enforced by the operating system."

Client groups are groupings of client systems so that you can apply NFS permissions—root access, for example—to the group as a whole rather than to individual systems. For example, if you have a set of computers from which you do system administration and you want all these systems to have root access to the NFS server, then you can create a client group, say *admin_nodes*, and assign root access to the NFS export. Click on the **Client Groups** tab to create client groups and add or remove systems from those groups.

11.4.1.3 Exporting Directories (Creating NFS Shares)

To export a directory via NFS on Windows 2000, you create what is called an NFS share. To create an NFS share,

1. Open Windows Explorer.
2. In the details pane, right-click on the directory you want to share.
3. Click **Sharing**.
4. Click **NFS Sharing**.
5. Click **Share this folder** and, in the **Share name** text box, type a share name. See Figure 11–9.

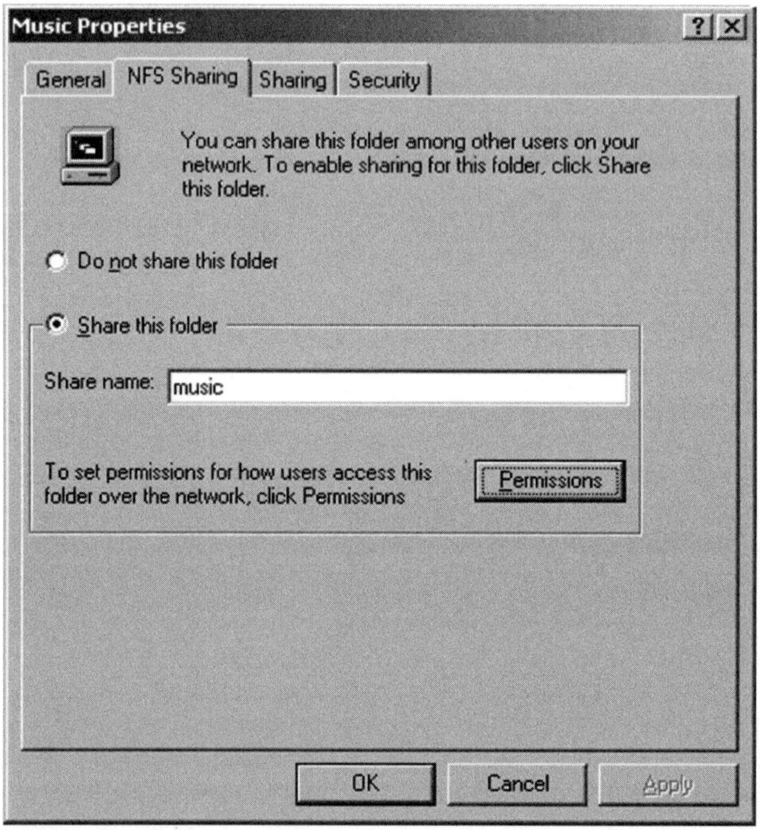

Figure 11–9 Creating an NFS Share.

You can also use the *nfsshare* command to create an NFS share. In fact, you must use this command if you want to prevent anonymous user access to your share. You cannot do this with Windows Explorer. See SFU Help for more information on the *nfsshare* command.

11.4.1.4 Permissions

You can then set the permissions for individual clients or a client group by clicking on **Permissions** on the **NFS Sharing** tab. When you do so, you get the **NFS Share Permissions** window, like the one in Figure 11–10. This window shows the NFS share path at the top and the list of systems granted access and the type of access at the bottom.

To add either individual client or client groups to the list, click the **Add...** button. You will get a window like the one in Figure 11–11. In my example, I created a client group called *admin_nodes* using the SFU MMC, as described earlier in "Logging, Locking, and Client Groups." I added two systems to *admin_nodes*: *hpux1* and *aix1*. Any permission I add to this client group affects both machines. To grant *admin_nodes* root access, you would select the group and click the **Add** button. Then, in the **Type of Access** box, select **Root**.

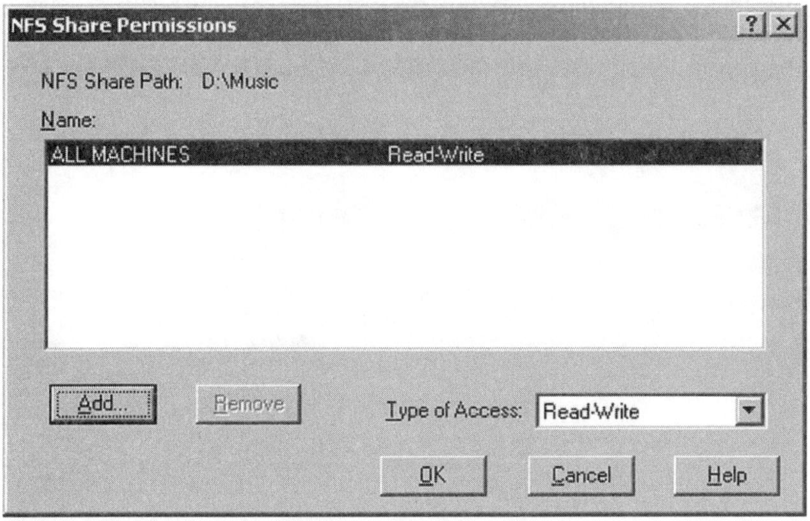

Figure 11–10 The NFS Share Permissions window.

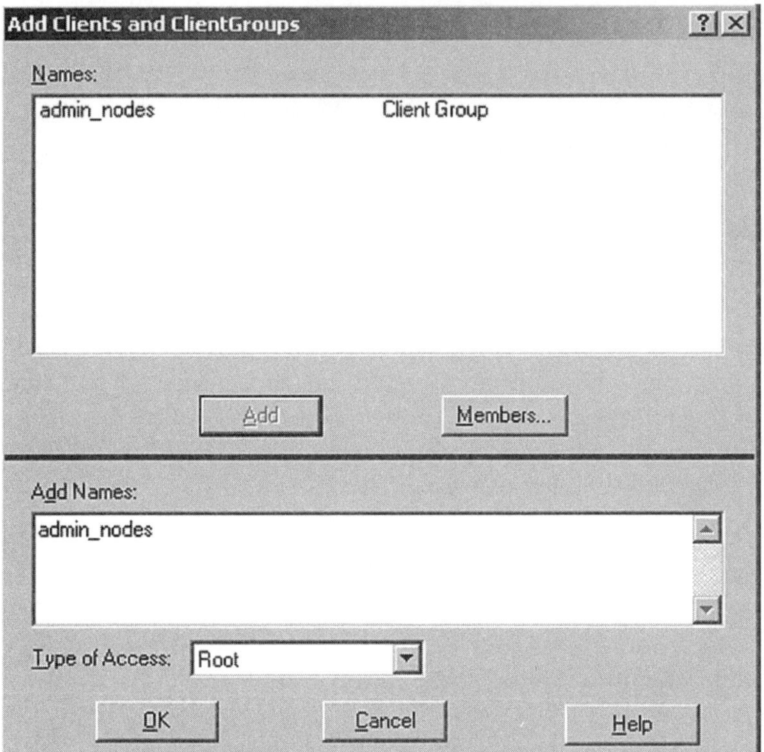

Figure 11–11 Adding a client group to the client list. In this example, the client group *admin_nodes* is being granted root access permission.

Figure 11-12 shows that, while all machines have read-write access, the *admin_nodes* client group has root access. If a user is logged in as *root* on a system other than one in the *admin_nodes* client group, that user will be mapped to the *anonymous* user and will have read-only access.

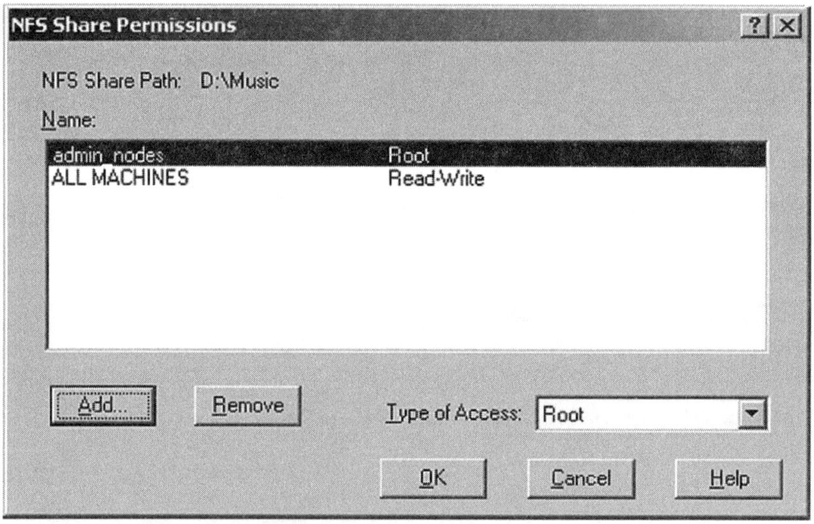

Figure 11–12 NFS Share Permissions with a client group.

11.4.2 Configuring the HP-UX Client

The HP-UX NFS client can mount NT file systems using either standard mounts or *automounts*. Only the *root* user can make standard mounts. A standard mount usually takes place at system startup and remains in effect until the administrator explicitly performs an unmount. Sites generally use standard mounts for constantly used directories, such as those containing key applications. Automounts are mounts that take place when needed, for example, when you change directories to an NFS file system. These mounts usually disappear after about five minutes of inactivity and are generally used for less frequently used directories.

11.4.2.1 Standard Mounts

To configure a standard mount using SAM,

1. Run SAM.
2. Select **Networking and Communications**.
3. Select **Networked File Systems**.
4. Select **Mounted File Systems**.
5. Choose **Actions→Add Remote File System→Using NFS...**

6. If the NFS client is not already enabled, you will get a message asking you if you wish to enable it. Select **Yes** to proceed.
7. Fill in the necessary information in the **Add Remote File System** dialog box. (See Figure 11–13.)

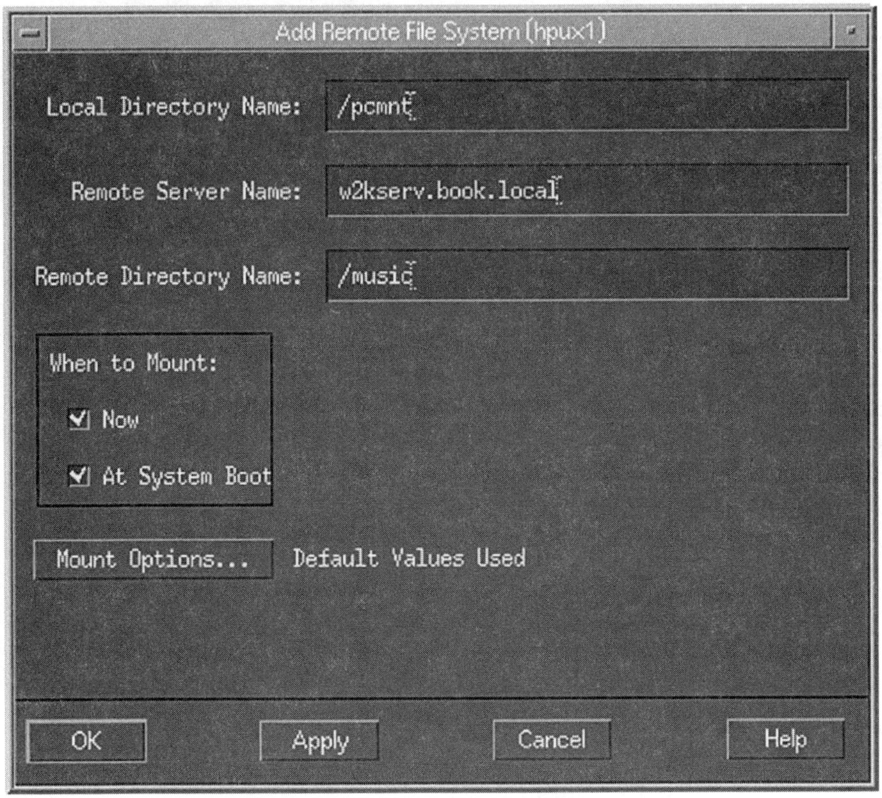

Figure 11–13 The Add Remote File System dialog box.

In my example, I created a mount point on *hpux1* called */pcmnt*. This is the value of the Local Directory Name box. Earlier, I had created an NFS share on *w2kserv* called *music*, whose path name was *D:\music*. Therefore, Remote Server Name is *w2kserv.book.local* and the remote directory name is */music*. Actually, the remote directory name is *D:\music*, so what I supplied here is the share name preceded by a slash (/). Pressing OK will execute the *mount w2kserv.book.local:/music* command with the default option values and will ensure that the mount will also take place at system boot. The primary default mount options are listed in Table 11–1.

Table 11–1 Default Primary NFS Mount Options

Option	Signifies
rw	Mount the directory read/write.
suid	Allow mounted programs that have setuid permission to run with the permissions of their owners, regardless of who starts them. This includes setuid programs owned by root.
hard	Causes the client to keep trying to access the server if it goes down.
intr	Often used with hard mounts, specifies that a user can interrupt a retry of an unavailable NFS resource using CTRL-C or the kill command.
fg	Mounts are tried in the foreground continuously until they succeed.
devs	Allows the mounting of device files.
timeo=7	The timeout, in tenths of a second, for NFS request.
retrans=4	The number of times an NFS request is retransmitted after it times out.
rsize=8192	The number of bytes the NFS client requests from the NFS server in a single read request.
wsize=8192	The number of bytes the NFS client sends to the NFS server in a single write request.

There are also additional cache options you can consider. See Hewlett-Packard's *Configuring and Administering NFS* for more information.

Once you mount a file system in this manner, you can see the results by executing the *mount* command. For example:

```
# mount
/ on /dev/dsk/c0t6d0 defaults on Wed Dec 13 14:58:15 2000
/pcmnt on w2kserv.book.local:/music defaults,NFSv3 on Wed Dec 13
14:59:48 2000
```

Note that the word *defaults* appears in the output to indicate the default options listed above. Also, note that the mount succeeded using NFS protocol version 3, the default protocol on both HP-UX NFS and Server for NFS.

> Remember: In order to perform a standard mount in HP-UX, you must be the root user.

11.4.2.2 Automatic Mounts (Automounts)

Automatic mounts, generally referred to as *automounts,* occur only when you access an exported directory and stay in effect while in use. After a period of inactivity, usually five minutes, the mount goes away. For a long time, the Automounter utility enabled automounts. More recently, a new utility called AutoFS improves on the old Automounter. For one thing, it can mount directories using NFS protocol version 3, as well as version 2. Automounter used only in version 2. The old Automounter created mounts under the */tmp_mnt* directory and then made symbolic links to the actual mount points, often confusing users. With AutoFS, the configured mount points and the actual mount points are the same. HP-UX 11 by default employs Automount, but you can migrate to AutoFS easily.

Configuring either Automount or AutoFS can get very complex, and for more information, consult HP's *Configuring and Administering NFS*. One thing that makes it particularly confusing is the use of the term *map*. Both NIS and the automount utilities use the term *map,* and you can integrate both NIS and automount. For example, with both Automounter and AutoFS, you can use what is known as the `-hosts` automounter map. The `-hosts` map causes the utilities to mount all the exported directories from any NFS server on the network when someone accesses any of those exported directories. To use this map, you add the following line to the automounter master map file, */etc/auto_master*:

```
/net -hosts nosuid
```

Or, the automounter master map file might itself be an NIS map! Hence confusion.

I tested the use of the `-hosts` automounter map and found that it works well. On my Windows 2000 NFS server, I exported (as described earlier in this chapter) a directory called *music* and a directory called *home*. I then configured the local */etc/auto_master* file on *hpux1* to include the line shown above, and then started AutoFS with the */usr/sbin/automount* command. I was then able to change directories to the */net/w2kserv/music* directory and then the */net/w2kserv/home* directory on demand. Again, consult *Configuring and Administering NFS* for more information.

11.5 Conclusion

NFS file sharing in a mixed environment can involve a variety of configurations. For example, you can have NFS servers on HP-UX, Windows 2000, or both. You can use local authentication or NIS. Windows 2000 can be an NIS server but not a client. If you use NIS, which will be your server, HP-UX or Windows 2000? I think you are beginning to get the idea. For my tests with NFS, I had Server for NIS running on Windows 2000 (*w2kserv*) and an NIS client running on HP-UX (*hpux1*). The name service switch on *hpux1* consulted NIS first for *passwd* and *group* information, and files first for other information (except for *hosts*, which used DNS first).

11.5.1 User Mapping

Key to the successful working of NFS, wherever it's configured, is the correct use of the User Mapping Service. First and foremost, you need to use Advanced Mapping in this service to map the *root* user on HP-UX systems to the Administrator account on Windows 2000. Even if you export directories with root access, you must map these accounts in order for the permissions to work properly. The combination of mapping the root and Administrator accounts and the exporting of directories with root access provides administrators appropriate rights.

For other user accounts, it helps to have your HP-UX user names and Windows 2000 user names match each other exactly. If you create an account on Windows 2000 with Server for NIS running, this is done for you automatically, provided you ensure that the UNIX attributes tab is configured properly. For example, see Figure 11–14.

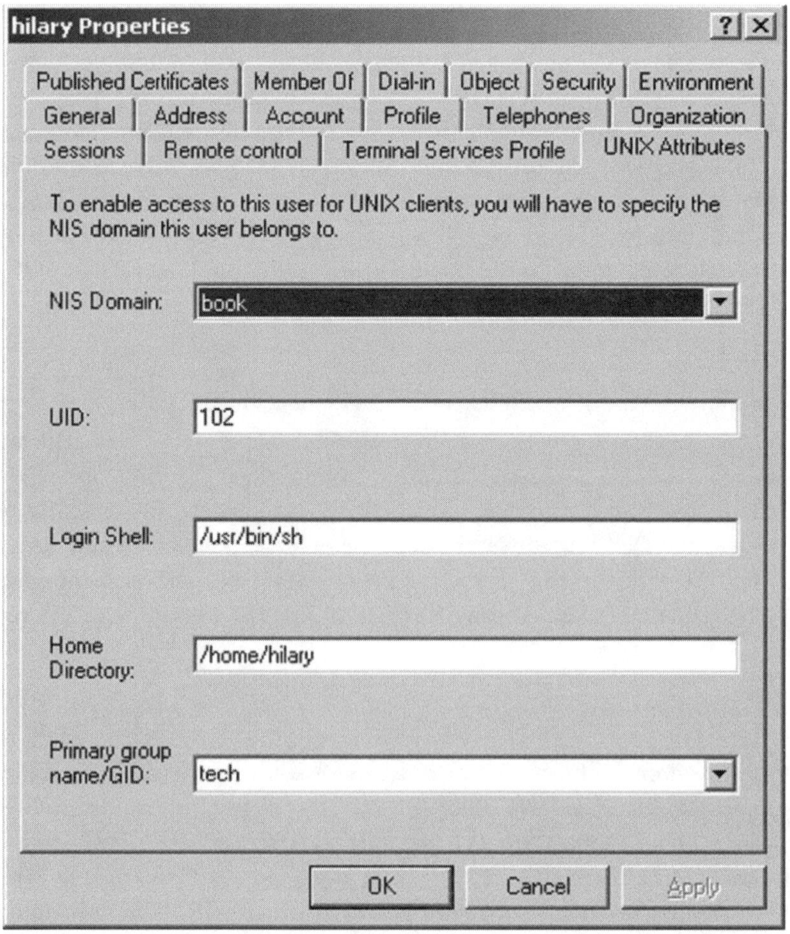

Figure 11–14 Enabling the NIS user. Select the user in Active Directory Users and Computers, right-click, and choose Properties. Then click the UNIX attributes tab.

I created the account *hilary* using Active Directory Users and Computers. I then opened that user's Properties to get to the UNIX attributes tab. You have to enable a new user for NIS by selecting the appropriate NIS domain name, which I did with this user. I also chose a Primary Group called *tech*, which also existed in NIS. As a result, whenever user *hilary* accessed an NFS resource, User Mapping automatically generated a mapping between the HP-UX user (as defined in NIS) and the Windows 2000 user. If a user's UNIX account name and Windows 2000 account name differ, then you must use Advanced Mapping to manually map the names (as done with the root and Administrator accounts).

11.5.2 Exporting Directories

After ensuring that User Mapping is correct, export your directories with the appropriate options, particularly if you need root access. Also, remember that, unlike regular Windows shares, NFS shares are case-sensitive. For example, if you export a directory with an NFS share name called *Home*, the client must mount the directory with the share name *Home*, not *home*.

11.5.3 Local Permissions

To ensure proper access to directories, be sure that the local file system permissions are correct. On Windows 2000, this means that you should export directories only from NTFS volumes. Even if you have exported and mounted file systems with read/write permission, the local file system permissions may still prevent users from working properly with their mounted files and directories.

11.5.4 Overall Experience

Both Client for NFS and Server for NFS on Windows worked well, though the client's connection time with the HP-UX NFS server was a bit slow (two to three seconds), and this was on an isolated network. However, read and write performance was satisfactory after connection.

I did find, however, that having Windows 2000 configured as an NFS server was often tricky, involving the coordination of Server for NIS, User Name Mapping, and Server for NFS. For HP-UX users who need more than occasional access to files stored on a Windows 2000 server, it might be better to use a CIFS client on the HP-UX system, something we will look at in the next chapter.

This chapter in no way provides a comprehensive description on using NFS for file sharing between HP-UX and Windows systems. For more in-depth information, see the Help pages that accompany Windows Services for UNIX and Hewlett-Packard's *Configuring and Administering NFS*.

References

1. Marshall Kirk McKusick, Keith Bostic, Michael J. Karels, and John S. Quarterman, *The Design and Implementation of the 4.4BSD Operating System.* (Addison-Wesley, 1996).
2. Hal Stern and Mike Loukides, *Managing NFS and NIS.* (O'Reilly, 1997)
3. Uresh Vahalia, *UNIX Internals: The New Frontiers.* (Prentice Hall, 1996).

CHAPTER 12

CIFS File Sharing

The Common Internet File System (CIFS) is a file and print sharing protocol that runs natively on Windows-based computers. Originally called the Server Message Block (SMB) protocol—which many still refer to it as—CIFS is a NetBT application, enabling file and print sharing using the NetBIOS API running on top of the TCP/IP protocol suite. Because it is IP-based, CIFS can run across routers and WANs, making it a useful file sharing tool for the Internet. In functionality, it resembles NFS but differs considerably in its actual implementation.

12.1 CIFS Versus NFS

We looked at NFS in Chapter 11, "NFS File Sharing." As stated in *The Design and Implementation of the 4.4BSD Operating System* (McKusick, et. al.), pp. 312, 313

- The protocol is designed to be stateless. Because there is no state to maintain or recover, NFS can continue to operate even during periods of client or server failures. Thus, it is much more robust than a system that operates with state.
- NFS is designed to support UNIX file system semantics. However, its design also allows it to support the possibly less rich semantics of other file system types, such as MS-DOS.
- The protection and access controls follow the UNIX semantics of having the process present a UID and set of groups that are checked against the file's owner, group, and other access modes. The security check is done by file system-dependent code that can do more or fewer checks based on the capabilities of the file system that it is supporting. For example, the MS-DOS file system cannot implement the full UNIX security validation and makes access decisions solely based on the UID.

- The protocol design is transport independent. Although it was originally built using the UDP datagram protocol, it was easily moved to the TCP stream protocol. It has also been ported to run over numerous other non-IP-based protocols.

In contrast to these points, let's start with the fact that Common Internet File System (CIFS) is both connection-oriented and state-full. It is connection-oriented in that it requires an SMB session to be set up before any file system command is issued. It is state-full in that the client maintains sufficient state information to recover from a server outage at the point of failure. CIFS is designed to be a cross-platform protocol, but being the native file sharing mechanism for Windows-based systems, it meshes easily with Windows file systems. The protection and access controls follow the Windows schema of having the server issue a request for credentials from the client that can be used for the entire SMB session. This contrasts with NFS, where each request is independent of others, with credentials accompanying each request. (Also important here is the fact that the *client* determines these credentials; the server accepts them without question.) Finally, while CIFS requires a connection-oriented transport protocol, such as TCP, NFS commonly runs over the connectionless User Datagram Protocol (UDP).

Other differences include the simple fact that NFS supports file sharing only, while CIFS supports file sharing, print sharing, and messaging. Also, CIFS supports *opportunistic locks* (*oplocks*). An SMB application can obtain an oplock on a file and then read ahead and buffer the file's contents locally, which can improve performance. NFS does not support oplocks. In fact, it does not work well with any kind of locking, for, as stated in Hal Stern and Mike Loukide's *Managing NFS and MIS*, p. 134, "Locking is a stateful operation and does not mesh well with the stateless design of NFS."

12.2 The Case for CIFS

You can examine these and other technical differences to decide which of these technologies is "better." In fact, there are folks out there who will do just that. However, beyond the technical reasons, there is also a lot of hype about the merits or deficiencies of NFS and CIFS. Those who simply don't like Microsoft (including the vendor who invented NFS, who will remain nameless) will often trash CIFS because of its Microsoft origins. CIFS vendors, including Microsoft, will often deride NFS as being old technology and out of step with the needs of the Internet. However, I will make the case that using a CIFS-based technology is a better way to go to achieve interoperability than NFS. And I do so simply from an administrator's point of view.

In my experience, Windows-based systems completely dominate the business desktop. UNIX remains strong in the server market: as database servers, application servers, file servers, Web servers. The only area where I've seen UNIX-based systems dominate the desktop is in the scientific and engineering workplace, often called *technical* computing. The desktops in this environment run CPU- and graphics-intensive applications whose performance needs are met only by RISC-based UNIX systems. (But even here, more and more vendors of such applications are porting, or even rewriting, their applications for Windows NT and Windows 2000.)

So, from the administrator's viewpoint, if you want to share files from a few UNIX servers, what do you do? Install an NFS client on all your Windows clients? Or do you install a CIFS server on your few UNIX servers? Which would require the least amount of administrative overhead? While there may be sites that would choose to standardize on NFS (and this would work well), I would rather install some kind of CIFS on the UNIX servers. Once you do so, UNIX client systems can continue to access their data via NFS, and the Windows-based clients can access the same data via CIFS, their native file sharing protocol. You have far fewer installations this way, and you have fewer systems to administer. UNIX systems, because of their wonderful memory model, can easily accommodate multiple protocol stacks. In the case of CIFS, they simply have to accommodate the functionality of the layers above the transport layer: the session, presentation, and application layers.

12.3 CIFS Implementations

The SMB protocol, upon which CIFS is based, first made its appearance in Microsoft's LAN Manager product in 1987. A year later, it appeared in IBM's OS/2's LAN Server. In 1992, SMB became an Open Group standard and has been a part of Windows for Workgroups, Windows 95, Windows 98, and Windows NT networking as each operating system made its appearance in the marketplace. In 1994, Microsoft released the SMB server source code to AT&T, who in turn ported the code to UNIX and made it available to UNIX vendors. Initially known as Advanced Server for UNIX (ASU), this product was adopted, modified, and renamed by various vendors, including Hewlett-Packard and Digital Equipment Corporation (DEC). In 1996, Microsoft changed the name of SMB to CIFS—though the terms are frequently used interchangeably—and submitted its specification to the Internet Engineering Task Force (IETF) as an Internet-Draft.

The Open Source movement has produced free software, called Samba, which is a CIFS product designed for UNIX systems. The origins of Samba go all the way back to 1991 as a project of Andrew Tridgell, a graduate student at the time in the Computer Sciences Laboratory at Australian National University. Currently spearheaded by a small group called the Samba Team, this freeware is available for nearly all UNIX implementations. It is open source software, so its licensing is subject to the GNU General Public License. (See Chapter 1 for information on GNU.)

In 2000, Hewlett-Packard released a new product, CIFS/9000, which implements both a CIFS server and a CIFS client on HP-UX 11. The CIFS/9000 Server is based on Samba, version 2.0.6, and provides file and print services to CIFS clients, including Windows 95, 98, NT, 2000, and HP-UX machines running CIFS/9000 Client software. The CIFS/9000 Client enables HP-UX users to mount as UNIX file systems shares from CIFS file servers, including Windows servers and HP-UX machines running CIFS/9000 Server. The CIFS/9000 client also offers an optional Pluggable Authentication Module (PAM) that implements the Windows NT LAN Manager (NTLM) authentication protocols. When installed and configured within HP-UX's PAM facility, PAM NTLM allows HP-UX users to be authenticated against a Windows authentication server.

12.4 CIFS/9000 Server in a Windows 2000 Domain

To illustrate connecting HP-UX systems with Windows 2000 systems, we will now describe a configuration using CIFS/9000. Given the close relationship this product has with Samba, much about using Samba will come forth as a result of this overview. In this way, you can extrapolate what needs to be done to employ CIFS in other UNIX offerings.

12.4.1 A Vision

If you have a Windows 2000 domain and want to introduce a CIFS/9000 server into this domain, it makes sense to have the Windows 2000 domain controller authenticate requests for resources. The main purpose for doing so is to avoid having to maintain two separate password databases. A client requests a CIFS/9000 resource, and the CIFS/9000 server passes authentication to the domain controller. As we saw in Chapter 11 with NFS, it helps to have user account names match each other; otherwise, you have to create a user-mapping file for account names that differ.

It is common, then, for sites to configure their users so that their UNIX account names and their Windows account names match. However, even though authentication takes place at one location—that of the domain controller—you still must maintain two separate user databases: one for UNIX and one for Windows 2000. If you add a user to the UNIX environment, you must add an equivalent user to the Windows 2000 domain. *But*, what if you run Server for NIS on the domain controller? That way, you can create new accounts for both environments in one location with Active Directory Users and Computers. (See Chapter 10, "Windows Services for UNIX," for a description of Server for NIS.) By combining CIFS/9000 (configured to use domain security) with Server for NIS, you can effectively unify your HP-UX and Windows 2000 user databases. Can this work? Let's see.

12.4.1.1 Configuring CIFS/9000 Server

Complete instructions on setting up the CIFS/9000 server are in Hewlett-Packard's document *Installing and Administering the CIFS/900 Server*. However this document describes mostly the enhancements HP has made to Samba and refers the reader to another book, *Using Samba*, by Robert Eckstein, David Collier-Brown, and Peter Kelley, for more specific information on actually using Samba itself, which CIFS/9000 essentially is. While there are numerous possible CIFS/9000 server configurations, and while your site will probably necessitate a customized solution, I would like to offer the following tips to assist you in setting it up:

1. Follow the instructions found in *Installing and Administering the CIFS/9000 Server* on how to install CIFS/9000.
2. Before configuring anything in the *smb.conf* file, create a dummy user called *smbnull* with no home directory and with group membership of *other*. This is described in the CIFS/9000 Release Notes and is designed to prevent problems of file access from Windows 2000 clients, among other things.

3. Set the *guest account smb.conf* variable to *smbnull* in the global section of the *smb.conf* file. (With CIFS/9000, this file is found in the */etc/opt/samba* directory.)
4. Modify *smb.conf* to support, if necessary, the following features: ACL support, case sensitivity for the Client and Server for UNIX Extensions, DOS attribute mapping, print services, and internationalization. See *Installing and Administering the CIFS/9000 Server* for more information.
5. Before starting the Samba daemons, add your CIFS/9000 system to the Windows 2000 domain:
   - Go into **Active Directory Users and Computers**, select your domain, and then select **Action→New→Computer**. You will get the **New Object–Computer** window, as shown in Figure 12–1. Fill in the necessary information, check the **Allow pre-Windows 2000 computers to use this account** box, and then click on **OK**.

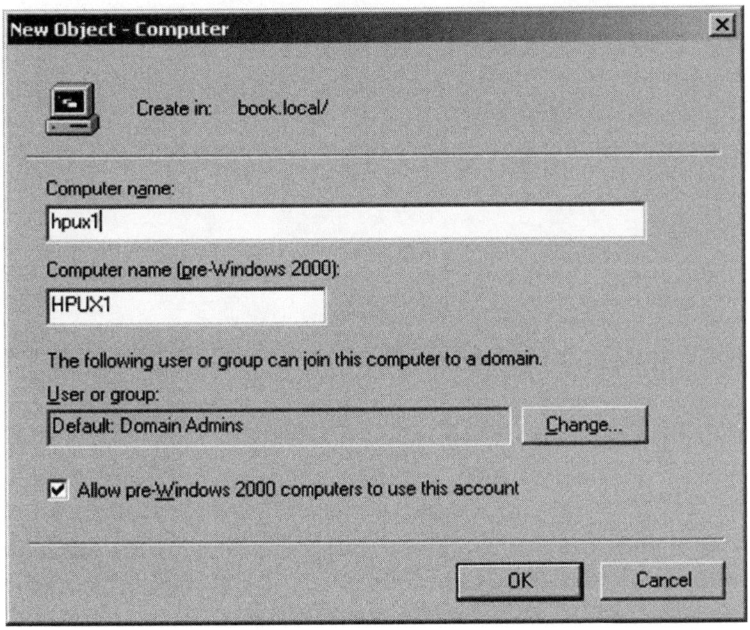

Figure 12–1 Adding a CIFS/9000 server to a Windows 2000 domain.

   - Then, on the CIFS/9000 Server, issue the *smbpasswd* command. For example,

```
# smbpasswd -j book.local -r w2kserv
```

Supply the Windows 2000 domain name as the argument to the *–j* option and the name of your domain controller as the argument to the *–r* option. This command will create a system password and store it in the */var/opt/samba/private* directory as a file with a name in the following format: *domain_name.server_name.mac*. In my example, the name is BOOK.LOCAL.HPUX1.mac. (The *mac* extension means that this is a machine account.)

6. Edit your *smb.conf* file and specify the following variables:
   - security = domain
   - netbios name = *server_netbios_name*
   - workgroup = *domain_name*
   - password server = *domain_controller_name(s)*
   - encrypt passwords = yes

   For example, my *smb.conf* contains the following entries for these variables, as well as for a couple of others:

```
[global]
     workgroup = BOOK.LOCAL
     netbios name = HPUX1
     security = DOMAIN
     encrypt passwords = Yes
     password server = w2kserv
     username map = /var/opt/samba/usermap
     guest account = smbnull
     read only = No
     case sensitive = yes
```

   As you can see, I specify the file */var/opt/samba/usermap* to contain mappings of user accounts whose names differ between the two operating systems. In my test environment, all my user account names match, with the exception of *root* and *administrator.* So, in this file, I have only one entry:

```
root = administrator
```

   I also specify *smbnull* for the guest account and case sensitivity.

7. Start the Samba daemons *smbd* and *nmbd*. With CIFS/9000, you do so by executing the following command:

```
# /opt/samba/bin/startsmb
```

There are other steps you might need to take, such as registering your server with Windows Internet Naming Service (WINS). Windows 2000 still supports WINS. Using WINS can make your life a lot easier. In *smb.conf,* you can specify your WINS server with the *wins server* parameter, to which you supply either the DNS name or IP address of your WINS server.

12.4.1.2 How It Works

We now have our CIFS/9000 a member of a Windows 2000 domain. By configuring *smb.conf* the way we have, we specify that client requests to the CIFS/9000 server will first be authenticated by the Windows 2000 domain controller. On top of all that, we have our Windows 2000 domain controller running Server for NIS.

In my environment, this setup works quite well. If I log into a Windows 2000 client as an everyday user, say, *dylan*, the domain controller authenticates me, as you would expect. Then, when I browse the network, I click on the *book.local* domain icon. One of the servers I see is *hpux1*, my CIFS/9000 server. Double-clicking on that icon shows me a list of shares available. In my initial configuration, the only share I see is one called *dylan*. Where did it come from?

By default, CIFS/9000 provides a special share definition called *homes* in *smb.conf.* If a user's home directory exists on the CIFS/9000 server, it will create a temporary share configured with the parameters under the *homes* definition so that the user can access that home directory. How does it determine the home directory? Either by scanning */etc/passwd* or consulting an NIS map. In my case, the user *dylan* is defined in an NIS map maintained by Server for NIS. I created this user using Active Directory for Users and Computers, being sure to set the UNIX Attributes so that *dylan* was defined in NIS as well. See Figure 12–2.

Therefore, upon logging in as *dylan*, CIFS/9000 sees that *dylan's* home directory is */home/dylan*. *Provided that this directory actually exists on the CIFS/9000 server,* then a share with the name *dylan* is created. Here is an important point. All Windows 2000 users whose home directories are to be served by CIFS/9000 must actually have those directories created for them by the *root* user. For example, when creating a new user account called *lucy,* I used Active Directory Users and Computers to do so. However, I also had to issue the following commands as *root* on *hpux1*, my CIFS/9000 server:

```
# cd home
# mkdir lucy
# chown lucy:tech lucy
# ls -l
total 6
drwxrwxr-x   3 dylan     tech          1024 Dec 22 05:30 dylan
drwxrwxr-x   4 hilary    tech          1024 Dec 21 22:19 hilary
drwxrwxr-x   2 lucy      tech            24 Dec 22 05:54 lucy
```

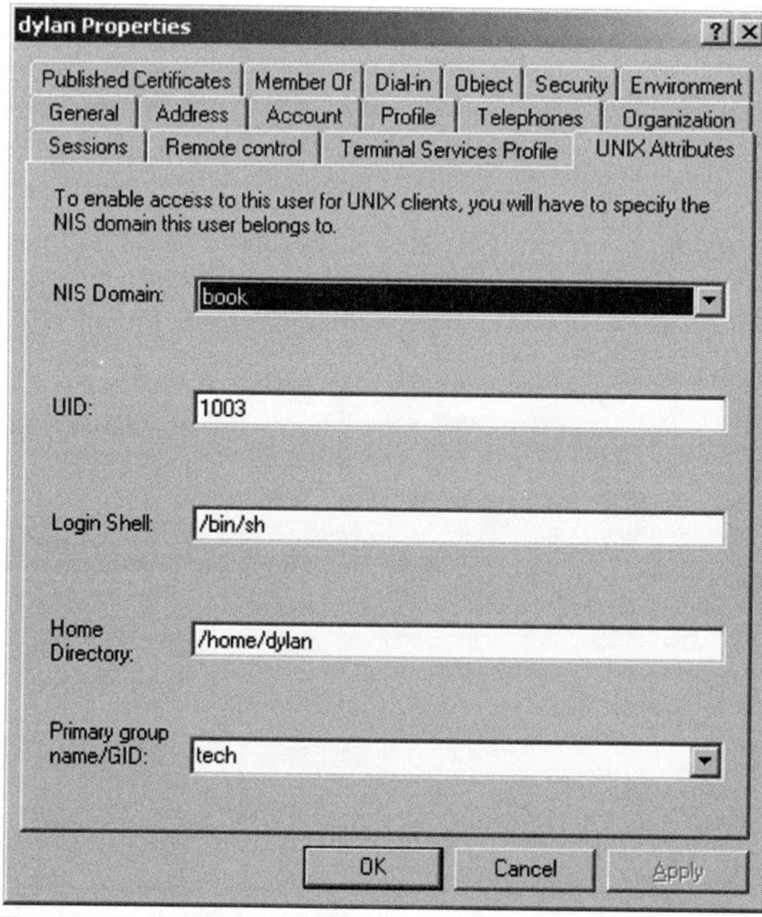

Figure 12–2 Ensuring a Windows 2000 user is defined in NIS. Server for NIS makes this possible.

With what I've described so far, we have two home directories for users: one defined in the user's UNIX Attributes and residing on an HP-UX system, and another as yet undefined but defaulting to the root directory of the Windows 2000 system they are logging onto. If you want to unify your home directories, specify the appropriate CIFS/9000 share in the Profile page of Active Directory Users and Computers, as shown in Figure 12–3. When the *dylan* users logs on, there will be a Z: drive pointing to his home directory on the CIFS/9000 server. Also, when he opens a command prompt, it will open to this share.

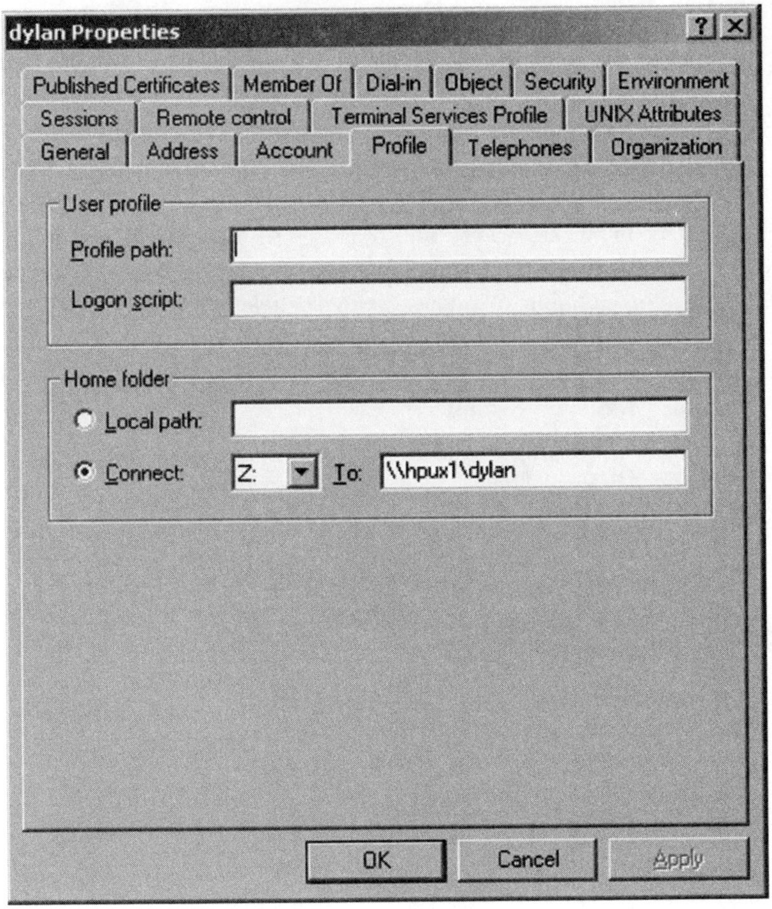

Figure 12–3 Specifying a home directory as being a CIFS/9000 share.

The scenario just described works quite well but should be viewed as a proof-of-concept only. There are probably a number of gotchas here. But the point is that by combining CIFS/9000 with Server for NIS, you can achieve a great deal of interoperability. For one thing, you have only one authenticating authority: the Windows 2000 domain controller. For another, you can have both your Windows users and their NIS counterparts specified in a single location. You can also have a single home directory whether the user logs on from a Windows system or an HP-UX system. In our example, the user *dylan* logged on from Windows 2000. However, if that user logs on to *hpux1* (an NIS client), then his user information, including account name, home directory, and login shell, are obtained from Server for NIS, and he gains access to his system normally. This combination is certainly worth further study!

12.5 CIFS/9000 Client in a Windows 2000 Domain

Now we can go in the other direction. By using the CIFS/9000 client, we can access files located on a Windows 2000 system. While *smbclient* is installed with the CIFS/9000 package, the client portion is not Samba-based. As we did previously with the CIFS/9000 server, we will create a scenario of using the client and leave the complete description of the product to HP's official documentation, *Installing and Administering the CIFS/9000 Client.*

In this scenario, we have some engineers who still need to use HP-UX workstations to run their CAD application. While they use these workstations periodically during the day, they do most of their work on PC workstations running Windows 2000. Their PC home directories are located on a Windows 2000 server. Occasionally, while working on the HP-UX workstations, they want to access their PC home directories without using something like FTP or Telnet. To make this possible, we will use the CIFS/9000 client.

12.5.1 Sharing the Home Directories

First, see Figure 12–4. Notice that we have changed the home directory for the user *dylan* to reflect that it now resides on *w2kserv.*

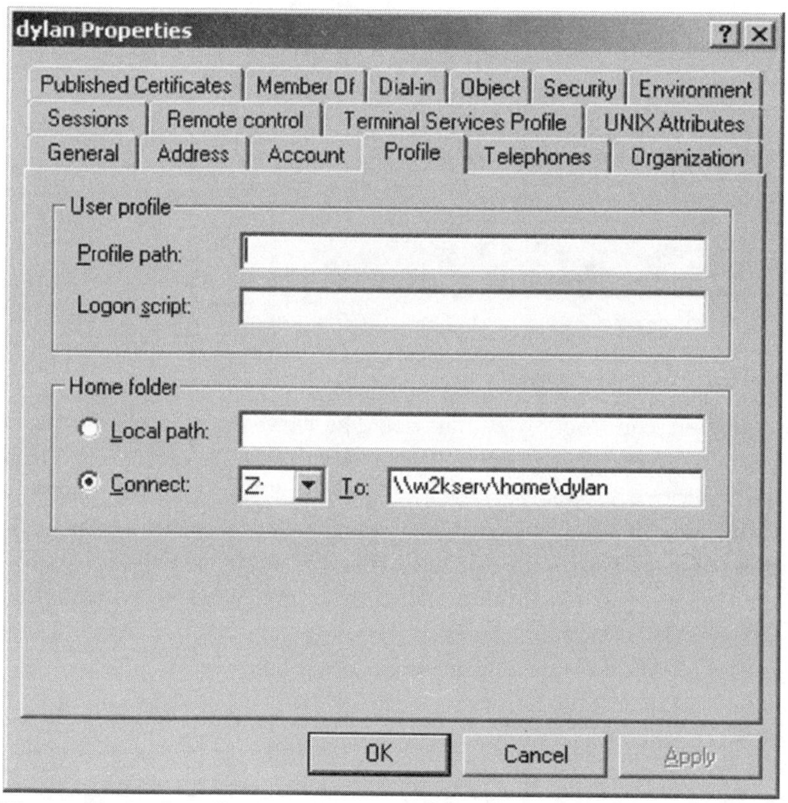

Figure 12–4 Specifying a home directory as being a Windows 2000 server share.

So, from whatever Windows 2000 client *dylan* logs on to, his home directory will be found in the Z: drive, which actually resides on *w2kserv*. The next step, then, is to share the *home* directory. We could share each individual's home directory, but that could create an excessive number of shares, depending on how many users you have. Also, CIFS/9000 does not support automounting, so if you had multiple users of an HP-UX workstation, you would have to make several static mounts for each workstation.

In order to share one directory, namely *home*, in a way that everyone has access to the home directory on the Windows 2000 server, you have to give Full Control permissions to Everyone when you create the share. See Figure 12–5.

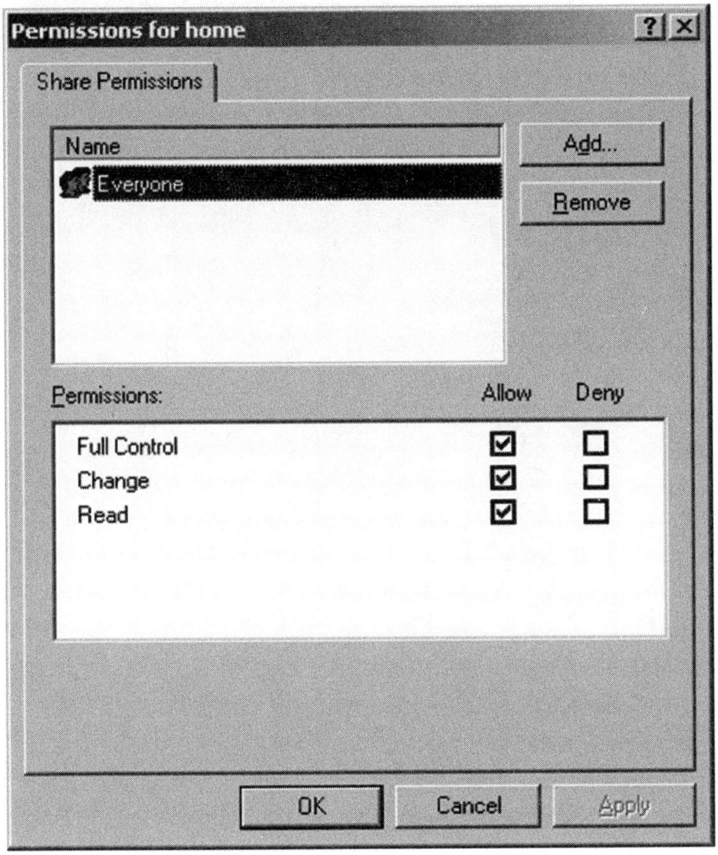

Figure 12–5 Granting Full Control to Everyone for the home share.

At first, there appears to be a problem here. If we give Everyone the Full Control share permission, do we not compromise the security of home's subdirectories? In other words, might not user *dylan* be able to change the contents of user *hilary's* home directory? It is certainly possible. However, in order to secure each user's home directories, we must ensure that those directories reside on NTFS volumes and then assign the appropriate NTFS permissions. Done properly, all CIFS/9000 clients will be able to access the *home* share, but each subdirectory within that share will be protected by NTFS permissions.

In our example, we secure the *dylan* subfolder of the home directory by right-clicking on its icon, choosing **Properties**, and then clicking the **Security** tab (see Figure 12–6).

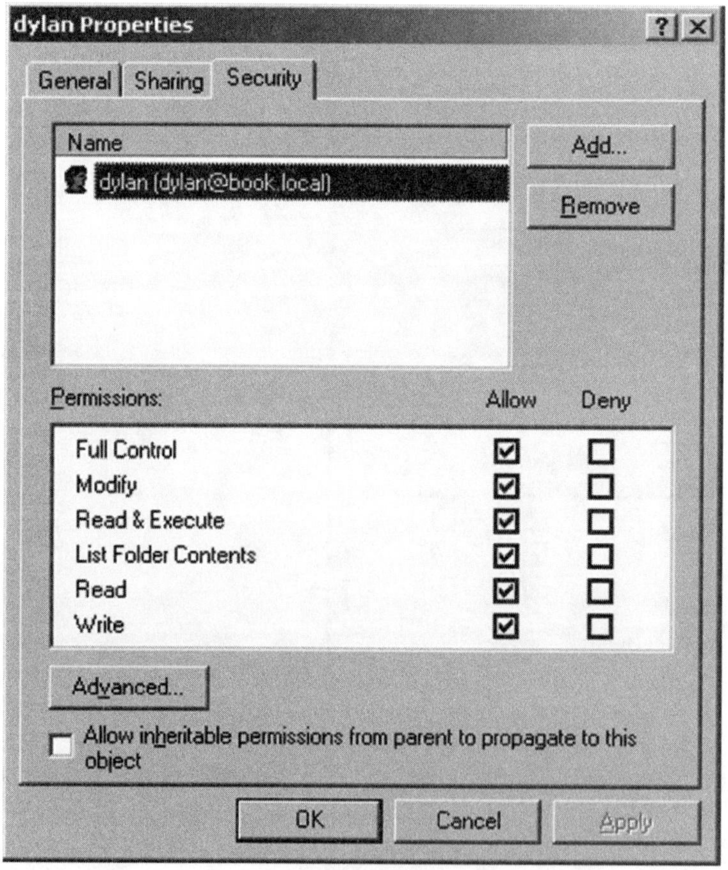

Figure 12–6 Securing a folder with NTFS permissions.

Note that only *dylan* has permissions to control this folder. This will keep others from messing with this folder despite the fact that Everyone has Full Control permission on the *home* share.

12.5.2 Using the CIFS/9000 Client

Installing and Administering the CIFS/9000 Client provides instructions for installing the client. Once you do so, Hewlett-Packard recommends you set the value of only the *domain* variable in the configuration file, */etc/opt/cifsclient/cifsclient.cfg*, unless you need to do any localization. In my test environment, I of course set the value accordingly:

```
domain = book.local
```

After that, you simply start the CIFS/9000 client daemon by issuing the following command as the *root* user:

```
# /opt/cifsclient/bin/cifsclient start
```

Once the daemon starts, you can mount shares. You can do so from the command line using the *mount* command. However, if you want the mount to take place every time the system restarts, then you should configure the */etc/fstab* file something like this:

```
/dev/dsk/c0t6d0 / hfs defaults 0 1
w2kserv:/home /pchome cifs defaults 0 0
```

This shows that I have a file system (or share) on *w2kserv* called *home* that needs to be mounted on my local */pchome* directory at system startup. After making this entry, I can issue the following command to mount all the shares specified in */etc/fstab*:

```
# mount -aF cifs
```

Finally, I need to set the RUN_CIFSCLIENT variable in the */etc/rc.config.d/cifsclient* file:

```
RUN_CIFSCLIENT=1
```

So far, then, we have created the *home* share on *w2kserv* containing Full Control permission for Everyone. We have also secured the *dylan* subdirectory (or subfolder) using NTFS permissions. We configured and started the CIFS/9000 client on *hpux1*. Then, as root we mounted the share *home* to the local */pchome* directory. But in order to access the */pchome* directory, each user must first be authenticated by *w2kserv*. Unless you set up PAM NTLM to do your authentication (which we'll discuss a little later), you must use the *cifslogin* command. For example, note the following series of commands:

```
$ id
uid=1004(dylan) gid=1000(tech)
$ cd /pchome
sh: /pchome: Permission denied.
$ cifslogin w2kserv
Remote user dylan's password:
$ cd /pchome
$ ll
total 0
drwxrwxrwx   2 dylan     tech      131072 Dec 28  2000 dylan
drwxrwxrwx   2 dylan     tech      131072 Dec 22 12:16 hilary
$ cifslist -A
```

```
============================================================
server w2kserv:
============================================================
Remote Username: dylan                  Local Username: dylan
Share: \\W2KSERV\HOME
        rw /pchome
```

User *dylan*, though he exists both in the Windows 2000 domain and the NIS domain, cannot access the */pchome* directory until he issues the *cifslogin* command. He could have specified the name of a different Windows 2000 account as in *cifslogin w2kserv hilary*—had he known hilary's password. However, because he did not do so, *cifslogin* assumed that the remote user name was also *dylan*. Also, note in the above output that *dylan* seems to own the *hilary* home directory. This is because the *home* share has Full Control permissions for Everyone. But the NTFS permissions override the share permissions, so that *dylan* cannot write to the *hilary* directory if the NTFS permissions prohibit him.

12.5.3 PAM and the CIFS/9000 Client

We described PAM NTLM in Chapter 8, "User Authentication," and stated that by employing it you can avoid having to use *cifslogin*. Let's review how you do that.

1. Edit the PAM NTLM configuration file */etc/opt/cifsclient/pam/smb.conf*. You set the *workgroup* parameter, which is actually your Windows 2000 domain, and then you set the *password server* parameter, which is your domain controller name. In our example we have:

   ```
   #================= Global Settings =======================
   [global]
   # workgroup = NT-Domain-Name or Workgroup-Name, eg: REDHAT4
      workgroup = BOOK

   # Use password server option only with security = server or domain

   password server = w2kserv

   Domain user map = /etc/opt/cifsclient/pam/domain_user.map
   ```

   As I have done with my configuration file, you might want to specify a user map file with the *domain user map* parameter. My map file contains only one mapping: that of *root* to *Administrator*.
2. Edit the global HP-UX PAM configuration file */etc/pam.conf*. If you want NTLM authentication only for when a user logs in at the console running the Common Desktop Environment (CDE), change the *libpam_unix.1* entries to *libpam_ntlm.1* under the appropriate sections. For password authentication and change *without* password expiration support, change only the *Authentication management* (*dtlogin* and *dtaction*) and *Password man-*

agement (*dtlogin* and *dtaction*) sections. If you do want password expiration support, change the *Account management* (*passwd*, *dtlogin*, *dtaction*) section as well. Below is a example:

```
#
# PAM configuration
#
# Authentication management
#
login auth required /usr/lib/security/libpam_unix.1
su auth required /usr/lib/security/libpam_unix.1
dtlogin auth required /usr/lib/security/libpam_ntlm.1
dtaction auth required /usr/lib/security/libpam_ntlm.1
ftp auth required /usr/lib/security/libpam_unix.1
OTHER auth required /usr/lib/security/libpam_unix.1
#
# Account management
#
login account required /usr/lib/security/libpam_unix.1
su account required /usr/lib/security/libpam_unix.1
dtlogin account required /usr/lib/security/libpam_ntlm.1
dtaction account required /usr/lib/security/libpam_ntlm.1
ftp account required /usr/lib/security/libpam_unix.1
OTHER account required /usr/lib/security/libpam_unix.1
#
# Session management
#
login session required /usr/lib/security/libpam_unix.1
dtlogin session required /usr/lib/security/libpam_unix.1
dtaction session required /usr/lib/security/libpam_unix.1
OTHER session required /usr/lib/security/libpam_unix.1
#
# Password management
#
login password required /usr/lib/security/libpam_unix.1
passwd password required /usr/lib/security/libpam_ntlm.1
dtlogin password required /usr/lib/security/libpam_ntlm.1
dtaction password required /usr/lib/security/libpam_ntlm.1
OTHER password required /usr/lib/security/libpam_unix.1
```

Exactly how you configure PAM NTLM is up to you, but you need to be careful or else you might not be able to log in at all. It is probably best to configure it incrementally; that is, you might specify NTLM for CDE logins and actions only, make sure they work, and then configure *login* and *passwd*.

In Chapter 8, we also described PAM Kerberos. Consult that chapter for more detailed information. As you might recall, using PAM Kerberos is a little trickier. You need to have a user account set up on the Windows 2000 Key Distribution Center (KDC), create a keytab file on the KDC, transfer that file to the HP-UX system, merge the contents of that file with */etc/krb5.keytab*, synchronize clocks between the HP-UX system and the KDC, configure */etc/krb5.conf,* and then configure */etc/pam.conf.* To configure */etc/pam.conf* for CDE authentication only, change the *dtaction* and *dtlogin* under the Authentication Management section. For example,

```
# PAM Configuration
#
# Account Management
#
dtaction  account  required  /usr/lib/security/libpam_unix.1
dtlogin  account  required  /usr/lib/security/libpam_unix.1
ftp  account  required  /usr/lib/security/libpam_unix.1
login  account  required  /usr/lib/security/libpam_unix.1
su  account  required  /usr/lib/security/libpam_unix.1
OTHER  account  required  /usr/lib/security/libpam_unix.1
#
# Authentication Management
#
dtaction  auth  required  /usr/lib/security/libpam_krb5.1
dtlogin  auth  required  /usr/lib/security/libpam_krb5.1
ftp  auth  required  /usr/lib/security/libpam_unix.1
login  auth  required  /usr/lib/security/libpam_unix.1
su  auth  required  /usr/lib/security/libpam_unix.1
OTHER  auth  required  /usr/lib/security/libpam_unix.1
#
# Password Management
#
dtaction  password  required /usr/lib/security/libpam_unix.1
dtlogin  password  required  /usr/lib/security/libpam_unix.1
login  password  required  /usr/lib/security/libpam_unix.1
passwd  password  required  /usr/lib/security/libpam_unix.1
OTHER  password  required  /usr/lib/security/libpam_unix.1
#
# Session Management
#
dtaction  session  required  /usr/lib/security/libpam_unix.1
dtlogin  session  required  /usr/lib/security/libpam_unix.1
login  session  required  /usr/lib/security/libpam_unix.1
OTHER  session  required  /usr/lib/security/libpam_unix.1
```

Since setting up Kerberos authentication is more involved, you might consider using PAM NTLM instead, since Windows 2000 domain controllers can indeed authenticate with NTLM for mixed environments.

Also, since account management and session management is not defined under Kerberos, you don't have to configure the Account Management and Session Management functions. They are provided only for compatibility with the PAM specification. One thing to watch out for with PAM Kerberos is that there is no user-mapping file. Therefore, you need a user called *root* on the Windows KDC if you want that account to be authenticated by that name. Other possibilities for handling the *root* user is to keep the *su* command configured for UNIX authentication or to use */etc/pam_user.conf* for that account. See the *pam.conf man* page for more information.

As with the CIFS/9000 server, the client seems to work well with Server for NIS. Again, this effectively unifies the user databases of Windows 2000 and HP-UX. Otherwise, for both PAM NTLM and PAM Kerberos, you need user accounts defined in both environments. While NIS running on HP-UX can consolidate your UNIX accounts, Server for NIS can consolidate those accounts with Active Directory.

12.6 Conclusion

We've looked at CIFS file sharing in this chapter by focusing on HP's CIFS/9000, the server portion of which is based on Samba. We looked at both the server and the client and found that a Windows 2000 domain controller can do all the authenticating. For the server, we can specify in */etc/opt/samba/smb.conf* that the domain controller will do the authenticating. For the client, we can specify NTLM or Kerberos authentication. On top of all that, we see that Server for NIS can help us achieve a unified user database by combining NIS maps with Active Directory and can be used in conjunction with CIFS/9000. While there may be some details we haven't covered here, we have enough to provide a proof-of-concept on a couple of ways to use CIFS/9000.

References

1. Marshall Kirk McKusick, Keith Bostic, Michael Karels, and John Quarterman, *The Design and Implementation of the 4.4BSD Operating System.* (Addison-Wesley, 1996).
2. Richard Sharpe, Tim Potter, and Jim Morris, *Special Edition: Using Samba.* (Que, 2000).
3. Hewlett-Packard, *Installing and Administering the CIFS/9000 Client.* (Hewlett-Packard, 2000).
4. Hewlett-Packard, *Installing and Administering the CIFS/9000 Server.* (Hewlett-Packard, 2000).

CHAPTER 13

Miscellaneous Interoperability Topics

What remains is a look at some miscellaneous interoperability topics, namely, network attached storage, the X Window system, and printing. So far, we have examined the most pressing issues system administrators face when confronted with a mixed environment: how systems communicate, how they find each other, how their naming systems work, how users are authenticated, and how to share files. We conclude with a brief look at other interoperability topics, realizing that these can also be worthy of extensive description. They are, perhaps, material for another book. So, let's proceed, starting with a twist to an area of file sharing: Network-Attached Storage (NAS).

13.1 Network-Attached Storage

Since file sharing is such an important goal in UNIX and Windows interoperability, we must take a look at the concept of NAS. NAS is disk storage accessible via networking technologies such as Ethernet, Gigabit Ethernet, and ATM, rather than via channel technologies such as SCSI and Fibre Channel. Unrestricted by distance and connectivity limitations, NAS makes it possible for large numbers of clients to access files from anywhere on the network. NAS is achieved by connecting a file server running a stripped-down operating system optimized for network I/O to some kind of storage system. This operating system does nothing but serve files over the network. It does not run other services like Dynamic Host Configuration Protocol (DHCP), Domain Name System (DNS), Windows Internet Naming Service (WINS), or Network Information Service (NIS). Therefore, fast performance is a prominent NAS feature.

EMC Corporation was the first to coin the term *network-attached storage*, but Auspex was the first company to actually implement the concept. Today, the leading vendors of NAS are EMC and Network Appliance. Both companies provide NAS for UNIX (via NFS), Windows (via CIFS), and mixed environments. The goal for these and other vendors is to provide NAS that is easy to integrate in mixed environments, easy to manage, performs well, and is always available.

13.1.1 An NAS Example

To illustrate the NAS concept, let's look at the EMC Celerra file server. There are two components to the Celerra: the file server itself and the storage. The storage consists of a disk array called the Symmetrix, either contained in the same cabinet as the file server or existing in a separate cabinet. The file server connects to the disk array either over a SCSI or Fibre Channel connection. It connects to the network via 10/100BaseT Fast Ethernet, Gigabit Ethernet, Fiber Distributed Data Interface (FDDI), or Asynchronous Transfer Mode (ATM). Clients connect to the file server over the network via NFS or CIFS. Figure 13–1 illustrates these components.

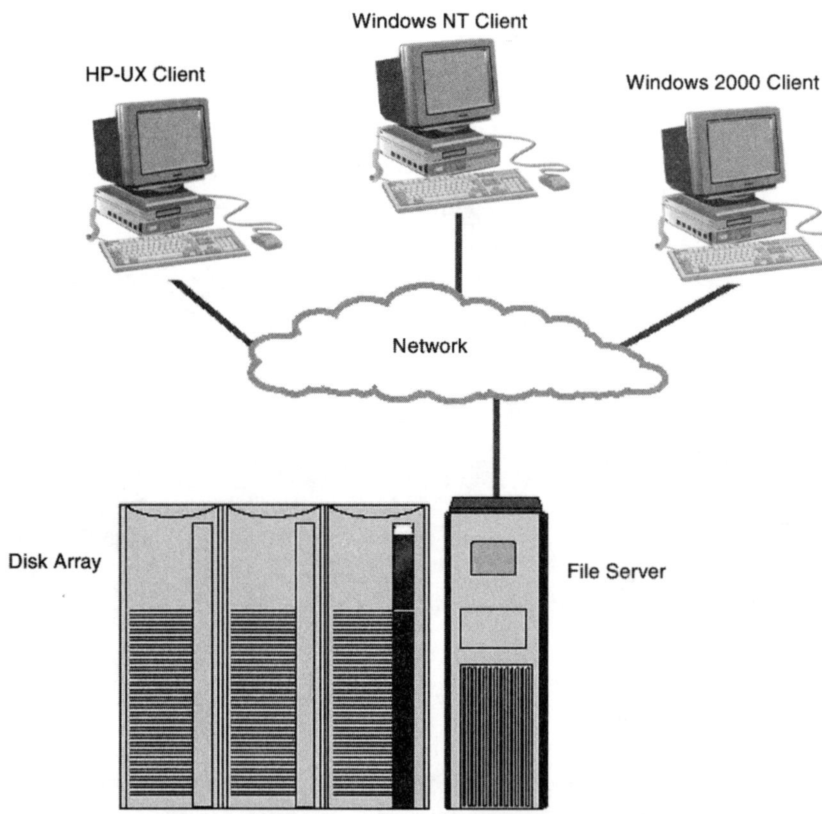

Figure 13–1 Components of Network-Attached Storage. This diagram shows the file server connected to a separate disk array. There are other file servers that share their cabinets with the disks, creating a single enclosure.

In addition to CIFS, the Celerra file server supports both version 2 and version 3 of NFS and both UDP and TCP as NFS transports. It also supports FTP and WebNFS, which lets you access NFS file systems using Web browsers, Java applets, and the Internet.

The file server components include *data movers* and at least one *control station*. The data movers run a small operating system called Data Access in Real Time (DART), while the control station runs a form of UNIX. The control station is used to configure the file server and provide management services. It plays no role in the actual delivery of data across the network. Each data mover runs DART and has an IP address for every interface it contains, as well as an IP address for each port in multiport NICs. You can also configure an Ethernet channel on multiport NICs, combining each port into a single trunk with a single IP address.

The file system created by the control station and shared by CIFS, NFS, and WebNFS is called UxFS, based on Berkeley's UFS. Conceptually, then, the way in which this file server works is illustrated in Figure 13–2.

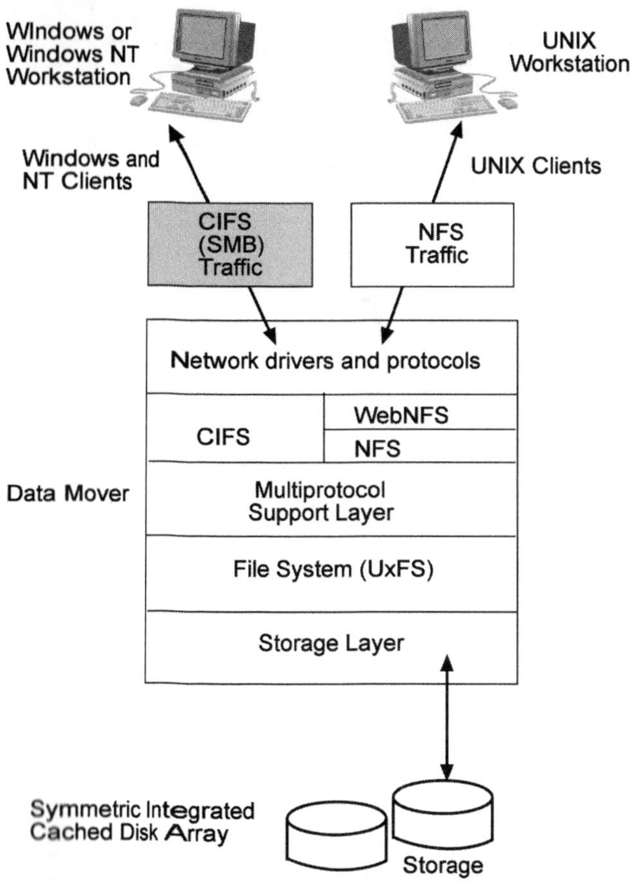

Figure 13–2 Functional layers of the Celerra file server.

NFS clients make requests to the file server's NFS server in the same manner as they always do: via Remote Procedure Calls (RPCs) containing the UID and GID of the user making the request. The file server's NFS server validates each request, using either local files or NIS. The CIFS server authenticates CIFS client requests with NTLM 0.12 authentication, not Kerberos, and thus must operate with Windows 2000 servers authenticating in mixed mode, that is, both NTLM and Kerberos. The Celerra file server does not do any CIFS authenticating but instead forwards authentication requests to domain controllers. Thus the file server runs as a member server only.

13.1.2 Benefits of NAS

NAS makes it possible for both UNIX and Windows clients to access the same data without the use of general-purpose servers. Thus performance is usually quite high. NAS can also provide a great deal more reliability and availability as well, particularly if the file servers connect to storage arrays such as the Symmetrix. NAS helps to eliminate data duplication by consolidating data on a single platform, making management and backup much easier. As long as the amounts of data used by organizations throughout the world continue to grow, and as long as there are heterogeneous clients needing to access this data, NAS is a very attractive form of UNIX and Windows 2000 interoperability.

13.2 The X Window System

One important way for UNIX and Windows 2000 systems to interoperate is to employ the X Window System. Originally developed for UNIX systems by MIT, the X Window System (X for short) is a graphical windowing system that separates an application from the display server. In other words, applications, known as X clients, can run in one place but have their displays located elsewhere on the network. These displays run X server software that accepts drawing instructions from the clients, creating little network traffic in so doing. Figure 13–3 illustrates the system. In this diagram we see what is known as X terminals, diskless systems dedicated to running X servers. By placing X server software on your workstation, you are in effect installing X terminal software emulation.

With X, you can have true application servers in your environment. In other words, you can have more powerful servers run applications for you; they simply display the application at your desktop. Running an application accessed via NFS or CIFS is not the same thing, because your local CPU is still doing the work when you run the program. By using X, the remote system does the processing while the local system does the displaying. A rough parallel to this way of doing things can be found in the World Wide Web, where a browser simply sends instructions to applications running on remote servers that process the input and display the results back to the browser.

The main benefit of using X in a mixed UNIX and Windows environment is that you don't have to worry about porting key applications from one platform to another. In the case of UNIX systems, X applications have been around for a long time, and porting them to Windows 2000 is costly and time consuming. Therefore, users who still need access to these applications, but who now have Windows 2000 workstations, can still get to them simply by installing an X server on their systems. These are available from vendors such as WRQ, developers of Reflection/X, and Hummingbird, makers of Exceed. For this book, I used a Windows 2000 version of Exceed and found that it performed quite well.

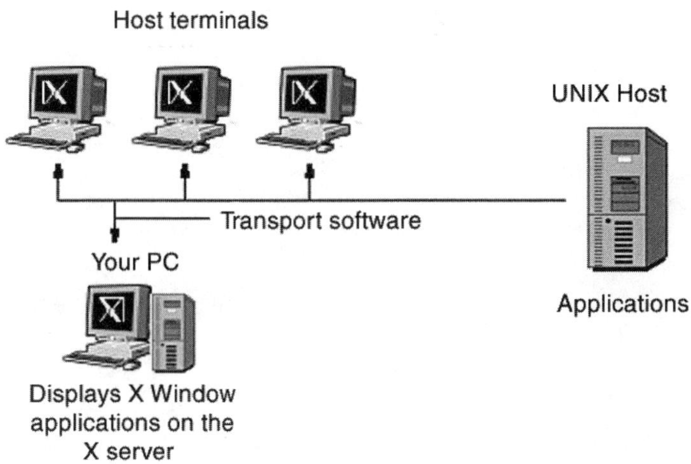

Figure 13–3 How X works.

Once you have an X server running on your Windows 2000 system, you can start X clients running on a UNIX system in a number of ways. One is to execute them using the utilities we covered earlier in the book: Telnet, Rexec, Rsh, and so on. Usually, X server vendors will supply their own versions of these utilities. Another way is through the use of X Window Display Manager Control Protocol (XDMCP). When used in broadcast mode, this tool provides the user with a list of available UNIX systems that a person can log on to. Figure 13–4 shows a chooser listing the systems available for logon.

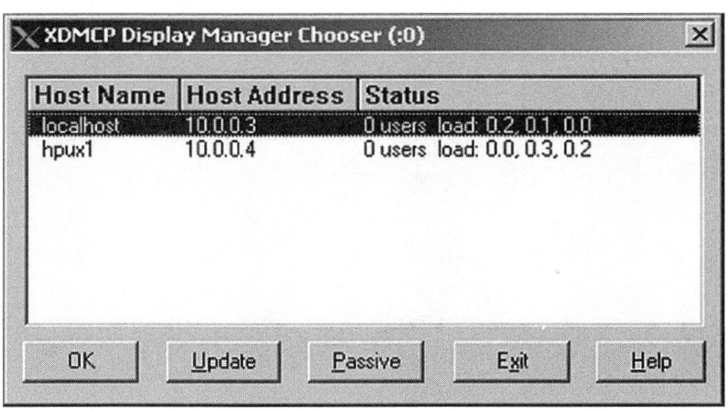

Figure 13–4 The XDMCP Display Manager Chooser.

Once you select a system, the remote system displays the login screen as if you were seated at that workstation. In the case of HP-UX systems, the *dtlogin* process will display the login screen, as shown in Figure 13–5. Notice that the entire login screen displays in a Microsoft Window. Once you log in, you get the same look and feel of your HP-UX system, though you may have to install additional HP fonts along with your X server software to get precisely the same look. Alternatively, you can use an HP-UX system as a font server. You can then toggle between both HP-UX and Windows 2000, using the Taskbar and/or the ALT-TAB keyboard sequence.

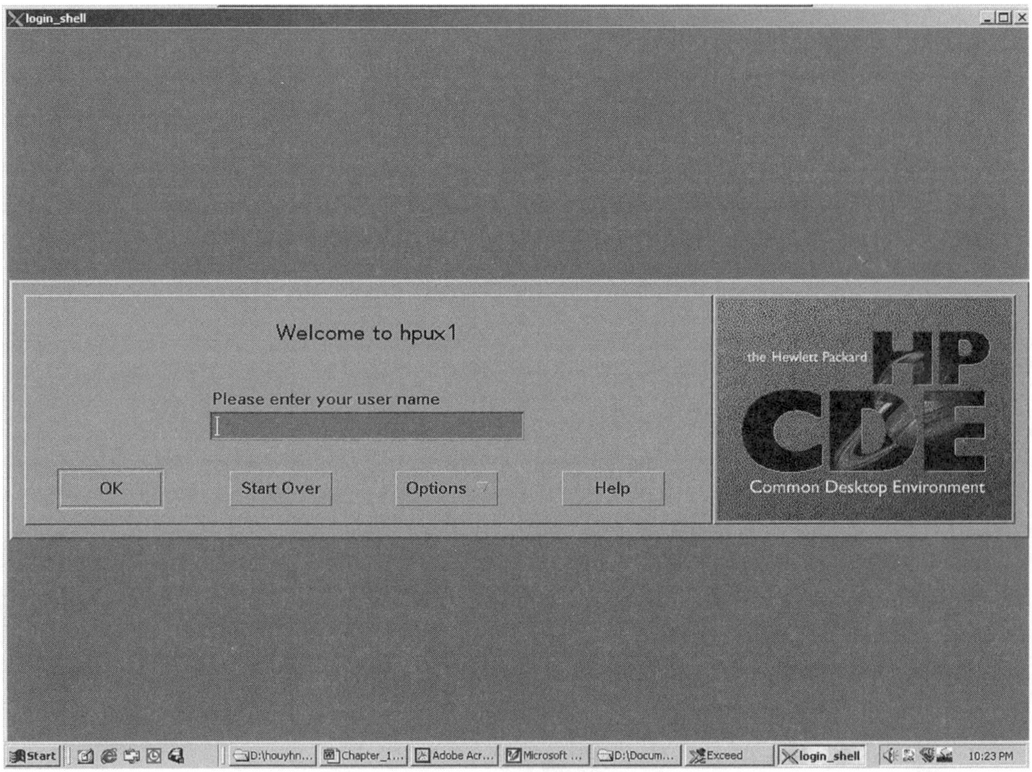

Figure 13–5 The CDE login screen provided by XDMCP. Note the Windows 2000 Taskbar at the bottom of the window.

Windows desktops are the rule in the business world and are gradually taking over those of scientific and engineering environments. Often in the past, the latter would see two workstations on a user's desk—a UNIX system for high-end work and a Windows system for documentation, email, and personal productivity applications. Alternatively, they would use some form of X to do the opposite of what we've just described, namely, turning the Windows GUI into an X client for display to the UNIX workstation. Such has required third-party software such as WinCenter from Network Computing Devices.

The Open Group, through the X.Org Consortium, maintains the existing code base for the X Window System and promotes its development and standards. You can get a lot of good information about X by consulting their Web site at *www.x.org*. You can also get information about X at the Web site of the XFree86 Project at *www.xfree86.org*. Whether obtained from these sources or from vendors, X can help you achieve interoperability not only for Windows and UNIX systems, but for other platforms as well.

13.3 Printing

There are several permutations of configuration for printing in mixed HP-UX and Windows 2000 environments. For medium-to-large sites, network printing takes the form of using a printer with an HP JetDirect card. For HP-UX systems, you must install the HP JetDirect software separately in order to do this. For Windows 2000 systems, you either need to install the Data Link Control (DLC) protocol (through **Local Area Connection Properties** box) or use the Standard TCP/IP Port Monitor (SPM). Windows 2000 print servers can contain the printer drivers for Windows clients to print to JetDirect cards, but HP-UX systems must have the appropriate interface model scripts installed locally. Printing to JetDirect printers is one simple way for both Windows 2000 and HP-UX clients to share printers. Another way is to print with locally attached printers using technology based on the old line printer daemon (LPD).

13.3.1 HP-UX Print Server with Locally Attached Printer

First, you must attach your printer to the HP-UX system and—if you're smart—use SAM to configure your printer. You will also make your life easier if you attach an HP printer, since HP-UX comes with interface model files for their printers. Start SAM, and then select **Printers and Plotters→LP Spooler→Printers and Plotters→Actions→Add Local Printer/Plotter**. After selecting the appropriate interface (usually parallel), SAM will ask you for such things as the printer name and model. As I have said, having an HP printer makes things simple, as you can see in the box that pops up after pressing the **Printer Model/Interface** button (see Figure 13–6). Just make sure you pick the right model script for your printer. Once you add your printer, SAM will list it for you, and you can see it listed with the *lpstat –a* command.

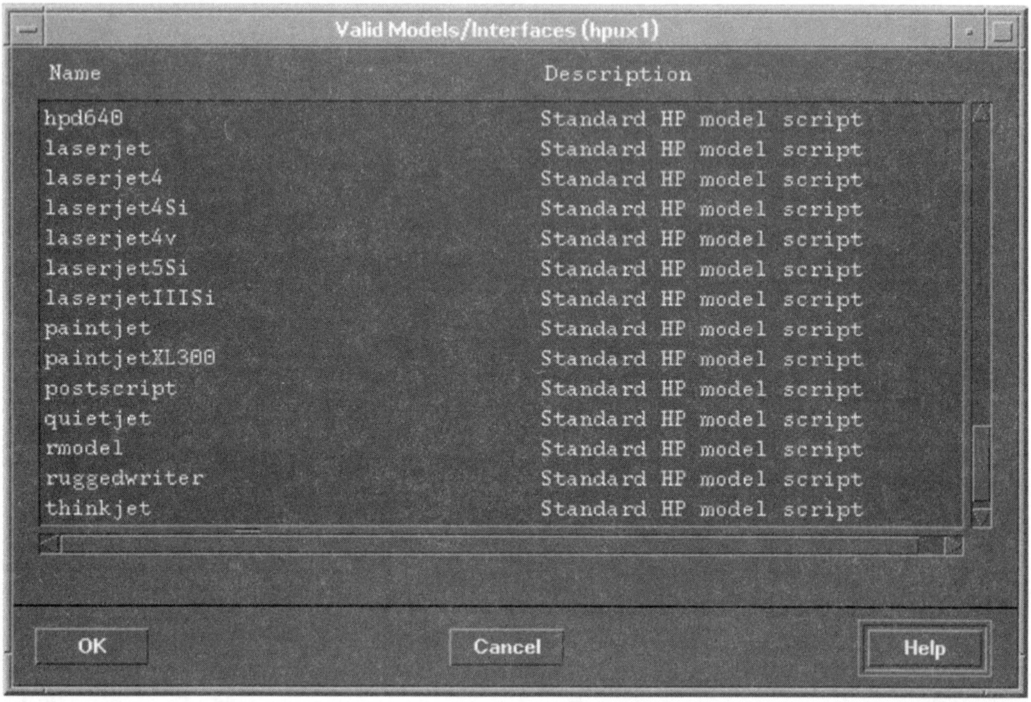

Figure 13–6 Model scripts available on HP-UX systems.

In order for you to print to this printer from Windows 2000, you must install Print Services for UNIX. This service is on the installation CD and can be installed by going into the Control Panel and running **Add/Remove Programs→Add/Remove Windows Components**. You will find it under **Other Network File and Print Services** (see Figure 13–7).

Once you do install Print Services for UNIX, run **Start→Settings→Printers→Add Printer**. You will get the Add Printer Wizard. Click **Local printer** and clear the **Automatically detect my printer** check box. On the next screen, you click on **Create a new port** and then select **LPR Port**, as seen in Figure 13–8.

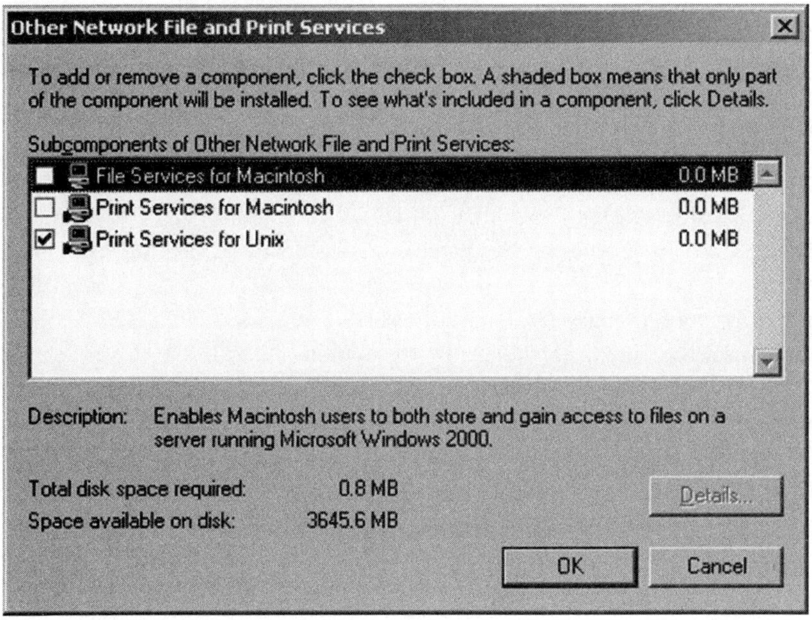

Figure 13–7 Installing Print Services for UNIX.

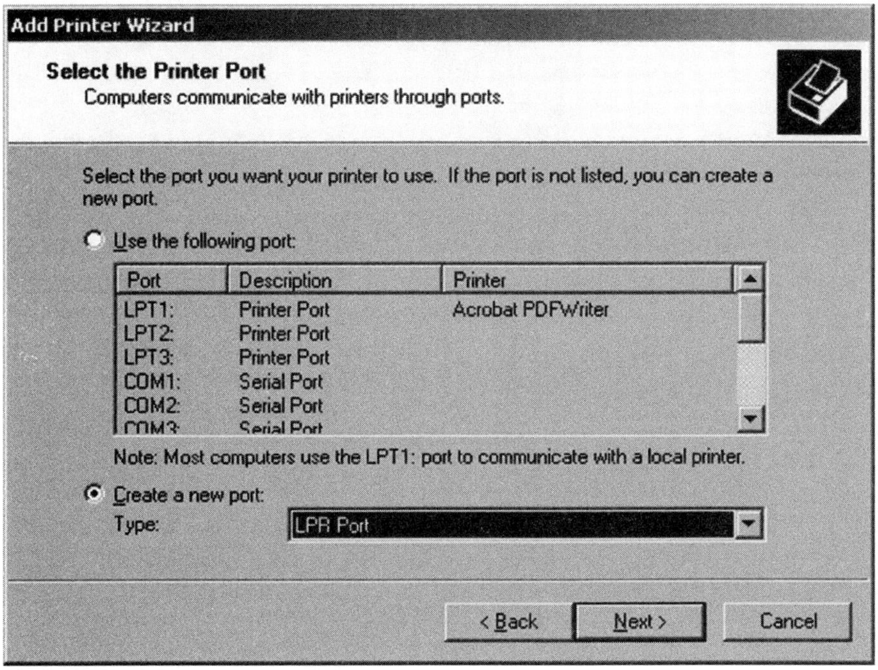

Figure 13–8 Creating an LPR port.

Click **Next**, and then provide the name or IP address of the HP-UX print server and the name of the printer you want to print to. You then will be instructed to install the appropriate printer driver. Many of HP's print drivers are already on the installation CD. If the driver you're looking for does not exist, then check Hewlett-Packard's Web site. Once you install the driver, you are ready to begin printing from Windows 2000 to HP-UX.

Print Services for UNIX supports printing only to UNIX computers running the LPD service (for example, Berkeley Software Distribution [BSD] UNIX computers). HP-UX is System V-based, but its implementation of *lp* combines BSD and System V features, making it compatible with LPD requests.

Sometimes, Printer Control Language (PCL) print jobs from Windows 2000 clients to HP-UX print servers fail after printing junk. This is because the Windows 2000 PCL driver sends a raw PCL file to the HP-UX spooler queue, which by default is not set up to handle raw output. You can fix this by editing the interface file. For example, the interface file on my test system, *hpux1*, was */var/spool/lp/interface/hpdj648c*, created when I added the printer using SAM and named after the printer. This is simply a text file. I changed the *outputmode* variable to read *raw* instead of *cooked*. As a result, the Windows 2000 system printed my PCL files just fine.

13.3.2 Windows 2000 Print Server with Locally Attached Printer

Printing in the other direction is even simpler. First, as in the previous configuration, you install Print Services for UNIX. Then, connect the printer to the Windows 2000 print server. If your printer is Plug-and-Play compatible and the driver already exists on the system, you simply make sure the printer is turned on during reboot or hardware scan. Then, you configure the HP-UX system to print to the Windows 2000 system.

When you run **SAM→Printers and Plotters→LP Spooler→Printers and Plotters**, you select **Add Remote Printer/Plotter** from the **Actions** menu. Then you fill in the screen, something like Figure 13–9.

Something to watch out for is that when you add a printer to Windows 2000, the default name is often long and contains spaces. Be sure to give the printer a nice, short name like *dj648c*. This will prevent any confusion for the HP-UX system. Once you add the remote printer, you can start printing files from applications or the command line. There is no need to specify an interface script name, since the Windows 2000 printer driver will do all the processing.

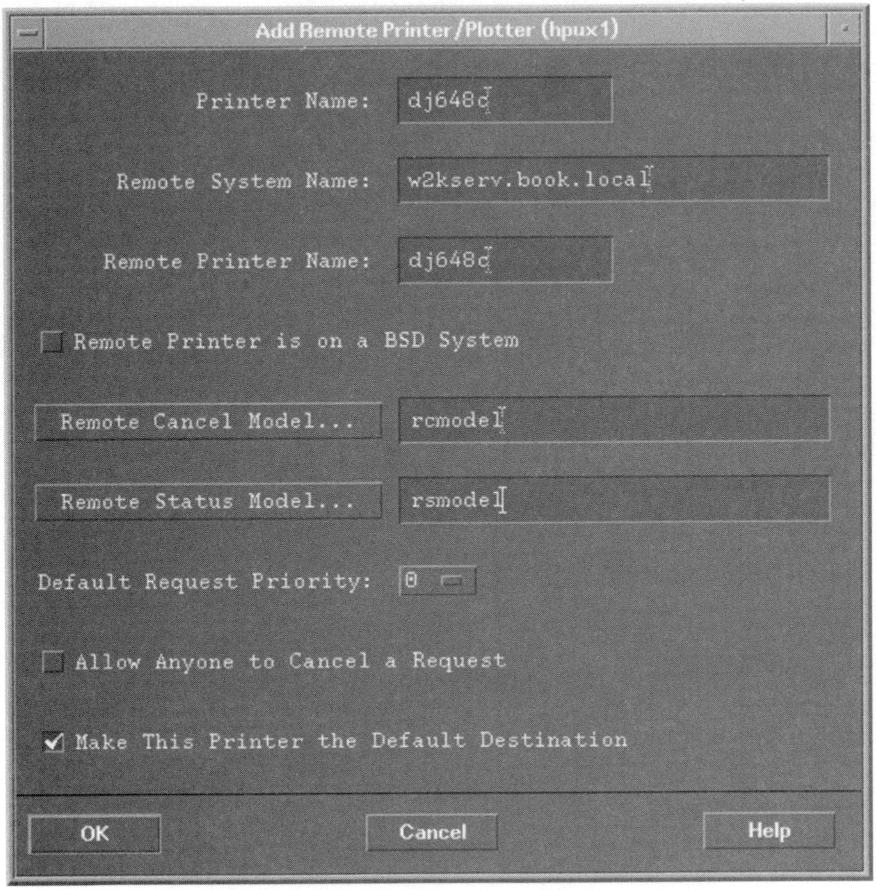

Figure 13–9 Configuring a remote printer on HP-UX using SAM.

13.4 Conclusion

So, we end with a brief look at other interoperability tools. NAS will play an increasingly important role in mixed environments and will supplant many server-based solutions. Managing X Window can be quite complex, but it offers a way to continue using UNIX-based systems even if you migrate your environment to Windows 2000. Inter-platform printing can take many forms, but the traditional method of attaching printers to a print server of some kind is easily assimilated in mixed environments. However, most sites have ways to print over the network to printers containing JetDirect cards, regardless of the operating system in which the job arises.

Thus, we end this book. Certainly, we did not look at every aspect of UNIX and Windows 2000 interoperability in all its details. Such would have produced a large, unwieldy book. However, I think we achieved the objective of providing some practical advice to systems administrators in managing the most common tasks they face in a mixed environment. I hope you found this book useful.

References

1. Niall Mansfield, *The Joy of X: An Overview of the X Window System.* (Addison-Wesley, 1994).
2. Microsoft, *Microsoft Windows 2000 Server Internetworking Guide.* (Microsoft Press, 2000).

INDEX

J

K

L

M

N

O

P

R

S

T

X